The Er[nst]

Tax [Saver's]

Companion
1997/98

The Ernst & Young
Tax Saver's Companion 1997/98

⧉ ERNST & YOUNG

JOHN WILEY & SONS

Chichester • New York • Weinheim • Brisbane • Toronto • Singapore

In the preparation of this book, all reasonable efforts have been made to offer the most current, correct, and clearly expressed information. Nonetheless, inadvertent errors can occur and tax rules and regulations often change.

Further, the information in the text is intended to afford general guidelines on matters of interest to taxpayers. The application and impact of tax laws can vary widely from case to case, based upon the specific or unique facts involved. Accordingly, the information in this book is not intended to serve as legal, accounting, or tax advice. Readers are encouraged to consult professional advisers for advice concerning specific matters before making any decision and the authors and publishers disclaim any responsibility for positions taken by taxpayers in their individual cases or for any misunderstanding on the part of readers.

Amendments to the 1997 Finance Bill have been incorporated to 1 February 1997.

© 1997 Ernst & Young

Ernst & Young is authorised by The Institute of Chartered Accountants in England and Wales to carry on investment business.

The United Kingdom firm of Ernst & Young is a member of Ernst & Young International.

Published by John Wiley & Sons, Baffins Lane,
        Chichester, West Sussex PO19 1UD, England.
        Telephone 01243 779777
        E-mail (for orders and customer service enquiries):
        cs-books@wiley.co.uk
        Visit our Home Page on http://www.wiley.co.uk or
        http://www.wiley.com

British Library Cataloguing in Publication Data
A catalogue record for this book is available from the British Library

ISBN 0-471-97250-9

Printed and bound in Great Britain by The Bath Press
from camera-ready copy supplied by the authors.

ABOUT THE AUTHORS

Ernst & Young's tax professionals have been providing domestic and international tax planning and compliance services to individual and business clients for generations. Today, Ernst & Young is one of the country's leading international professional services firms, with offices in 670 cities worldwide and 26 cities in the UK. Clients include individual taxpayers, employees, partners, landowners, company directors and entertainers, as well as business entities of all sizes – from the largest to the smallest.

With approximately 1,300 tax professionals, Ernst & Young has one of the largest tax practices in the UK. This book draws upon the experience of many of those professionals for its contents.

Principal editors

Philip Davis
Dawn Nicholson

The editors would like to thank all those who have made contributions to this book and in particular:

Nigel Bradley	Tina McBrierley
Jonathan Bruce	Bill McHardy
Peter Clifford	Penny Mighall
Sandra Deboo	Graham Morgan
John Dougherty	Nigel Smith
Nigel Gill	Kay Sullivan
John Jones	Ken Timmins
Zainab Juhoor	Mark Waddilove
Paul Knox	Martin Whittaker
Glenn Leitch	Jenni Woolven
John Mackay	

Contents

How to use this book

The Ernst & Young Tax Saver's Companion 1997/98 is a year-end and year-round tax planner with easy-to-follow, money-saving tax strategies from one of the country's foremost tax authorities, Ernst & Young. This book, with its concise explanations of key provisions, can also be used for quick guidance on important personal and business transactions. It will be particularly useful when you are filling in your tax return.

The book is organised into three sections:

Part I, Tax strategies for individuals, contains chapters that tell you what income is taxable, what you can deduct from it, how to work out your capital gains and how you check your tax. All are important when completing your tax return. The tax return guide on page xviii gives you cross-references to those pages in the book which refer to the sections of your return. There is a chapter on capital gains tax and one on the tax-saving steps you may be able to take to cut your tax bill.

Part II, Tax strategies for businesses, explains many of the fundamental tax questions that confront the owner of any business. Chapters 7 and 8 explain how to choose your business structure, how to work out your taxable business income and what business deductions are available. Special attention is paid to the complex tax rules for sole traders and partnerships in Chapter 9 and the consequences of self assessment. Chapter 10 looks at paying the tax on your business income. Chapters 11 and 12 focus on planning suggestions that can save money for businesses and the people who run them, and also what you should think about when you dispose of your business.

Part III, How to improve your financial future, contains a wealth of information on how to ensure that you and your family are protected from the financial risks you face, how to plan sound investment strategy and how to secure a comfortable retirement. The final chapter on estate planning offers advice on gifts, trusts and inheritance tax planning to ensure your family keeps as much of your estate as possible.

Among its many benefits, this book offers the following special features:

Tax Savers Highlighted throughout every chapter in the book are numerous Tax Savers – specific strategies and recommendations that can help you cut your tax bill.

Tax Alerts These highlight recent changes in the tax law that you should know about and tax pitfalls of which you should be aware. If you are aware of a new development in the law before the end of the year, you can often take timely and appropriate action and save yourself money.

Tax Filing Tips Cross-references in the text to the relevant sections of your tax return guide you through the completion of the new self assessment tax return form.

Special chapters on year-end tax planning for individuals and businesses The prudent taxpayer must make decisions before 5 April about a number of important tax questions – for example, whether to generate income now or defer it to next year and whether to pay a deductible expense this year or in the future.

Important information on the tax aspects of 'life-cycle events' These are the occasions, transactions and eventualities that most of us will have to deal with at some time during our lives. A special index outlining where you find information on 'life-cycle events' discussed in this book follows this introduction.

Clearly presented rules on the tax law for individuals, estates, gifts and businesses Included in each section are examples that show you how the rules work and strategies to help you plan better.

The Ernst & Young Tax Saver's Companion 1997/98 contains the following additional features that will be of year-round use to individuals and business people alike:

An overview of self assessment This section provides a brief guide to the main elements of the new self assessment regime which will commence from the tax year 1996/97.

Changes in tax law you should know about This section highlights some of those changes which are referred to throughout the book and which are proposed by the 1997 Finance Bill.

Up-to-date tax tables showing the appropriate tax facts for the 1996/97 tax year (which you will need to check your 1996/97 tax bill) and for the 1997/98 tax year (which you will need in your forward tax planning).

Tax calendar A month-by-month reminder of important tax action dates for individuals and businesses.

Index to life-cycle events

This special index can be used to locate pages that contain important information on the tax aspects of 'life-cycle events' – those milestones that most adults will be facing at one time or another during the course of their lives. By reading this information, you'll get off to a good start in understanding and planning for the tax consequences associated with various life-cycle events.

1997/98 personal tax calendar – Key tax dates

APR '97

5 Final date for using capital gains tax and inheritance tax annual exemptions for 1996/97.

1996/97 tax year ends.

Final date to make election to transfer married couple's allowance for 1997/98.

Final date for mortgage interest election between husband and wife for 1996/97.

6 Income tax returns for 1996/97 issued.

30 Inheritance tax due on gifts made between 6/4/96 and 30/9/96.

MAY '97

31 Employees must receive form P60 for 1996/97 (details of pay and tax deducted) from their employers by this date.

JUNE '97

1 Interest starts to run on outstanding 1 December 1996 assessments (1995/96 taxed income and capital gains assessments).

JULY '97

6 Employees must receive form P11D for 1996/97 (return of expenses and benefits) from their employers by this date.

31 Due date of payment of second interim tax payment for 1996/97.

AUG '97

SEPT '97

30 Date for submission of 1996/97 tax return if Revenue calculation of tax is required.

OCT '97	NOV '97	DEC '97
5 If no tax return issued for 1996/97, notify Revenue if chargeable to tax for that year.		
JAN '98	**FEB '98**	**MARCH '98**
31 Date for submission of 1996/97 tax return with self-calculation of tax. Due date of payment of balance of tax for 1996/97. Due date of payment of first tax payment on account for 1997/98.	28 Unpaid tax for 1996/97 will be subject to a 5% surcharge.	Check PAYE Notice of Coding for 1997/98 when issued. Consider in relation to 1991/92 if claims should be made for: • errors or mistakes • additional personal allowances • relief against double assessment • double tax relief • delayed remittances of overseas income or gains.

1997 tax return completion guide

INCOME AND GAINS IN THE YEAR TO 5 APRIL 1997

Sections in 1997 Tax Return	Relevant pages of this book
Income from employment	4-19
Income from share schemes	26-37
Income from self-employment	xxiv, 127-50
Income from a partnership	141-50
Income from land and property	24-26
Income from overseas	12, 14-16
Income from trusts/settlements	37-39, 92-93
Capital gains	42-46
Residence matters	96-99
Income from savings/investments	26-32
Income from pensions	19-20
Income from Social Security benefits	22-23
Other income	37-40
Pension contributions, etc	58-65
Other reliefs due	65-78
Allowances due	55-58
Tax due for the year	79-90, 129-130

Top tax
planning tips

1 Use the tax allowances available to your family to best effect. Consider transferring ownership of assets to your spouse to achieve a spread of income that will use all their personal allowances and lower tax rates. In particular allocate your investments to make full use of the lower rate of tax (20%) payable on savings and dividend income by all basic rate taxpayers since 6 April 1996. If you are over 65 bear in mind the income thresholds at which you and your spouse qualify for higher allowances. Transferring an asset to your spouse has no tax cost and can reduce capital gains tax when the asset is sold (note restrictions which apply for transfers by parents to minor children).

2 If you have investments which stand at a profit and which you do not intend to sell, you can use your capital gains tax allowances by 'bed and breakfasting' an appropriate part of your shareholdings. You can reduce your future capital gains on an eventual sale.

3 Make sure you know how best to exploit the benefits your employer provides for you by fully understanding them. For example, if you can exercise your approved share options within the Revenue-approved time limits you can save up to 40% tax.

4 Think whether you can replace personal debt with business debt or mortgage debt which can attract tax-deductible interest. If you have spare cash consider reducing your home mortgage. The after-tax return on investing it is unlikely to produce income in excess of your mortgage payments.

5 Ensure that any income gifts you make to charity are tax deductible through a Deed of Covenant or Gift Aid and that instead of selling taxable assets to make gifts you make gifts of the assets themselves. The charity can then sell them tax-free. Make sure you claim your higher rate income tax deduction from the Revenue.

6 If you can employ your spouse in your business, then any earnings paid to them may be sheltered by their personal tax allowances, if they have little or no other taxable income.

7 If you participate in an approved employer pension scheme consider making tax deductible additional voluntary contributions.

8   For family companies carefully consider remuneration versus dividends as a way of enjoying profits. Dividends can avoid PAYE and National Insurance contributions but if paid instead of earnings may reduce pension and other benefits.

9   Start your planning early. This allows you time to take advantage of strategies that may not be available later in the year because of changes in the law, or because it takes several months to realise the maximum benefits, or because there is insufficient time to implement a strategy.

10 Make your contributions to a pension plan early in the tax year. The combination of making early contributions and compounding will make your money grow faster than if you wait until the last minute, particularly as these investments are tax-free.

11 Consider tax-favoured assets for your investment portfolio (eg, TESSAs or PEPs). When comparing the return from tax-free investments with others, use the after-tax return on taxable investments.

12 Take the time to work out the value of your estate and the potential inheritance taxes. Their size may surprise you and simple tax planning can save significant taxes for your family. If you can afford it, make gifts to your children during your lifetime but do not give away anything you may possibly need in the future. Make sure you make a will, so that your assets pass to the person you intend when you die.

13 If you have a shareholding in an unquoted company, note that any transfers of these shares may attract inheritance tax relief at 100%. Investment in unquoted rather than quoted shares could therefore give you a considerable advantage if and when you want to make gifts of any assets. Unquoted shares for the purpose of this relief include those quoted on the USM and AIM. Remember, however, that these are very high risk investments so make sure they fit your risk profile first.

An overview of self assessment

THE BASICS

This section provides a brief guide to the main elements of the new self assessment system. It is designed to give the reader a general grasp of the issues involved, and it should not be regarded as replacing specific advice on an individual's position. More detail is provided in the relevant sections of this book.

Self assessment will initially affect at least nine million people – all those individuals who usually receive tax returns. Companies are due to follow on to the system later – the latest indications are that self assessment for companies will start around the beginning of 1999.

'Self assessment' began as a reform of the tax administration system putting the onus on the taxpayer to work out his or her own tax. But to enable taxpayers to manage, the rules for the taxation of self-employment income, income from property, and investment income have all been significantly altered. In the end, every taxpayer will have a single tax bill payable in three instalments. But converting from the old system (which happens in 1996/97) is not going to be easy.

THE BACKGROUND TO SELF ASSESSMENT
What is self assessment?

In previous years an individual taxpayer filled in his or her tax return showing details of income earned and reliefs or expenses claimed. The Inland Revenue then worked out what tax was due and sent the taxpayer a bill (unless all the tax due had already been collected, for example by deduction at source or from wages and salaries through the PAYE system) or a refund. Essentially self assessment means that the taxpayer will have to take responsibility for this final step – working out the tax due – although the Revenue are still prepared to do the computational work, provided the taxpayer sends in his return earlier than he has had to in the past.

Because previously different kinds of income were taxed under different rules and at different rates and times, the switch to self assessment has meant that the tax system itself has had to be substantially reformed in order to give people the chance to be able to cope. So this is much more than simply a change in the time limit for putting in your return. Even if you are taxed mainly under PAYE, the time at which you pay tax on your other income will alter, and you may find yourself paying tax on it earlier than at present.

How will it work?

Everyone who receives a tax return will be able to choose whether to return it by 30 September this year (in which case the Revenue will work out the tax bill) or to work out the tax bill themselves, in which case the return has to be sent back by 31 January 1998. There will be a twelve-month period in which the return can be corrected for obvious mistakes. After that the year is closed unless the Revenue has formally opened an enquiry on it.

The tax return must be filed by the relevant date (30 September or 31 January) otherwise the penalty regime, which is largely automatic, will swing into action. If you receive a return, and do not have all the information ready by the filing dates, you must still complete the return using estimates (clearly marked as such) where necessary. You can then remove the estimates when further information becomes available.

Taxpayers won't have to check tax bills for each different source of income as they do at present, but in return for this greater simplicity tax has to be paid on account in two instalments, the first on 31 January in the tax year itself and the second on 31 July following the end of the year. These instalments will each be based on 50% of the income tax liability for the previous year. Thus for 1996/97 you should (if you are expected to have a residual liability after taking account of tax deducted eg, under PAYE) have made your first payment on 31 January, and will be due to pay the second amount on 31 July this year (1997).

The final payment will be due on 31 January 1998. This will include any capital gains tax plus any further tax due on income (or any repayment of tax which has been overpaid).

Taxpayers can reduce payments on account if they believe their income has reduced in comparison with the previous year. There are de minimis limits so that, if you only have a small amount of income taxable under self assessment (for instance if your income is mainly dealt with under PAYE) you do not have to make payment on account.

EMPLOYERS AND SELF ASSESSMENT

Why are employers affected?

Many employers pay expenses on behalf of their employees. Some of these expenses may be taxable on the employee, while others are not. Employers also often provide their staff with benefits, and again some of these are taxable (cars) while others are not (most subsidised meals). Under the previous system these were a matter for discussion between the employer and the Revenue and details of taxable benefits were simply recorded in the form P11D which the employer sends to the Revenue.

Under self assessment the employee has to provide this information to the Revenue, either so that the Revenue can work out the tax bill, or as part of the employee's own computation of the tax due. This includes the tax value of the benefit which previously the Revenue would have worked out. But of course it is the employer who holds most of the information.

What do employers have to do?

Employers now have to provide each employee with the details of what benefits and expenses he or she receives as well as providing this information to the Revenue. Because the employee may wish to put in a return by 30 September, this information has to be made available to him by 6 July.

The employer has to provide not just the details of the benefits but also their tax value, otherwise the employee will not know what figure to put on the return. The new rules also place employers under obligations to make reports about benefits given to their employees by third parties, and benefits which they provide to people who are not their employees.

Potential problems centre on how to obtain details of benefits from third parties – there is no obligation on the third party to give the employer this information – and on the tax value of a benefit. For example, if a company allows an employee to use a personal computer at home, how does the employer work out what the value of any private use was?

What does this mean for businesses?

The very largest employers should be able to cope with the increased information requirements. But there is widespread concern that smaller employers will find the information hard to provide without taking on staff and/or technology to do the work which was previously done by the Revenue.

Businesses also have to come to terms with the fact that information has for the first time to be provided to employees about the tax status of the company, which is relevant for some benefits and expenses.

When	What happens
6 April 1996	self assessment officially began
31 January 1997	first interim tax payment for 1996/97
6 April 1997 onwards	1996/97 tax returns issued
31 May 1997	employers must give P60 to employees
6 July 1997	employers must give P11D to employees
31 July 1997	second interim tax payment for 1996/97 due
30 September 1997	1996/97 tax returns due (Revenue to compute tax)
31 January 1998	1996/97 tax returns with tax computation due final tax payment for 1996/97 due first interim payment for 1997/98 due

SELF-EMPLOYED PEOPLE AND SELF ASSESSMENT

What has changed for self-employed people?

These are the people (about four million of them) who are arguably most affected by self assessment. Self-employed people can prepare accounts to any date in the year, and were previously taxed on the profits for the accounting period which ended in the preceding tax year. From 1997/98, tax will be charged on the profits for the accounting period ending in the current tax year.

For new businesses there is no problem. Everyone who started in business since 5 April 1994 is already taxed on the profits earned in the current year. But for existing businesses, previously on the 'preceding year' basis, special rules have been introduced to get through the 'transitional period'. Basically, these businesses will be taxed on the old system in 1995/96 (ie, the profits made in the accounting period ending in 1994/95 will be taxed) and on the new system in 1997/98 (ie, the profits made in the accounting period ending in 1997/98 will be taxed). But for 1996/97 – the 'transitional year' – there will be two years' worth of accounts (ending in 1995/96 and 1996/97) but only one year in which to tax the resulting profits. For this year only the tax bill will be one-half of the taxable profit for these two years taken together: see illustration 3 on page xxvii.

Does this mean I could reduce my tax bill this year?

Obviously if half of the profits for 1995/96 and 1996/97 are going to drop out of tax, people might have been tempted to move profitable transactions into the transitional period to try to avoid half the tax which would otherwise arise. The 1995 Finance Act introduced anti-avoidance provisions in an attempt to deter this. They have been substantially toned down from the first draft, but they are still formidable. And they contain the first ever fixed penalties for tax avoidance (as opposed to evasion).

What does this mean for businesses?

Businesses need to consider carefully the effect of their activities during the transitional period (generally the two accounting periods ending in 1996/97). Some actions may cause a cessation of the business for tax purposes, which can have unforeseen effects. Changes in business practice could trigger the anti-avoidance rules unless the taxpayer can show that tax avoidance was not a motive (and this is harder to do than it may seem).

Partnerships are particularly vulnerable, since the admission or exit of a partner, or changes in the way the partnership is financed, can affect the tax position.

HOW IS THE INLAND REVENUE CHANGING?

The essence of self assessment from the Inland Revenue point of view is a switch to a 'process now, check later' regime under which they will select returns for a more or less complete examination: between 5,000 and 10,000 of these enquiries each year will be totally random. So we can expect to see a much more audit-like approach by the Revenue.

The reform of the assessing machinery obviously frees up a considerable amount of manpower within the Inland Revenue. Much of this will be redeployed onto audit or investigation work, but up to 3,000 jobs will go. In his November Budget the Chancellor announced a further 2,000 people would be deployed onto investigation and audit work, so it is clear that the first self assessment returns are going to be subject to an unusually high level of scrutiny.

At the same time, the end of the system under which the Revenue guessed your income, assessed it, you had to appeal against the assessment and then argue about the true figures means that less time should be spent in essentially administrative tasks.

An optimistic view is that this new approach should be much less confrontational: after all, if a return is selected at random the Inspector can hardly start out from the premise that the taxpayer is hiding something. But the investigatory culture within the Revenue is very strong, and a more pessimistic view could be that Inspectors, encouraged by a performance-related pay culture, will use the very wide audit and information powers they have been given to browbeat taxpayers. The 'Spend to Save' package announced in the last Budget, and referred to above, seems to tilt the odds in favour of the pessimists.

SELF ASSESSMENT ILLUSTRATIONS
How self assessment will affect different classes of taxpayer

Illustration 1

Mrs Old is a retired widow. Her 1996/97 tax bill was £100.

Her income in 1997/98 consists of:

State pension	3,000	
Occupational pension	15,000	(PAYE £3,044.00)
Building society interest (net)	1,500	(Tax deducted £375.00)
National Savings income bond interest	950	

Tax Liability

Pension income	18,000
Untaxed interest	950
Taxed interest	1,875
Taxable income	£20,825

Tax on	Amount	Tax	Rate
	4,045	0.00	0
	6,925	1,385.00	20%
	9,855	2,266.65	23%
	£20,825	3,651.65	
Deducted at source		3,419.00	
Tax due		£232.65	

She will need to pay:	
On 31 January 1998	0.00
On 31 July 1998	0.00
On 31 January 1999	232.65
	£232.65

(Payments on account are not required as the tax bill for the previous year, £100, is less than the de minimis limit under which payments on account are not required, £500.)

Illustration 2

Mr Big is self-employed and his tax bill in 1995/96 was £15,000. His only income is from his business. He is not married.

In 1996/97 his taxable profits are: £75,000

Tax Liability	Amount	Tax	Rate
Tax on	3,765	0.00	0
	3,900	780.00	20%
	21,600	5,184.00	24%
	45,735	18,294.00	40%
	£75,000	£24,258.00	

Mr Big will have to pay:

For 1996/97

On 31 January 1997	7,500.00
On 31 July 1997	7,500.00
On 31 January 1998	9,258.00
	£24,258.00

and for 1997/98 payments on account will be required as follows:

On 31 January 1998	12,129.00
On 31 July 1998	12,129.00

Illustration 3

How businesses are taxed in 1996/97

Blocks & Co prepares accounts to 30 June.

Taxable profits for each year of account are:

30.6.1994	20,000
30.6.1995	25,000
30.6.1996	35,000
30.6.1997	40,000

The tax bill for 1995/96 is based on taxable profits of 20,000 (previous year).

The tax bill for 1997/98 is based on taxable profits of 40,000 (current year).

The tax bill for 1996/97 is based on taxable profits of 30,000* (transitional).

*ie,	25,000
	35,000
	£60,000 x 50% = £30,000

Changes in the tax law you should know about when planning in 1997

The 1997 Finance Bill was published on 3 January 1997 following the Budget on 26 November 1996. The following is a summary (as of 1 February 1997) of some of the main provisions which could be of relevance to you in your tax planning. The Bill is subject to change before it is enacted (which is most likely to occur in April) and you should therefore remember that the following points may be modified.

INCOME AND GAINS TAX

Rates and allowances

The changes in rates and allowances contained in the Bill can be found in the table at the end of this section.

Rent a Room relief

Those who take lodgers into their home will benefit from an increase of £1,000 in the 'Rent a Room' relief threshold taking it to £4,250 per annum. This will take effect from 6 April 1997.

Reinvestment relief

The rules determining the availability of reinvestment relief for investment in companies with subsidiaries will be extended to those with overseas as well as domestic subsidiaries. In addition, the test to determine 'qualifying companies' will now be dependent on the activities of the group as a whole rather than the activity of each individual company.

Venture Capital Trusts (VCT)/Enterprise Investment Schemes (EIS)

The relaxation of the rules to determine which companies qualify for re-investment relief has also been extended to VCT and EIS investments. Even if one of the subsidiary companies carries on non-qualifying activities, it will not prevent the parent company from qualifying for VCT and EIS investment, provided that this does not constitute a substantial part of the group's activities as a whole.

At present a VCT is required to invest at least 70% of its subscription capital in qualifying shares and securities within three years of launch, irrespective of when the capital was raised. This condition has proved difficult to satisfy and has thus been changed to allow venture capital houses a three-year investment window for the proceeds of each new issue.

All of the above measures will assist the private sector in encouraging new sources of investment. It will also widen the scope of available tax efficient vehicles for the investor.

Taxation of securities
'Qualifying Corporate Bonds' (QCBs) are generally exempt from capital gains tax (individuals) or corporation tax (companies).

Where an individual holds a bond which is not a QCB, he should pay capital gains tax on any gain arising from disposal. In the past, individuals have exchanged shares for bonds which were not QCBs, taking advantage of certain favourable tax rules to defer any taxable gain. At a later date these bonds became QCBs (without triggering a tax charge) and so the potential gain deferred fell out of the charge to tax. From 26 November 1996, any such conversion will give rise to a taxable capital gain, but this will not be deemed to have crystallised until the bond is disposed of.

Employee matters
Scale charges for company-provided fuel have been substantially increased. Car and mileage allowances paid under the Fixed Profit Car Scheme (FPCS) have also been increased.

Tax relief available under Profit Related Pay Schemes (PRP) is to be phased out over two years starting on 1 January 1998. The current tax-free ceiling of £4,000 will be reduced to £2,000 from 1 January 1998 and to £1,000 from 1 January 1999. No relief will be available from 1 January 2000.

Measures are to be introduced to extend the scope of PAYE (effective from 26 November 1996) and NIC (effective from 5 December 1996), to unapproved employer share incentive and share option schemes. The current exemption afforded to all such employer schemes will be retained for Inland Revenue approved employee share schemes only.

As expected, legislation is to be introduced to make the relief for expenditure on travel to work, or away from the normal place of work, both 'simpler and fairer'. Site-based employees will be allowed to deduct all costs of travelling from home to their place of work. The allowable reimbursement in all cases where the employee is eligible to make a claim will be calculated as the additional cost of travel over and above the costs incurred by the employee when travelling to their normal place of work.

National Insurance
There are minor changes in the contribution rates which will be effective from 6 April 1997. The 1997/98 rates are detailed in the table at the end of this section.

INVESTMENTS, TAX SHELTERS AND PENSIONS
Life insurance reform of policy holder taxation
On 27 November 1996, the Inland Revenue issued a Consultative Document putting forward proposals for a major review of the taxation treatment of life assurance policies. The Revenue have invited comments by 30 April 1997.

One of the most significant proposals is to remove the current practice of certifying at the time when they are taken out that the proceeds from some regular premium policies are not taxable. An 'exit test' would be introduced. Payments arising from a life policy will be subject to no further tax provided certain stipulated conditions are met at the time of payment.

Other proposals include:

■ new rules for attributing gains to policy holders and for charging them to tax

■ a new exemption for gains arising on death

■ provisions for policies held under trust preventing gains escaping tax.

Although no specific reference is made to certain insurance policies, such as Guaranteed Income Bonds, comments are also invited on the appropriateness of bringing them within the proposed new regime.

It is also not known at this stage whether any changes that become law in the future will be made retrospective as far as any existing life insurance policies are concerned.

Pensions scheme – earnings cap
The earnings cap on which contributions and benefits are based under approved occupational and personal pension plans is to be increased from £82,200 in 1996/97 to £84,000 in 1997/98.

INHERITANCE TAX
The threshold above which inheritance tax is payable has been raised to £215,000, effective from 6 April 1997.

Agricultural Property Relief has been extended to farmland dedicated to wildlife habitats with effect from 26 November 1996. Land and buildings dedicated under the Government's Habitat Schemes will consequently qualify for inheritance tax relief in the same way as land and buildings actively used for farming.

ANTI-AVOIDANCE LEGISLATION
Some of the main provisions of relevance to personal tax planning involving offshore structures have been the subject of recent debates in the courts. The ambiguity of these provisions has led to uncertainty over many years whether they are capable of applying if the transfers abroad take place before the transferor acquires UK 'ordinarily resident' status. It is proposed that amendments will be made to these provisions to clarify their application and ensure they work effectively. For income arising from 26 November 1996, the legislation will apply to all individuals, whether or not UK ordinarily resident when the transfer is made, but only where a tax avoidance motive exists.

The Government has also indicated its intention to set up a joint working group to review the whole area of anti-avoidance legislation.

1996/97 and 1997/98 tax tables

INCOME TAX RATES 1996/97 AND 1997/98

Rate	Taxable income bands	Tax on band	Rate	Taxable income bands	Tax on band
%	*1996/97*	£	%	*1997/98*	£
20	£1-3,900	780	20	£1-4,100	820
24	£3,901-25,500	5,184	23	£4,101-26,100	5,060
40	Excess		40	Excess	

The rate of tax applicable to discretionary and accumulation and maintenance trusts for 1996/97 is 34% and remains at that rate for 1997/98.

Savings income and dividend income is limited to tax of 20% for basic rate taxpayers in 1996/97 and 1997/98.

CAR AND FUEL BENEFITS

Car benefit 1996/97 and 1997/98

Company cars are taxed on the basis of 35% of the list price of the car when it was new, subject to an £80,000 ceiling. The annual benefit reduces:

- by one-third if annual business mileage between 2,500 and 17,999
- by two-thirds if annual business mileage is 18,000 miles or more.

Where a car is four or more years old at the end of the tax year the benefit will be reduced by a further one-third. It will also be reduced by contributions the employee makes for private use.

Fuel benefit

| | 1996/97 | | 1997/98 | |
	petrol	*diesel*	*petrol*	*diesel*
Engine size	£	£	£	£
1400cc or less	710	640	800	740
1401 - 2000cc	890	640	1,010	740
Over 2000cc	1,320	820	1,490	940
Without a capacity	1,320		1,490	

Reduced to nil if the employee refunds the cost of the whole of the fuel used for private journeys.

INCOME TAX RELIEFS
Principal reliefs

	1996/97 £	1997/98 £
People under age 65		
Personal allowance	3,765	4,045
Married couple's allowance *	1,790	1,830
People aged 65 to 74		
Personal allowance	4,910	5,220
Married couple's allowance *	3,115	3,185
People aged 75 and over		
Personal allowance	5,090	5,400
Married couple's allowance *	3,155	3,225
Income limit for age allowance	15,200	15,600

Other reliefs

Additional relief for single parent *	1,790	1,830
Widow's bereavement *	1,790	1,830
Blind person	1,250	1,280
Mortgage interest loan limit*	30,000	30,000
Life assurance premiums	12$\frac{1}{2}$%	12$\frac{1}{2}$%

(Pre 14 March 1984 contracts only)

* Relief given at 15% in 1996/97 and 1997/98.

Personal pension schemes

Age on 6 April	% of NRE *
35 or less	17.5
36 - 45	20.0
46 - 50	25.0
51 - 55	30.0
56 - 60	35.0
61 or over	40.0

Retirement annuity schemes

Age on 6 April	% of NRE*
50 or less	17.5
51 - 55	20.0
56 - 60	22.5
61 or over	27.5

* net relevant earnings, subject to maximum of £82,200 in 1996/97 and £84,000 in 1997/98.

Enterprise investment scheme 1996/97 and 1997/98

Maximum investment	£100,000
Income tax relief given at	20%

Maximum carry back to previous tax year is lower of £15,000 or half the amount invested on or before 5 October.

Eligible for capital gains tax reinvestment relief for gains on disposals from 29 November 1994.

CAPITAL GAINS TAX

Gains are taxed at the individual's marginal income tax rate. In the case of discretionary and accumulation and maintenance trusts the rate is 34% in 1996/97 and 1997/98 and in the case of life interest trusts 23% in 1997/98 (24% in 1996/97).

Annual exemptions	1996/97	1997/98
Individuals, personal representatives and trusts for disabled persons	6,300	6,500
Other trusts (maximum depending on number of trusts created by same settlor since 1 June 1978)	3,150	3,250

INHERITANCE TAX
Rates

1996/97	*1997/98*
First £200,000 @ NIL	First £215,000 @ NIL

Excess @ 40% (death) 20% (lifetime)

Exemptions 1996/97 and 1997/98

		£
Annual gifts per donor		3,000
Small gifts per donee		250
Gifts on marriage:	from parent	5,000
	from grandparent	2,500
	from others	1,000

Gifts to individuals and certain trusts made more than seven years before death are tax-free.

Charge on gifts within seven years of death

Years since gift	0-3	3-4	4-5	5-6	6-7
% of full charge	100	80	60	40	20

NATIONAL INSURANCE CONTRIBUTIONS
From 6 April 1997

Class I
NOT CONTRACTED OUT

Total weekly earnings	Employee	Employer
Below £62.00	NIL	NIL
£62.00 - £109.99	2% on	3%*
£110.00 - £154.99	first £62	5%*
£155.00 - £209.99	plus 10%	7%*
£210.00 - £465.00	on next	10%*
Over £465.00	£403	10%*
* on all earnings		

CONTRACTED OUT

Total weekly earnings	Employee	Employer First £62	Balance over £62 (COSR Schemes**)	Balance over £62 (COMP Schemes***)
Below £62.00	NIL	NIL		
£62.00 - £109.99	2% on	3%	NIL	1.5%
£110.00 - £154.99	first £62	5%	2%	3.5%
£155.00 - £209.99	plus 8.4%	7%	4%	5.5%
£210.00 - £465.00	on next	10%	7%	8.5%
Over £465.00	£403	10%	7%*	8.5%*

* On earnings over the upper earnings limit the contracted-out rate for employers reverts to 10%.

** COSR = Contracted-Out Salary Related

***COMP = Contracted-Out Money Purchase

Class IA	Employer contribution of 10% on amount of taxable benefit for employer-provided car and fuel
Class II	Self-employed earning £3,480 or more per annum Flat rate of £6.15 per week
Class III	Voluntary Flat rate of £6.05 per week
Class IV	Self-employed 6% of profits or gains between £7,010 and £24,180

NIC compensation for Statutory Maternity Pay
Proposed rate for 1997/98 6.5%

UK Retail Price Index

BASE: 13 JANUARY 1987 = 100

Source: Office for National Statistics

	Jan	Feb	Mar	Apr	May	Jun	Jul	Aug	Sep	Oct	Nov	Dec
1982			79.44	81.04	81.62	81.85	81.88	81.90	81.85	82.26	82.66	82.51
1983	82.61	82.97	83.12	84.28	84.84	84.84	85.30	85.68	86.06	86.36	86.67	86.89
1984	86.84	87.20	87.48	88.64	88.97	89.20	89.10	89.94	90.11	90.67	90.95	90.87
1985	91.20	91.94	92.80	94.78	95.21	95.41	95.23	95.49	95.44	95.59	95.92	96.05
1986	96.25	96.60	96.73	97.67	97.85	97.79	97.52	97.82	98.30	98.45	99.29	99.62
1987	100.00	100.40	100.60	101.80	101.90	101.90	101.80	102.10	102.40	102.90	103.40	103.30
1988	103.30	103.70	104.10	105.80	106.20	106.60	106.70	107.90	108.40	109.50	110.00	110.30
1989	111.00	111.80	112.30	114.30	115.00	115.40	115.50	115.80	116.60	117.50	118.50	118.80
1990	119.50	120.20	121.40	125.10	126.20	126.70	126.80	128.10	129.30	130.30	130.00	129.90
1991	130.20	130.90	131.40	133.10	133.50	134.10	133.80	134.10	134.60	135.10	135.60	135.70
1992	135.60	136.30	136.70	138.80	139.30	139.30	138.80	138.90	139.40	139.90	139.70	139.20
1993	137.90	138.80	139.30	140.60	141.10	141.00	140.70	141.30	141.90	141.80	141.60	141.90
1994	141.30	142.10	142.50	144.20	144.70	144.70	144.00	144.70	145.00	145.20	145.30	146.00
1995	146.00	146.90	147.50	149.00	149.60	149.80	149.10	149.90	150.60	149.80	149.80	150.70
1996	150.20	150.90	151.50	152.60	152.90	153.00	152.40	153.10	153.80	153.80		

Glossary

Additional Voluntary Contributions (AVCs)	Contributions in excess of a member's compulsory contributions, if any, to a company pension scheme.
Administrators	The persons the law appoints to administer your estate if you die without a will.
AIM	The Alternative Investment Market. A mechanism to trade shares which have no full Stock Exchange listing.
Annuity	A series of payments, which may be subject to increase, made during a specified period or until the death of the person receiving the annuity.
Appropriated/ Appropriation	As it relates to share schemes: The date on which the shares are allocated by the trustees to the employee.
Balance sheet	A summary of the value of a business at a given date.
Bare trust	A simple form of trust where the trustees can retain assets and apply them for a child's benefit in minority only, or where the beneficiary is legally incapacitated. In all cases (other than the latter) the trustees must pay over assets at the age of majority.
Bed and breakfasting	An arrangement whereby assets (usually shares) are sold and then are repurchased shortly thereafter.
Beneficiary	As it relates to a trust or estate: The person for whom trust or estate assets are held and for whose benefit they must be applied.
Bonus issue	Free additional shares issued to existing shareholders of a company.
British Government Stock (Gilts)	Loans to the Government which are guaranteed to be repaid, at £100 for each

£100 of nominal stock, at various maturity
dates. They pay interest at a fixed rate.
Index-linked gilts provide interest and
capital repayment linked to any increase in
the Retail Price Index.

Capital conversion plans   A lump sum investment is gradually
transferred into a ten-year 'qualifying' life
policy, for example, where the proceeds will
be tax free after 7.5 years (subject to the
outcome of the consultative Inland Revenue
document on life insurance policy taxation).

Cohabitants   Persons who live together without being
married to each other.

Contracting out   An arrangement whereby employees can opt
out of participation in the State Earnings
Related Pension Scheme and make up those
benefits through a personal pension plan.

Convertible stock   A debt instrument from a company which
pays a fixed rate of interest to the purchaser
who has the right (but not the obligation) to
convert the stock into the underlying shares
usually of the issuing company.

Debentures   Fixed interest securities issued by limited
companies which may be quoted on the
Stock Exchange.

**Decreasing
term assurance**   Life assurance where the cover gradually
decreases as the years go by.

Depreciation   An accountancy term for measuring wear
and tear on business assets.

Disclaimer   A person may decline to accept a gift which
somebody tries to make to him. This can be
done by a deed of disclaimer.

Discretionary trust   A trust where the trustees decide who
receives the income and capital.

Donee   The person who receives a gift.

Donor   The person who makes a gift.

Earnings cap   Remuneration limit on which certain
pension benefits and contributions are
calculated.

**Enhanced
scrip dividends**

Dividends which may be taken either as cash or additional shares, but where the value of such additional shares exceeds the cash dividend.

Executors

The persons you appoint by your will to administer your estate.

Free standing AVCs

Contributions by company pension scheme members to a pension contract separate from the main scheme.

Futures

A contract binding two parties to a sale or purchase at a known future date, at a price fixed when the contract is effected.

Goodwill

The value of a business not attributable to fixed assets.

Guaranteed growth bond

Similar to a guaranteed income bond except that no income is paid but a guaranteed rate of appreciation is returned along with the capital at maturity.

Guaranteed income bond

A single premium insurance policy which gives a guaranteed income each year for a specified period. Upon maturity, the capital is returned.

Guardian

A person you appoint in your will to take care of your minor children.

Hybrid Pension scheme

A company pension scheme where benefits are based on the better of, for example, final pay or the pension that the accumulated fund can buy.

Index linked

An investment which rises in line with an index such as the Retail Price Index or National Average Earnings.

Indexation allowance

An inflation allowance given against chargeable gains by reference to increases in the Retail Price Index.

**Interest in
possession trust**

A trust where some person or persons has a right to income payments but where the trustees may decide who receives capital.

Intestate succession

The general legal rules which apply to your estate to determine who receives your assets if you leave no will.

Lease premium	Arrangement whereby a lump sum payment is made to a landlord as consideration for a lease being granted.
'Legal Rights'	Rights under Scots law which provide for obligatory gifts to certain members of your family if you die.
Options	Financial instruments for which payment gives a right but not an obligation, to buy or sell something at an agreed price on or before a specified date.
Pension mortgage	A mortgage where the lender anticipates the borrower drawing enough from the tax-free cash lump sum in a personal pension plan or retirement annuity policy to repay the debt.
Personal pension plan	A pension scheme under which the self-employed or those employees not members of a company pension scheme can make pension provision. Such plans first became available from 1 July 1988.
Power of attorney	A legal document giving a nominated person authority to deal with your assets.
Qualifying Corporate Bonds (QCB)	Tax favoured corporate debt instruments. Most loan stock issued by UK companies will be regarded as QCBs.
Retirement Annuity Contract	Similar to personal pension plans but not available after 30 June 1988. Contributions are payable gross before any tax relief is given, regardless of the purchaser being employed or self-employed.
Rights issue	New issue of shares for cash initially available only to existing shareholders. Rights to acquire shares not taken up by shareholders may be sold or may lapse.
Scrip dividends	Additional shares issued to existing shareholders in lieu of a dividend distribution.
Settlor	A person who creates a trust or a person who has contributed assets to a trust.
Share options	A right to acquire shares at some time in the future at a price fixed at the date that right is granted.

Single premium bonds Life insurance policies, with no fixed term, which invest the contributions into a wide variety of investment funds.

Staggered vesting Benefits under personal pension plans (and retirement annuity contracts) which are able to be drawn at different times.

Surrender As it relates to insurance: Cancellation of an insurance policy by the payment of a surrender value.

Traded Options Buying and selling options themselves.

'Transfer of value' The amount by which your aggregate assets are reduced when you make a gift.

Trustee A person who administers a trust for the benefit of beneficiaries and has legal ownership of the assets.

Unquoted shares Company shares not quoted on the Stock Exchange (NB. for the purposes of the tax legislation, companies quoted on the Alternative Investment Market (AIM) are not regarded as quoted companies).

Work in progress The value of work completed but unbilled, at any given date.

Tax strategies for individuals

PART

I

"How can I pay less tax?" Hardly a day goes by when an accountant or tax adviser isn't asked that question. Indeed, there are numerous tax-saving strategies people can use to lower their tax bills. We have organised this section of the book in the way we think you should approach the challenge.

Step 1, is to determine what portion of your income is subject to tax and what is not. Income, of course, is not just the money you get in your wage packet or salary. It also includes interest, dividends, rent, royalties, pensions, annuities or maintenance payments among many other things.

Step 2, is to calculate the expenses you have incurred during the year and other amounts which can be deducted from your income before calculating your tax. We have included many suggestions for maximising your claims to allowances and therefore lowering the amount of tax you have to pay.

Many consider **Step 3,** checking the calculation of your tax, the trickiest part of the process. It can involve several calculations and there are pitfalls for the unwary. You will also have to make certain decisions – for example, if you pay pension premiums, whether you should elect to treat them as paid in the previous tax year. Some of these decisions can help to lower the tax you pay.

Finally, **Step 4,** represents both the end and a new beginning. The well-informed taxpayer can take steps at the end of the tax year that can reduce or postpone taxes until a later year. We have included a chapter on year-end planning opportunities which also illustrates how you can start planning so that less tax will have to be paid in future years.

This is the first year when you will prepare your tax returns under the new self assessment regime which begins in 1996/97. If you want to be aware of what will be required of you, you should refer in particular to *'An overview of self assessment'* at the beginning of this book and to Chapter 4.

1 Tax on income

WHAT INCOME IS TAXED?

Income tax is levied on your 'taxable income', in a 'tax year', which runs from 6 April one year to 5 April the next. This book deals with the rules which apply to your income for the 1996/97 tax year which runs from 6 April 1996 to 5 April 1997.

Your 'taxable income' is determined by subtracting authorised deductions from the income you receive which is subject to tax. These deductions are for the most part tax allowances and certain out-of-pocket expenditures.

Which types of income are subject to tax?

All income received, including that from the following sources, is normally subject to tax and has to be included in your income tax calculations:

- salaries, wages, commissions, tips and any other payment from your job, plus the value of certain employee benefits
- payments for consultancy, freelance or spare-time work
- income from a business
- your share of income from a partnership, whether or not it is distributed to you
- income from pensions and annuities
- interest from savings and investments
- dividends from shares and distributions from unit trusts
- rents and royalties
- income from an interest in an estate or trust
- certain maintenance payments and social security benefits
- income from certain life insurance policies.

Certain types of income, however, are tax-free, meaning no tax will be charged on it. Some examples are:

- sums paid by your employer under a profit-related pay scheme (up to certain limits)
- certain earnings from working abroad
- certain employee benefits
- certain payments when you lose a job
- certain maintenance payments and social security benefits
- income from a Personal Equity Plan
- interest on National Savings Certificates

- proceeds from most life insurance policies
- most grants and scholarships for education.

Details of which sources of income are subject to tax and the special rules applying to each type are given in the remainder of this chapter.

Certain receipts do not count as income and so are not subject to income tax. The main ones are:

- gifts and presents you receive (as long as they are genuine gifts, not in return for work you have done)
- winnings from competitions, lotteries or gambling
- if you receive money from selling something this does not normally count as income (but you may be liable to capital gains tax – see Chapter 2)
- if you inherit money from someone who dies, it does not count as income (but it may be liable to inheritance tax – see Chapter 15). However, any income you get from investing inherited money, income from investments you inherit, income from a trust set up under a will, and income paid to you during the period of administration of a will are all subject to the income tax rules in this chapter.

What you can deduct

After you have calculated your total income subject to tax, you are ready to make the deductions necessary to establish your 'taxable income' on which tax is calculated. Other reliefs then reduce your income tax liability.

Chapter 3, *'Tax Reliefs'* describes many of these reliefs, deductions and exemptions, but most of those which apply to a particular type of income (eg, expenses in your job) are described in this chapter along with the respective type of income.

The order in which the deductions are made can have different tax results. Generally you may subtract allowable deductions in whichever order results in the greatest reduction of your liability to income tax, but you must deduct personal reliefs after other deductions.

Some deductions are automatic but others must be claimed, often within strict time limits, and you should make sure you know what the time limits are and how to make a claim so that you don't lose out on allowable deductions. A checklist is given in Chapter 6.

WAGES, SALARIES AND OTHER EARNED INCOME
What you have to include

As a general rule, you must include in your total income everything you receive as payment for services you provide. This includes wages, salaries, commissions and tips. The main exception to this is profit-related pay which your employer pays you under a scheme which is approved by the Inland Revenue. You can receive up to 20% of your pay (up to a maximum of £4,000) from such a scheme in each tax year, and this amount will be completely free of tax (but see *'Changes in the tax law you should know about when planning in 1997'*).

Benefits in kind

If you are paid 'in kind' with goods, services or vouchers, for example, you normally have to include the 'cash equivalent' of such a benefit in your total income. However, some benefits are tax-free, and people earning less than £8,500 a year may not have to pay tax on others – see page 7.

The following are some of the more common forms of benefits in kind that are normally subject to tax:

1 *Car provided for personal use* If your employer provides you with a car you are taxed on an amount which is basically 35% of the car's list price when new, though there may be reductions to this depending on your business mileage, the age of the car and whether you pay your employer anything for your private use. The list price includes the cost of accessories but not those which are special modifications made for disabled drivers. There is a further tax charge on a pre-set scale if your employer also provides you with fuel for personal use. See the tax tables at the beginning of this book for details.

2 *Company vans* If your employer allows you to use a company van up to a gross vehicle weight of 3,500 kilograms for private travel, you are taxed on a notional income of £500 (or £350 if it is more than four years old at the end of the tax year). If the van weighs more than 3,500 kilograms you are only taxed if you use it wholly or mainly for private travel. The tax charge is then based on the running costs of the vehicle and its market value when first made available to you. However, no charge is made for occasional private use.

3 *Mobile telephones* If your employer provides you with a mobile telephone which is available for your private use you are taxed on a notional receipt of £200.

4 *Provision of living accommodation and connected expenses* If your employer provides you with living accommodation and it isn't necessary for you to live there to perform your duties effectively, you are taxed on the annual value of the property. This will normally be the rent paid in the case of leased accommodation or the gross rateable value where your employer owns an interest in the property. If the cost to your employer of providing the property exceeds £75,000 there is an additional charge based on this excess. Any heating, lighting, cleaning, maintenance, decoration costs or other similar expenses met by your employer are also subject to tax.

5 *Beneficial loans* If your employer lends you more than £5,000 and does not charge you interest, or charges interest at less than the 'official rate' (a rate published from time to time by the Inland Revenue), you are taxed on the difference between the amount of interest you actually pay and the amount you would have paid if interest had been charged at the 'official rate'.

6 *Rights to acquire shares* If your employer provides you with any rights to acquire shares in the company, when you exercise that right you are taxed on the value of the shares less any amounts you pay for the shares. However, there are concessions for certain Inland Revenue approved share schemes. These are described further in this chapter under *'Employee share schemes and trusts'*.

7 *Medical insurance* If your employer provides you with private medical insurance you are taxed on the cost of the premium he pays (unless it only covers you whilst working abroad).

8 *Vouchers and credit tokens* If you receive a voucher or token which can be exchanged for goods or services you are taxed on the expense incurred by your employer in providing it for you.

Tax-free benefits in kind

Certain fringe benefits you receive from your employer are specifically excluded from taxation. These include:

1 *Car parking expenses* The provision of a car parking space at or near your place of work is not subject to tax.

2 *Canteen facilities* The benefit of being provided with meals available for staff generally in any canteen is tax-free.

3 *Child care* If your employer operates a workplace nursery that meets the Revenue requirements you are not taxed on the benefit. Your employer will confirm whether the workplace nursery qualifies or not.

4 *Scholarships* A scholarship paid from a company trust fund or scheme which is coincidentally paid to an employee's child is tax-free provided it is not paid by reason of the parent's employment. Not more than 25% of scholarship awards made can go to families of employees.

5 *No-additional-cost service* If you receive services from your employer which are regularly offered to his customers and your employer incurs no additional cost in providing those services for you, you do not have to include their value as part of your income. Example: air flights for airline employees.

6 *Medical check-ups* You are not taxed on the cost of a routine medical check or medical screening paid for by your employer.

7 *Meal vouchers* These are tax-free provided they can be used for meals only and are not worth more than 15p per day.

8 *Pension schemes* If your employer has a pension scheme you are not subject to tax on the contributions which he makes directly for your benefit, provided that the plan is approved by the Revenue. You may be able to make contributions into the scheme up to 15% of your salary. Such contributions will be a tax-efficient deduction from your taxable salary. If your employer has no pension plan or you choose not to join it, you can make provision yourself by taking out a personal pension plan. See under the heading *'Pension contributions'* in Chapter 3 for more details on contributions to pension plans which qualify as tax deductions.

9 *Sports facilities* If your employer provides sports facilities or other recreational facilities which are available to his employees generally you will not have to pay tax on this benefit.

10 *Incidental expenses incurred on business trips* If your employer reimburses you for incidental personal expenses such as newspapers, telephone calls home and

laundry which you incur when you are away from home on business, you will not have to pay tax on the reimbursement provided it does not exceed the limit. This is £5 for every night spent away from home on business in the UK and £10 for every night spent abroad. If reimbursement exceeds these limits, the whole sum, and not just the excess, becomes taxable.

11 *Liability insurance* The cost of directors' and employees' liability insurance paid by your employer is not taxable, or is a deductible expense, if paid by you. This applies to costs in meeting work-related liabilities (or the cost of meeting any uninsured liabilities) and applies to expenses incurred up to six years after the employment has ended.

12 *Training expenses* You are not taxed on the benefit you obtain if your employer pays expenses you incur in pursuing certain training courses provided:

- you are under 21 when the course begins, or
- you are acquiring new skills needed for your job which will improve your effectiveness.

Expenses can include:

- fees and the cost of books
- travel to and from the course
- the reasonable costs of meals while you are there.

If your employer encourages you to take paid leave to attend a full-time UK course of the above nature which lasts four or more weeks, expenses in the above categories which you incur personally can be subtracted from your wages before working out your tax liability.

The text above mentions just a few examples. You should consult with your employer to find out how to treat a particular item.

Employees earning £8,500 or less

Provided you are not a company director, if you are paid at a rate of £8,500 a year or less you are not liable to tax on many benefits provided by your employer such as a car, van, or mobile telephone. Exceptions are living accommodation and vouchers or credit tokens on which you will be taxed. In working out whether your earnings exceed this limit you must, however, include the value of any benefit that would be taxable if your earnings exceeded the limit.

Ex gratia payments

If you receive a lump sum payment in connection with the termination of your employment, the first £30,000 may not be subject to tax. This applies in particular to payments of compensation for loss of office, to redundancy payments even if they exceed the sum which your employer is obliged by law to pay you, and to payments in respect of death or disability due to an accident.

A termination payment is not exempt if:

- your employment contract entitles you to receive it, or

- it is common practice for an employer to make an ex gratia payment to a particular class of employees, or
- it is made on, or in anticipation of, retirement or death.

Employee share schemes and trusts

You do not have to include as income the value of certain share options granted to you under approved share option schemes.

Approved executive share options granted to you before 17 July 1995 fall into this category. Provided that the option is exercised between three and ten years from the date of the grant, and at least three years after any previous qualifying exercise of options, any gain attributable to the shares on exercising such options is not charged to income tax but any gain realised when the shares are sold will be subject to capital gains tax. The gain from exercising options granted under such schemes after 17 July 1995 is subject to income tax unless the aggregate value of all shares subject to approved options held by you at the time of granting new options is £30,000 or less.

You may also have share options granted under an approved savings-related share option scheme. Under this scheme you save into a Save As You Earn account for either three or five years to fund the price of buying the shares at the end of the savings period when the share option is exercised. Again the grant or exercise of such options is not liable to income tax.

In an approved profit-sharing scheme shares are 'appropriated' to an employee but are held by trustees on his behalf. The value of the shares at the time of 'appropriation' is not subject to tax and no tax liability arises when they are released to the employee provided the shares have been held by the trustees for three years. This time limit was reduced from five years by the Finance Act 1996 and if you are in such a scheme you should check with your employer how the change impacts on you.

In all cases the shares are subject to capital gains tax when they are sold. Where the gain on exercise of options has already been charged to income tax, the share value at exercise is treated as the cost of the shares when sold for the purpose of working out the amount subject to capital gains tax.

Shares acquired under a savings-related share option scheme or released from a profit sharing scheme can be transferred into a single company Personal Equity Plan (PEP) within ninety days of the exercise of the option or the release without incurring a capital gains tax liability. The maximum market value that can be transferred in this way is £3,000. As shares held within a PEP do not incur any tax liabilities, this can be an excellent way of avoiding tax on any increase in value of shares allotted to you.

Tax Saver

If the ninety-day period spans the end of one tax year and the beginning of another you may be able to transfer shares to the value of £6,000 – two years' worth of PEP allowances – by transferring £3,000 before 5 April and £3,000 after 6 April.

P60 and P11D Forms

Shortly after the end of the tax year your employer will provide you with a form P60 which will show your total earnings for the tax year and any tax which he has deducted. If you earn £8,500 or more and have received benefits-in-kind he must also, by 6 July following the end of the tax year, provide you with a copy of form P11D which he submits to the Revenue, or a similar statement showing the value of the benefits on which you will be taxed.

Expenses in employment

This section covers a variety of expenses that you can claim on your tax return. Expenses which are allowed are subtracted from your income before working out your tax – so they reduce the amount of tax you have to pay.

The general rule is that you can deduct an expense in employment provided that you have incurred it wholly, exclusively and necessarily in the performance of your employment duties. That includes expenses of travelling in the performance of your duties but does not, for example, include the cost of travelling from home to your place of work. The Inland Revenue take a very narrow view of what may be deducted under this general rule, but with careful and proper planning you may be able to deduct more than you think.

Expenses reimbursed by your employer

Any expenses which your employer pays to you or reimburses to you should be included as income from your employment unless your employer has been granted a dispensation (see below). Your employer will not have received a dispensation for any general allowance ('round sum') for entertaining or other expense that is paid to you. Expense payments also include any expenses which you have settled by means of a credit card in your employer's name.

Tax Filing Tip

You must claim a deduction in the Employment (Page E2) section of your tax return for the amount of these expenses.

Dispensations

To save your employer work, if he satisfies his Tax Inspector that expenses he pays or reimburses are allowable business expenses, the Inspector may issue him with a notice of nil liability for these expenses, ie, a notice that he does not need to include them on the annual returns he makes to the Inland Revenue. Nor need you, as his employee, show them in your income tax return. As a result, you do not need to claim the expenses as a deduction. Usually dispensations will be given for travelling and meal costs at approved rates for absences on business journeys and they may cover other things such as reimbursement of business telephone calls, etc. You should check with your employer whether a dispensation is in force for any expense which you incur and which he pays or reimburses.

Travelling and subsistence expenses

Travelling expenses are only deductible for business journeys which involve travelling from one place of work to another. Journeys from home to your normal place of work are not usually business journeys. However, if you are required to work elsewhere on a particular occasion and you go there straight from home or return directly home after such a trip, you can deduct the lower of the expenses actually incurred and those which would have been incurred if the journey had started and finished at your normal place of work.

It is more difficult to decide whether you have a normal place of work if you are required to work at different locations such as your customers' premises or building sites. Where you have no normal place of work but work on site at different places from time to time, you cannot deduct the travel from home to the site. If, however, you are required to travel as an integral part of your job (for example a travelling salesman) and don't have any normal place of work, you are allowed to deduct the expenses. For site workers the cost of the journey in travelling between sites is allowed.

Tax Alert

The rules on travel expenses are to be relaxed from 6 April 1998 so that tax relief will be given for the additional cost of a business journey rather than the lesser of cost of travel from home and the cost of travel from the normal place of work. It will also allow site-based employees to claim the cost of travel to the site.

If you are temporarily working away from your usual work place and the distance involved makes it necessary for you to stay overnight, you can claim a deduction for accommodation and meal costs. You can also claim expenses for meals when you are engaged on a business journey but not otherwise. Remember you cannot deduct any personal expenses incurred other than the 'Incidental expenses' discussed earlier, on page 6, whether on a business journey or not.

Motoring expenses

If you use your own car on your employer's business you can claim deductions for the actual expenses you incur which relate to your business use of the car. You have to keep detailed records of your motoring expenses and your business and private mileage.

You are also entitled to deduct a 'capital allowance' on the cost of the car. In the first year this is calculated at 25% of the cost of the car, and in subsequent years at 25% of the balance, eg:

	Allowance	*Balance*
Car cost	£10,000	–
capital allowance – year 1	£2,500	£7,500
capital allowance – year 2		
£7,500 x 25% =	£1,875	£5,625
capital allowance – year 3		
£5,625 x 25% =	£1,406	etc

The maximum allowance in a particular year is limited to £3,000.

The capital allowance deductible from your taxable income is only that proportion of the allowance which reflects the business use you make of the car. For example, if your total mileage in the tax year is 12,000 miles of which 4,000 miles were for business, you can claim one-third of the capital allowance as a deduction. But when you sell the car, if the proceeds exceed the 'written down value' (ie, the initial cost less the capital allowances to date), you will be charged tax on the difference. Effectively, some of the capital allowances previously given will be clawed back in the year in which you sell the car.

If you obtain a loan to buy the car which you use in your employer's business and on which capital allowances are available, you can also claim relief for the interest due on the loan within three years of the end of the tax year in which you took out the loan. In this case you do not need to show that acquiring the car was necessary for the performance of your duties. The relief is restricted to reflect the business use of the vehicle.

For some employees, keeping the necessary records of their business trips can be quite burdensome and many employers operate a 'fixed profit car scheme' under which they reimburse their employees a flat rate mileage allowance at a scale approved by the Inland Revenue. Where the fixed profit car scheme is in operation, you do not need to pay tax on the expenses reimbursed. You can opt out of the fixed profit car scheme and claim relief for actual expenses incurred if you prefer.

For employees using their own vehicles, whose employers have not entered into the 'fixed profit' car scheme, the Finance Act 1996 included provisions to enable such employees to also use the tax-free mileage rates to calculate the tax due.

Employees have the choice between Schemes A and B below.

A Flat rate allowance for all engine sizes

Miles	Pence per mile 1996/97	1997/98
Up to 4,000	38½p	40p
Over 4,000	21p	22½p

B Alternative scale based on engine size

Engine size (cc)	Up to 4,000 miles		Over 4,000 miles	
	1996/97	1997/98	1996/97	1997/98
Up to 1000 cc	27p	28p	16p	17p
1001 – 1500 cc	34p	35p	19p	20p
1501 – 2000 cc	43p	45p	23p	25p
Over 2000 cc	61p	63p	32p	36p

The fixed profit car scheme allowance includes capital allowances due on your car. It does not, however, cover any interest relief due on borrowing to buy the car so make sure you claim any deduction due for this on your tax return.

Working outside the UK

If the duties of your employment are performed entirely abroad, you can deduct the cost of your travel from any place in the UK (including your home) to take up the overseas employment. You can also deduct the cost of your return when it ends. This applies provided that your employer is resident in the UK, or if non-resident, you are 'domiciled' in the UK. (The concept of domicile is explained in Chapter 5.) If you work partly in and partly outside the UK, you are allowed to deduct the cost of journeys borne by your employer provided that the journeys are made wholly and exclusively for the purpose of performing duties which can only be performed outside the UK or, the cost is that of returning to the UK afterwards. In addition, where your employer provides board and lodging or reimburses its cost, a deduction should be available.

If you work outside the UK for a continuous period of 60 days or more, you can claim a deduction for the costs of up to two outward and homeward journeys by your spouse and children in any tax year. Again your employer must pay or reimburse the cost and the journeys must be undertaken during your absence working abroad. Your children must be under the age of 18 at the beginning of a journey in order to qualify for relief.

Spouse travelling with you

Other than under the special rules given above for employees working abroad, you will not normally receive a deduction for the travelling and subsistence expenses of your spouse accompanying you on a business trip. Exceptionally, if you can show that there is some practical reason why those expenses are also wholly, exclusively and necessarily incurred in the performance of your duties, some relief may be allowed, eg, if you are in very poor health so that it would not be reasonable to expect you to travel alone, or if your spouse were required jointly to host a series of business entertaining occasions. Merely attending functions will not suffice.

Relocation expenses

If you move home to start a new job or transfer within your employer's organisation and your employer pays some of your removal expenses, you will not be taxed on the amount he pays if it is an 'eligible expense' (see below) and it is within the limit of £8,000.

Removal expenses which are eligible for deduction are:

- expenses of disposing of your old home
- expenses of acquiring your new home
- expenses of an abortive acquisition
- expenses of moving your furniture and belongings
- travelling and subsistence expenses
- bridging loan expenses
- duplicate expenses.

Expenses of disposal You must have had ownership of all or part of your former home in order to claim these expenses. They consist of:

- legal expenses
- penalties for redeeming your mortgage
- fees of estate agents, etc
- advertising expenses
- disconnection charges for gas, electricity, telephone, etc
- insurance, maintenance and security costs for the home while unoccupied
- any rent paid.

Expenses of acquisition Again you must acquire ownership or part ownership of your new home. The allowable expenses are:

- legal expenses
- arrangement fees connected with a loan
- insurance in connection with the loan
- survey fees
- land registry fees
- stamp duty
- connection charges for gas, electricity, telephone, etc.

Expenses of an abortive acquisition The expenses of acquisition listed above are also allowable even if you did not complete your purchase because of circumstances outside your control.

Costs of transporting furniture and belongings These include:

- insurance for the removal
- packing and unpacking costs
- temporary storage charges
- detaching and attaching domestic fittings.

Travelling and subsistence expenses Allowable expenses consist of:

- you and your family visiting the new area for reasons connected with the move
- travelling between your old home and your new job
- subsistence costs
- the travelling costs of your family from your old home to your new home and related subsistence costs.

Bridging loan expenses To qualify you must own all or part of your old home and your new home. If the new loan exceeds the market value of your interest in your old home, interest payable on the excess is not eligible.

Duplicate expenses The expenses allowable under this category are expenses incurred on the purchase of domestic goods which replace goods used at your old home but which are not suitable for use at your new home.

Note that you cannot claim deduction for council tax paid on your old home while it is lying empty.

The total value of all the removal expenses and benefits you can receive tax-free under the above categories from your employer is £8,000. Any excess is subject to income tax.

You cannot claim a deduction for :

- mortgage or housing subsidies (even though the house you moved to is in a higher-cost area)
- interest payments for the mortgage on your existing home
- costs of joining new clubs
- losses on partly-used season tickets
- any loss on the sale of your old home
- penalties on school fees for giving insufficient notice of withdrawing your child from school, etc.

Professional fees
If you have to pay fees to a professional body in order to carry on your profession or which are relevant to your work, you can deduct the subscription from your earnings.

Tax Saver

Your professional body will tell you whether it has been approved by the Inland Revenue and how much you can claim.

Business entertainment
Generally, you can claim entertaining expenses as an employment expense in the same way as you can any other expense. You must show that you are obliged to entertain for business reasons; entertaining personal friends or business acquaintances for social reasons is not an allowable cost. You can deduct the cost of your own meal where the entertaining includes such costs.

The deduction applies only to specific entertainment costs which your employer meets or reimburses to you; if he gives you a general ('round sum') allowance (ie, a fixed sum) to cover entertaining, this will not be regarded as a deductible expense. You cannot deduct the cost of entertaining your own colleagues.

Keeping records
You should keep careful records of expenditure which you incur and which you wish to deduct for tax purposes. The Inland Revenue may ask you to provide supporting information such as copy invoices or other evidence that you incurred the expense.

Foreign earnings deduction
If you go to work abroad but are counted as tax-resident in the UK, you will remain liable to UK tax on what you earn abroad. You will normally be regarded

as tax-resident in the UK if your period of full-time employment overseas does not include a complete tax year.

However, if you work abroad for more than a year, you can claim a deduction equal to 100% of your overseas earnings, as long as any visits you make to the UK during your period overseas meet certain conditions. This means the whole of what you earn abroad would be free of UK tax, though it may be taxed abroad.

In order for your period abroad to count as a 'qualifying period' and to secure the 100% deduction:

- the 'qualifying period' (ie, from the day you first went to work abroad up to the day you finally return home) must be 365 days or more
- you must not make a visit to the UK of more than 62 days
- the number of days you have spent in the UK must not be more than one-sixth of the total number of days since the beginning of the qualifying period. This test is applied at the end of each stay abroad (ie, each time you visit the UK).

If a visit to the UK means you exceed one of these limits, all your foreign earnings so far will be liable to UK tax. A new qualifying period can start to run from a different date of departure, so the entire qualifying period is not necessarily lost.

Tax Alert

There is legislation which enables the Inland Revenue to challenge any arrangements whereby the earnings for a qualifying period may be artificially weighted when compared with the earnings received outside that period or from an associated employment.

A day of absence from the UK is one on which you were out of the UK at midnight and therefore includes the day of departure from the UK but not a day of arrival. If you make more than one return visit to the UK during a potentially qualifying period of absence, you should keep a cumulative record of the total length of the period since you first went abroad and the total number of days you spend in the UK. It is important you check your 'one-sixth limit' has not been exceeded.

Example:

You left the UK on 1 November 1995 to work abroad.

You returned for holidays from 20 March to 10 April 1996 and from 1 August to 21 August 1996.

You complete your overseas assignment and return home on 24 December 1996.

	Days in UK	Days out of UK	Cumulative days in UK	Cumulative days in period	1/6th test
Abroad 1 Nov 95-20 Mar 96		140	0	140	0
UK 20 Mar 96-10 Apr 96	21				
Abroad 10 Apr 96-1 Aug 96		113	21	274	45
UK 1 Aug 96-21 Aug 96	20				
Abroad 21 Aug 96-24 Dec 96		125	41	419	69

Your total qualifying period is 419 days. No visit to the UK exceeds 62 days.

The number of days in the visit from 20 March to 10 April is 21 so when you return on 1 August you have not spent more than one-sixth of the total period of 274 days in the UK.

When you return on 24 December your total days spent in the UK will be 41 which is still less than one-sixth of the total period of 419 days. Note: the one-sixth test is only applied at the end of a period spent overseas, not at the end of a period spent in the UK.

Therefore the whole of what you earned abroad would be free of UK tax.

Keep a very careful note of your days in and out of the UK and check them carefully before you make any return visit to the UK. You can regulate your time in the UK to minimise your tax. Losing the 100% deduction could be a very expensive mistake.

Checking tax due on income from employment

The UK has one of the most sophisticated and effective systems in the world for collecting tax on income from employment. It is known as the Pay As You Earn system or more generally, PAYE. For many taxpayers, the PAYE system works so efficiently in collecting tax from wages and salaries each pay day that the correct amount is collected by the end of the tax year. In these cases it is not necessary to complete a tax return at the end of the year unless required by the Inland Revenue. However, if you receive benefits in kind from your employer, or if your PAYE code was not correctly calculated, the tax deducted under PAYE may not be correct and you will need to complete a tax return to determine the amount of tax overpaid or underpaid.

Code numbers

The key to the accurate operation of PAYE is the code number the Inland Revenue sends you on a Notice of Coding. Each time your employer pays you he uses the code number to refer to tax tables which tell him how much of the payment is taxable. A second set of tables then tells him how much tax is due on the taxable amount.

Your code number is a matter for agreement between you and your Inspector of Taxes. Your employer must deduct the amount of tax appropriate to the code he has been given by the Inland Revenue. If he is not notified of a code, he is obliged to operate an emergency code which assumes that the only deduction you are entitled to is your personal allowance. If this code is being used you may find that too much or too little tax is deducted.

The value of the code number reflects the deductions which are available to be set against the wage, salary or pension liable to tax. The code number can, therefore, be adapted to collect any tax due on untaxed sources of income such as benefits in kind or even any interest received gross. This is done by deducting the income or the value of benefits from your allowances. Similarly, if you are due extra deductions the allowances given in your notice of coding can be increased. Where you have two or more employments, all the allowances will normally be set against the income from one of them, leaving the others to be taxed in full.

Your code number is one-tenth of your net allowances rounded down, followed by a suffix letter. The letter shows the personal allowances to which you are entitled (eg, L means you are a single person and H means you get the personal allowance plus either the married couple's allowance or additional personal allowance). When the amounts of personal allowances are changed, employers can immediately adjust codes to the new rates by referring to the suffix. There are some other codes which are used in special situations:

Code	Meaning
OT	There are no allowances to be set against income.
NT	No tax should be deducted from your earnings.
BR	Tax is to be deducted at basic rate only.
DO	Tax is to be deducted at the 40% rate.
K (prefix)	An amount will be added to rather than deducted from your taxable income.

K codes require further explanation. Sometimes items from which tax cannot be deducted at source exceed your personal allowances. Typically this might arise if you receive benefits in kind such as a car. For pensioners it may arise if you receive a State pension and an occupational pension. In such cases you may have a negative code (a K code) which works by producing an amount which is added to your actual pay to arrive at your taxable pay.

Some adjustments to your notice of coding may be difficult to understand. This is the case with allowances which are given at a fixed rate. For example, with the married couple's allowance relief is given at 15% for 1996/97 and 1997/98. The allowance will be shown in full (£1,790: 1996/97 and £1,830: 1997/98) on your Notice of Coding, but if nothing else were done you would get relief on this amount at your highest rate of tax. Therefore there will also be an Allowance Restriction shown. For 1996/97 and 1997/98 these will be £671 and £636 respectively if you are a basic rate taxpayer, or £1,119 and £1,144 respectively if the Inland Revenue expect you to be a higher rate taxpayer. These reductions leave you with a reduced allowance which, multiplied by 24% (23%: 1997/98) or 40% respectively, give the correct tax deduction of £268.50 for 1996/97 and £274.50 for 1997/98.

Another confusing entry arises if the Inland Revenue collect unpaid tax for an earlier year through your notice of coding. To collect £100 of tax they will need to restrict your allowances by £416 (£435: 1997/98) if you are likely to be a basic rate taxpayer or by £250 if you are likely to be a higher rate taxpayer.

The adjustments to your notice of coding just described involve an estimate of your likely top tax rate. Because it is an estimate you should always check its accuracy at the end of the tax year. If your tax rate was higher or lower the wrong amount of tax will have been deducted under the PAYE system.

Checking your notice of coding

As the Inland Revenue will rely on the PAYE system to deduct the correct amount of tax, it follows that you should check your notice of coding when it is issued. If you disagree with it, write to your Inspector of Taxes immediately.

Starting a job and changing employment

If you are starting a new job and have not previously been in employment during the tax year, your employer will ask you to provide certain information and complete a declaration on Form P46 to enable the issue of a code number for you. Until this is done, the employer will use the emergency code mentioned above so it is in your interest to complete the form as quickly as possible.

When you leave an employment you will receive a form P45. The form is in four parts, one of which your former employer will send to the tax office immediately you leave and parts two and three of which you should give to your new employer. The remaining part is for you to keep to help you complete your tax return under self assessment. The P45 contains a record of the last entries on your former employer's payroll records and normally provides the starting figures for a new employer, thus ensuring that PAYE continues to operate smoothly even if you change jobs in the middle of a tax year.

Checking your final tax

If the Inland Revenue think that you have underpaid or overpaid tax they will issue a tax return. If you want the Tax Inspector to calculate the tax overpaid or underpaid you must send back the completed tax return by 30 September. If you calculate the tax due yourself, the return must be sent back to the Inspector no later than 31 January if you are to avoid a penalty.

If, after the end of the tax year, you believe you have paid the wrong amount of tax under the PAYE system and have not been sent a tax return you should ask the tax office to send you one.

If you have overpaid tax you should receive a repayment once the Tax Inspector has received and checked the tax return. If you have underpaid tax you will be required to pay over the unpaid tax by 31 January following the end of the tax year. If the sum involved is up to £1,000 the Inland Revenue should adjust your code number for the following year so that the unpaid tax is collected along with the tax due on your following year's income. In this case you should ensure your return reaches the Inspector by 30 September.

If you do not want any underpaid tax collected through your tax code you will need to inform the Inspector and pay the tax no later than 31 January.

PENSIONS

Employers' pensions and personal pensions

Pensions which you receive from employers' approved pension schemes to which you have belonged and from retirement annuity contracts and personal pension plans which you have taken out, are liable to tax in the same way as earnings and should be entered on your tax return on page 4 of the main body of the tax return. The same applies if you receive a widow's or dependant's pension paid under these schemes.

All such pensions are taxed under the PAYE system (see above), so if your tax coding is correct the right amount of tax should be deducted.

For more details about employers' pensions and personal pensions, see Chapters 3 and 14.

State pensions

Under the UK social security system everyone is entitled to a State retirement pension provided they have an adequate National Insurance contribution record and have reached the State pension age of 65 for a man or 60 for a woman (the State retirement age for women is being increased to 65 but will be phased in gradually between the years 2010 and 2020). There are various types of State pension, all of which are chargeable to income tax and must be included on your tax return. These include the basic pension, additional pension from the State earnings-related pension scheme (SERPS), the age addition for people over the age of 80, and graduated pension for those who paid graduated contributions between April 1961 and April 1975. In addition, if your State pension is increased because you have deferred retirement beyond the normal State pension age or if your pension is increased to provide for a spouse or a childminder, this too is subject to income tax. However, additional sums paid for child dependants are tax-free. The entitlement to State pension is based on each individual's own contribution record but some women are entitled to a pension based on their husband's contribution record. Even if the pension received is based on the husband's contributions, a wife is still taxed on her State pension as her own income and not as her husband's.

Other State pensions include war pensions which are payable to those who have served in the armed forces and suffered disablement due to an injury or disease attributable to service. A war pension may be paid to a widow whose husband died from an injury or wound attributable to his service. War pensions are exempt from income tax.

Widows' pensions

Women aged between 45 and 65 when their husband died may be entitled to a widow's pension from the State. This too is subject to income tax. Widows under 45 who have children for whom Child Benefit is payable may be entitled to Widowed Mother's Allowance. This allowance is also taxable.

Tax Filing Tip

State pensions should be shown on page 4 in the main body of the tax return under the question dealing with UK pensions, retirement annuities and social security benefits.

NATIONAL INSURANCE

Class I contributions

People in employment pay Class I National Insurance contributions. The rate of Class I contributions varies according to the level of your earnings. The figures in brackets are the new 1997/98 rates applicable from 6 April 1997. In 1996/97 you do not have to pay any Class I contributions if your earnings are £60.99 per week or less (£61.99). If your earnings are £61 per week (£62) or more you pay 2% on the first £61 (£62) of your earnings and 10% on your earnings between £61 (£62) and £455 (£465) per week. If you have contracted out of the State Earnings-Related Pension Scheme (SERPS), then the 10% rate is reduced to 8.2% (8.4%). Contributions are deducted when your wage or salary is paid to you and the deductions are paid directly by your employer to the Inland Revenue along with any PAYE that has been deducted.

Your employer also has to pay a contribution which rises according to your earnings level over four different bands. Again, he pays no contribution if he pays you less than £61 (£62) per week and his maximum contribution is 10.2% (10%) on earnings of £210 (£210) and over per week.

National Insurance contributions are payable on most income that is liable to Schedule E taxation (broadly, the income of an employed person). Exceptions include certain payments in kind or where your employer provides board or lodging or services or other facilities, and payments by way of pension. Contributions are not payable on a redundancy payment or reimbursement of expenses actually incurred in your employment.

Class IA contributions

If your employer provides you with a car on which you are taxed as a benefit in kind, your employer must pay a Class IA contribution on the amount of the taxable benefit of the car and on any fuel benefit. The rate of the Class IA contribution is the same as the maximum Class I contribution for employers, ie, 10.2% of the taxable benefit for 1996/97 and 10% for 1997/98.

Class II contributions

If you are self-employed and aged between 16 and 65 for men (60 for women), you must pay a Class II contribution. Most people pay this by making a direct debit from their bank account to the Department of Social Security but alternatively you can be sent a quarterly bill. The normal rate of Class II contribution for 1996/97 is £6.05 per week (£6.15 per week for 1997/98).

If your earnings are under £3,430 for 1996/97 (£3,480 for 1997/98) you can apply to the Department of Social Security for a small earnings exception. You will not then have to pay Class II contributions.

You will also not be liable to pay Class II contributions for any complete week in which you are out of the country or in receipt of incapacity benefit or otherwise incapable of work throughout the week.

Class IV contributions

Class IV contributions are paid by the self-employed on the profits or gains from their trade or profession. They are collected by the Inland Revenue at the same time as they issue the Schedule D tax assessment. The rate of Class IV contribution payable for 1996/97 is 6% of your profits or gains between £6,860 and £23,660. For 1997/98 the rate remains at 6% and the limits are £7,010 and £24,180. You do not have to pay any contributions if your profits or gains are below the limit of £6,860 (£7,010 for 1997/98) or if you are a man aged 65 or over or a woman aged 60 or over at the beginning of the tax year. If you are under 16 you can apply for exception. Class IV contributions do not increase any entitlement to benefit and you should remember that any deduction which reduces your profit for tax purposes will also reduce your liability to Class IV National Insurance.

If you make a loss in your business and claim a deduction against your total income for tax purposes, you can use the loss in future years to reduce your liability to Class IV contributions. The loss will, of course, no longer be carried forward for income tax purposes. Losses which have not been relieved against total income and are carried forward for tax purposes are also carried forward for Class IV purposes and deducted from profits in future years before levying the charge.

If you are an employee as well as carrying on your own business, you may end up paying Class I, Class II and Class IV contributions. There is an overall maximum on the Class IV contributions which you need to pay in these circumstances which is the difference between £1,328.65 and the total of your Class I and Class II contributions in the tax year. These figures are the maximum for 1996/97 (£1,356.15 for 1997/98). If you are employed by a partnership and admitted as a partner part way through the tax year, you are particularly likely to find you are due a repayment of National Insurance contributions.

Class III contributions

Class III contributions are voluntary. The difference between National Insurance and income tax is that the payment of Class I, II and III contributions entitles you to certain social security benefits including State pension. In order to qualify for maximum benefits, you must have paid a certain number of contributions. Class III contributions can be paid by any person whose contribution record is insufficient to qualify them for full entitlement to basic retirement and widow's pension because, for example, they worked abroad for a few years. In 1996/97 Class III contributions are payable at the rate of £5.95 per week (£6.05 for 1997/98). You should contact the Department of Social Security first to check your contribution record and decide whether you need to pay Class III contributions or not.

Multiple occupations

If you have multiple employments or self-employments, National Insurance contributions are usually worked out separately in relation to each, so you may find that you pay a mixture of Class I, Class II or Class IV contributions. You are not required to pay more contributions overall in any tax year than a set maximum which in the 1996/97 tax year is £2,152.86 (£2,201.62 for 1997/98). If you have paid more than this you should claim a repayment from the Department of Social Security. If you know in advance that you will pay too much National Insurance, you can apply for deferral.

You obtain deferral of Class I contributions by applying on form CF379 to the deferral group of the Department of Social Security in Newcastle upon Tyne. You cannot usually obtain deferral for any of the tax year if you apply after 14 February in that year.

It may be impossible to anticipate precisely what your self-employed earnings during a tax year will be, but if it appears likely that your contributions will exceed the maximum limits, you can apply for deferral of Class II and/or IV contributions by sending a form CF359 to the deferral group of the Social Security office in Newcastle upon Tyne. If you are granted deferral of Class IV contributions the Inland Revenue will not collect any that ultimately fall due. They will, however, tell the Department of Social Security the amount of profits or gains that are liable to Class IV. These will be assessed directly by the Department of Social Security and will be due for payment within 28 days of demand.

Tax Alert

If you do not pay the correct amounts of National Insurance contributions, you may jeopardise your entitlement to Social Security benefits such as State pension or unemployment benefit.

SOCIAL SECURITY

The United Kingdom Social Security system provides benefits or assistance to claimants in a wide variety of circumstances. Many benefits take the form of cash payments or financial assistance. Some are liable to tax while others are tax-free. This section deals with the main benefits and outlines what you have to include in your tax return but if in doubt you should consult your local Department of Social Security office.

Because of the circumstances in which many social security benefits are paid, recipients will often have little other income and hence will not be liable to taxation. It is, however, important to know whether a benefit is taxable as this may affect the amount of tax repayment you can claim on other income or whether you are permitted to receive bank account interest without deduction of tax by the bank.

Non-taxable benefits include:

- attendance allowance
- council tax benefit
- disability working allowance
- guardian's allowance
- housing benefit
- one-parent benefit
- severe disablement allowance (weeks 1-28 inclusive)

- child benefit
- disability living allowance
- family credit
- industrial disablement
- maternity allowances
- incapacity benefit
- Christmas bonus for pensioners

Income support is taxable when paid to people who are unemployed or on strike; in other circumstances it is tax-free.

Most other social security benefits are taxable. This includes widow's benefit, industrial death benefit, statutory maternity pay, statutory sick pay and invalid care allowance. Incapacity benefit (which replaced sickness and invalidity benefit from 13 April 1995) is not taxable from weeks 1–28 inclusive but is taxable from week 29 onwards.

Job-seeker's allowance

Job-seeker's allowance is taxable. The Department of Employment keeps a record of the taxable part of each weekly benefit payment of job-seeker's allowance (and income support if applicable). They give you a Statement of Taxable Benefit when you start a new job or sign off, or alternatively after the end of the tax year. This enables the Department of Employment to determine how much tax is due on the job-seeker's allowance and the tax due is first of all set off against any PAYE repayment due on your earnings prior to the period of unemployment. If you owe tax, the Inland Revenue normally recover it by adjusting your PAYE code for a later tax year after you have found another job.

Tax Filing Tip

Taxable social security benefits should be reported on page 4 in the main body of the tax return under the question dealing with UK pensions retirement annuities and social security benefits.

MAINTENANCE PAYMENTS

If you receive voluntary maintenance payments or payments made under an agreement or court order which was made on or after 15 March 1988, you do not have to pay any tax on what you receive, nor do you have to enter the payments on your tax return.

However, if you receive payments under 'existing obligations' (see under '*Maintenance payments*' in Chapter 3) some or all of what you get may be taxable. If you are separated or divorced from the payer, the first £1,790 (in 1996/97, or £1,830 in 1997/98) paid to you in the tax year is free of tax, but the excess is taxable. If you are a child or step-child of the payer, the full amount is taxable. However, in either case:

■ if the payer has increased the amount of the payments since 6 April 1989, you do not have to pay any tax on the extra amounts, only the figure at that date,

■ if the payer has elected for the payments to be treated as 'qualifying maintenance payments' (see Chapter 3) you do not have to pay any tax on any of the maintenance you receive, nor do you have to enter the payments on your tax return.

Tax Filing Tip

You should report taxable maintenance or alimony on page 4 under the question dealing with such payments in the main body of the tax return.

INCOME FROM LETTING PROPERTY: SCHEDULE A BUSINESS
What you include as income

All property which you let (whether furnished or unfurnished) and irrespective of the type of lease, is treated as a 'Schedule A business' and all income and expenses are aggregated.

Unlike losses from other commercial businesses (see Chapter 9), any rental loss can only be set off against letting income in subsequent tax years.

Letting income includes any payment you receive for the use or occupation of property which you own. The value of payments 'in kind' is also treated as letting income. Include charges you make for gas and electricity.

Lease premiums

If you receive a premium for granting a lease of fifty years or less, part is treated as extra letting income and part is treated as a capital gain. You work out the amount treated as a capital gain by dividing the premium by 50 and multiplying by the number of years in the lease less one. To work out the amount subject to income tax, you subtract the capital gain from the amount of the premium.

For example, you receive £40,000 for a 30-year lease;

$$\text{Gain} = \frac{30 - 1}{50} \times £40,000 = £23,200$$

$$\text{Income} = £40,000 - £23,200 = £16,800$$

Deductible expenses

You are allowed to deduct expenses that you incur wholly and exclusively on property you let out. These include repairs, advertising, insurance, caretaker's wages, cleaning, property agents fees, rent collection costs, heat, light (gas and electricity) and general maintenance charges.

Be careful to distinguish ongoing repairs from 'dilapidations' which arose before you acquired the property or capital improvement expenditure, which you cannot deduct. Repair expenses are expenses incurred to keep your property in good rental condition. They include painting and decoration costs, roof repairs, plumbing repairs, etc. But if for example the repairs to the roof amount to installing a new roof, or improving it to a standard that is better than the original roof, you cannot deduct the cost. Instead you should treat the cost of improvements as part of the cost of the building in computing your capital gain when you sell it.

If you let furnished property you can also deduct an allowance for the use of the furniture. There are two ways of working this out. The easiest way is to deduct 10% of the rent received as reduced by water rates or other services paid by you which should normally be a tenant's liability, as a 'wear and tear' allowance. Alternatively you can adopt the renewals basis. Under this method you cannot deduct the original cost of furniture or equipment but you can deduct the cost of a replacement when the original item wears out and is discarded.

Holiday lettings

There are different considerations for people who let out holiday homes. To qualify as holiday lettings the property must be available for letting at a full commercial rent to the public generally for at least 140 days in a twelve-month period and it must actually be so let for a minimum of 70 days. It must not be occupied by the same people for more than 31 consecutive days during seven months out of the twelve-month period. Caravans are included as holiday lets. If your property qualifies you are treated as carrying on a trade. This is advantageous if your expenses exceed your rental income because you can set the loss off against your other income. You can also claim capital allowances for fixtures and fittings.

Tax Saver

If you rent furnished rooms in your own home you can choose to take part in the rent-a-room scheme under which the first £3,250 (1996/97) of gross rents are free of tax (£4,250 for 1997/98). This is advantageous if your rental income is less than the above limit, but you have the option to be taxed in the normal way instead. The relief is useful if you take in a lodger or if you live near a major sporting event, and rent out rooms in your house during the event.

Tax Filing Tip

Income from rent and property needs to be reported on your tax return under section Land and Property: page L1 and L2.

Interest relief

Loan interest incurred wholly and exclusively for the purposes of the letting business (whether UK or overseas property) is deductible, when incurred, as a letting expense. Previously such interest was only deductible against the net letting income when actually paid.

Tax Alert

If you pay rent to a landlord who is not resident in the United Kingdom you must deduct income tax at the basic rate from the rent and pay it over to the Inland Revenue unless specifically directed otherwise by reference to an agreement between the non-resident landlord and the Inland Revenue. This only applies to direct payments – if the landlord employs a UK-based property agent to collect the rent on his behalf, you can safely pay it without deducting the tax.

See Chapter 4 regarding the possible need to make payments on account.

INTEREST RECEIVED

What you include as income

Interest you receive from most bank or building society accounts (save for certain special accounts), from loans that you have made to others, and on Government securities and certain National Savings products is taxable. With effect from 1996/97, the tax rate on savings income is limited to 20% for basic rate taxpayers, though higher rate tax payers will remain subject to tax at 40%.

National Savings

National Savings products are sold by the Department of National Savings and are guaranteed by the UK Government. The terms of each product change from time to time but the following are the main tax features.

National Savings Certificates

These certificates earn interest annually which usually increases over a five-year period. No interest is paid until the certificates are cashed in at which time interest paid is tax-free and does not need to be included in your tax return. There are currently two types of certificates on offer at any one time. These will include an issue offering a fixed rate of interest, and index-linked certificates which will earn extra interest in line with the increase in the retail price index. Interest on all of these products is tax-free.

National Savings Income Bonds

Interest on income bonds is paid gross (without deduction of tax) on a regular monthly basis. The income is, however, taxable under the special rules described under *'Working out tax due on interest paid gross'* on page 31. Because the interest is paid gross, it is particularly attractive to people who are not liable to income tax, since it avoids the need to make a tax repayment claim from the Revenue and therefore also has a cash flow advantage.

National Savings Deposit and Capital Bonds

Interest is added to deposit bonds annually although it is not actually paid to the holder until the bond is encashed. The interest is, however, taxable and as it is paid gross it is also taxed under the special rules described under *'Working out tax due on interest paid gross'* on page 31.

National Savings Ordinary Account
The first £70 of interest paid in each tax year is free of tax and it does not need to be included in your tax return. Interest is paid gross and if you get more interest than the £70, the excess is taxable and must be shown on your tax return.

Premium bonds
Premium bonds entitle the holder to enter a regular draw for prizes. Any prize money paid under the premium bond scheme is free of tax.

Government stock
Interest paid on Government stock, known as gilt-edged securities, is paid in one of two ways. Where the gilt is purchased through the National Savings Stock Register the interest is paid gross (without deduction of tax) and taxed under the special rules described under *'Working out tax due on interest paid gross'*. Government stock purchased in any other way, eg, through a stockbroker, has basic rate tax deducted from the payment at source and is taxed in the way described under *'Working out tax due on taxed interest'*.

Pensioner's Guaranteed Investment Bond
This investment pays interest gross to investors who are aged 60 or over. The maximum holding is £50,000. The interest rate is very competitive and as it is paid gross, people who do not pay tax do not have to go through the process of reclaiming it. It is, however, subject to tax under the special rules described under *'Working out tax due on interest paid gross'*.

First Option Bonds
These are available to anyone aged 16 or over. The minimum purchase is £1,000 and the maximum £250,000 with a higher rate of interest being paid on holdings of £20,000 or more. On the first anniversary of each bond you receive taxable interest from which tax has been deducted at basic rate. You can decide whether to cash in the bond or retain it for a further year at each anniversary but no interest is paid on a bond encashed before its first anniversary.

Children's Bonus Bonds
Children's bonus bonds can be bought for any child who is aged under 16 and will go on growing in value until he or she is 21. Interest paid on the bonus bond is totally exempt from income tax.

Tax Saver

National Savings Certificates are an attractive tax-free investment and usually offer a competitive rate of return particularly to higher rate taxpayers, while being virtually risk-free. Generally, the interest rates paid on National Savings products are lower than those paid on building society accounts. However, you may find that these lower rates are more attractive when you compare them with the after-tax yield from other investments. If you have surplus funds to invest which you won't need for a five-year period, you should consider National Savings Certificates as an investment.

Tax Saver

National Savings Certificates are not automatically encashed at the end of their term and millions continue to be held by the public beyond their normal redemption date. At that time they will start to earn interest at a rate known as the general extension rate. Although this interest is also tax-free, the rate is usually very low and if you have old issues of National Savings Certificates you would be better to redeem them or roll them over into a current issue. Current issues frequently allow reinvestment of the proceeds of old issues in addition to the normal maximum subscription levels.

Tax Saver

Children's Bonus Bonds are a particularly attractive investment for someone who wishes to save on behalf of a child. It is a particularly good way for parents to provide for their children as interest paid on these bonds is not taxable income for the child, nor does it affect the parent's taxable income.

Bank and building society accounts

Interest paid on most savings and investment accounts run by banks and building societies is taxable and is paid after deduction of basic rate tax, as described under *'Working out tax due on taxed interest'.*

Tax Saver

If you know you are not liable to pay income tax (usually because your tax allowances are greater than your total income), you can register with a bank or building society to have interest paid gross (ie, without the deduction of any tax). This will save you having to reclaim the tax deducted at source. This is most likely to benefit children, the elderly and people who have no job, eg, non-working spouses. Ask at your bank or building society, Post Office or tax office for form IR110.

Tax-Exempt Special Savings Accounts: 'TESSAs'

TESSA accounts are offered by most banks and building societies and interest earned on the account is tax-free provided the capital is not withdrawn for the five-year term of account. Only one TESSA per person is allowed and investors must be over 18 years of age. The maximum investment over the five years is £9,000 but there is also an annual maximum that can be invested of £3,000 in the first year and £1,800 per annum thereafter. If the full £3,000 is invested in year 1, only £600 can be invested in year five. You can withdraw the interest but the payer will withhold an amount equal to lower rate tax on the amount withdrawn which is only released at the end of the five-year term where no capital has been withdrawn during the term. If you withdraw capital in the five-year period the account ceases to qualify as a TESSA and all interest earned earlier becomes taxable. However, you will have deferred paying the tax due on interest from previous years. From 1 January 1996 (when the first TESSAs matured), the 1995 Finance Act enabled those with maturing TESSAs to roll over the whole capital (but not interest) of the maturing account (within a six-month period) to a new 'follow-up' TESSA account, hence accelerating full investment in the new account.

Where less than the full £9,000 is invested, annual additions of up to £1,800 may be made until the follow-up TESSA is fully funded.

Tax Saver

Rates of interest on TESSAs are often higher than on other accounts with the same bank or building society. If you can afford to leave money on deposit for five years the tax-free return on a TESSA is excellent especially for higher rate taxpayers. Even if you have to close the account early, interest will still have accumulated faster than in a taxed account on the same amount and you may have deferred paying tax on it to a later tax year. Make sure you open a TESSA if you possibly can in preference to long-term savings in other types of account.

SAYE accounts

Interest on a SAYE account is free of tax. Only SAYE schemes linked to savings-related share option schemes (where maximum monthly contributions are £250) are now available. SAYE contracts taken out before 1 December 1994 do not need to be linked to savings-related share option schemes (see Chapter 2 under *'Employee share schemes and trusts'*).

Joint accounts

Interest arising from an account held in joint names of husband and wife is shared equally for tax purposes. Exceptionally, if you can show you own the capital in different proportions the income may be taxed in those proportions. Otherwise the Revenue will assume equal proportions.

Tax Saver

As either party to a joint account is normally able to withdraw the funds, opening a joint account can be a good way of ensuring that the spouse in a lower tax bracket pays part of the tax on the income, without the need for the other to give up total access to the funds (see Chapter 6).

Accrued income on stocks and bonds

If you buy or sell or make a gift of Government securities the price you pay or receive (or which you are deemed to pay or receive in the case of a gift) is divided into two parts. The first is the capital cost and the second is an element of income called 'accrued interest'. The latter represents a proportionate part of the next interest payment due. The same principle is applied to interest accruing on other securities such as company loan stocks, foreign government bonds, etc.

Income is prevented from being converted into capital gains by applying a special rule to the taxation of this 'accrued interest' element of the sale proceeds. The special rule does not apply if your total holdings in such securities do not exceed £5,000 in nominal value throughout the tax year. With effect from 6 April 1996, the rule does not apply if the deemed disposal arises on a death.

To work out your accrued income position look at the contract note which the stockbroker provides to you (which records the sale/purchase) and which will specify the number of days' interest added to or subtracted from the price you have paid or received. Alternatively, you will have to calculate this figure by working out the number of days that have passed between the date of sale/purchase and the interest payment date.

Example: You buy £10,000 of 10% Treasury Stock 2001 on 26 November 1996. Interest payments of £500 would normally arise on 26 February and 26 August. The price you pay when you buy the stock will be increased by £254, equal to 93 days of the interest which will be payable to you on 26 February 1997. This sum of £254 will be taxed as the income of the person selling the stock since it is attributed to his ownership between August and November. It is therefore regarded as a 'rebate amount' and deducted from the interest receipt of £500 which you receive on 26 February 1997. Hence you pay tax on £246.

If you had sold the stock instead and received the extra payment you would have an 'accrued income charge' in 1996/97 of £254 which you would include as income on your tax return.

The tax year in which the income is subject to tax is determined by the day on which the next interest payment is due. For example, if you sold 12% Exchequer Stock 1998 on 16 March 1997 the next interest payment date is 20 May 1997 so the accrued income is charged to tax in 1997/98 even though you must include it in your tax return to 5 April 1997. You offset all 'charges' and 'rebate amounts' for each tax year to determine if there is an overall charge under the accrued income scheme.

The capital gains tax cost or proceeds of sale of the securities affected are adjusted by a similar amount. However, as UK government securities and qualifying corporate bonds are exempt from capital gains tax, this only affects the tax position of corporate loan stock and non-UK government securities.

Annuities
If you buy a purchased life annuity, part of each instalment you subsequently receive is treated as a refund of capital and part as taxable income. The company paying the annuity will tell you how much is taxable and this is the amount you enter on your tax return.

Personal damages claims
If you are paid interest on a claim for damages in respect of personal injuries it is not regarded as taxable income.

Working out tax due on taxed interest

Most interest paid by banks and building societies and certain other sources has tax deducted at source. Banks, building societies and other financial institutions have from 6 April 1996 deducted tax at 20% from interest paid.

From 1996/97 the tax due on net interest is worked out in a similar manner to that for dividends (refer to *'Working out tax due on dividends and taxed savings'* later in this chapter).

If you are only liable to tax at the basic rate there will be no further tax to pay. If the whole of your taxable income (including the interest) in the tax year is too low for you to pay tax, you will be able to claim a refund.

If you are a higher-rate taxpayer, or if adding the gross amount of the interest to your taxable income puts you into the higher-rate bracket, you will have some extra tax to pay. As lower rate tax has already been paid on the interest, the extra tax will be charged at the difference between the 40% higher rate and the 20% lower rate – ie, at 20%.

Working out tax due on interest paid gross

The rules for existing sources of interest changed from 1996/97. In that year you will be assessed on one-half of the total interest arising in both 1995/96 and 1996/97. From 1997/98 you will be assessed on the interest credited to your account in the tax year. As in the case of taxed interest, from the 1996/97 tax year the rate of tax applicable has been limited to only 20% for basic rate taxpayers.

Tax Alert

Before you close an account in 1996/97 look at the interest received in 1995/96. If it is higher than the amount on which you are due to be assessed in that previous year (ie, the income of the year preceding that) the Inland Revenue will issue a further assessment on the higher amount. Careful timing of when you close accounts so this doesn't happen can save you tax.

If you opened a new account on or after 6 April 1994 under the new rules the tax you are liable for each year will be based on the actual amount of interest arising in that year.

Tax Alert

Strictly, the law says that for accounts which pay interest gross, each new deposit and withdrawal should be treated as if an account were opened or closed. In practice, the Inland Revenue treat bank accounts as a continuing source unless you request that the strict basis applies or unless particularly large sums are deposited or withdrawn. The transitional year rule for 1996/97 described above offers the potential for manipulating the sums on deposit on such accounts so that the interest arising in 1995/96 and 1996/97 is maximised. Only one-half of it is then assessed to tax. The Inland Revenue have announced that where they see evidence of existing sources of interest taxed on a current year basis having been

depleted, and interest sources taxed on a preceding year basis have been increased, so as to take advantage of this transitional provision, they will apply the strict basis to negate any tax advantage. You should, therefore, avoid manipulating your untaxed interest to take advantage of these provisions if you do not want to fall foul of these rules.

Furthermore, if you manipulate interest payments or rates as between tax years you should be aware that the Inland Revenue can employ anti-exploitation measures to prevent you taking advantage of the transitional rules mentioned above. Indeed, there can be a tax penalty of up to 5% for 40% taxpayers.

Tax Filing Tip

UK savings income which is taxable must be shown under the question dealing with income from UK savings and investments Tax Return: Page 3.

DIVIDENDS
What you include as income

Dividends are distributions of cash paid by a company to its shareholders. Companies can make non-cash distributions which are taxed in a similar fashion to cash dividends. You may also indirectly receive dividends through a trust or the estate of someone who has died. In most cases, such dividends are taxable as income but it is important to distinguish them from other income, as dividends attract a lower rate of income tax if you are a basic rate taxpayer.

Dividends carry a 'tax credit' of 20% which is treated as tax paid by the individual receiving the dividend. You must add this tax credit to the dividend to get the gross taxable income. See *'Working out tax due on dividends and taxed savings'*.

Some dividends, however, are treated as capital gain distributions. These include dividends paid when a company is wound up. More rarely payments are non-taxable if they are considered to be a return of capital. You should be informed by the company making the payment about their nature at the time when made.

Dividends included in trust income

If you receive the income of a trust, to which you are entitled as of right, the trust is disregarded and you are treated as if you received the income direct. You need to know how much of the trust income you receive consists of dividends in order to apply the tax rules described above. Usually the trustees will first offset expenses against the trust income before making the distribution but they will provide you with a Certificate of Income and Tax Deduction which will tell you how the income is made up.

Tax Filing Tip

You will need to enter this information on page 2 of your Tax Return and form T1.

If you receive income from a trust where the trustees have discretion whether to make payment to you or not, the above rule does not apply. Your income is simply a trust income distribution which will bear tax at the full tax rates attributable to your other income and not the preferential dividend rate.

Unit trusts

If you hold units in a unit trust you can receive income distributions in one of three ways – as a dividend distribution; as a foreign income distribution (or partly as both); or as an interest distribution. The first two types of distribution are taxed as dividends and carry a tax credit of 20%. An interest distribution on the other hand is paid net of basic rate tax (1996/97: 24%; 1997/98: 23%). The voucher accompanying the payment will tell you which type of distribution it is.

The tax situation is the same whether distributions are paid out to you or reinvested in the fund. If the first distribution you get from a unit trust includes an 'equalisation' payment, this is a return of part of the money you invested and is not taxable.

Stock dividends/enhanced stock dividends

A bonus issue of shares paid by a company is not taxable. But if a stock or scrip dividend is paid as an alternative to receiving a cash dividend, it is subject to income tax. The amount taxed depends on whether the market value of the stock dividend shares is substantially greater (ie, at least 15% greater) than the value of the cash dividend.

If it is not and the shares are accepted, the equivalent of the cash dividend is taxed as dividend income. If the market value of the stock dividend is more than 15% greater than the cash alternative, the amount subject to income tax is the market value of the shares on the first day they are dealt in on the Stock Exchange (or if they are unquoted their market value on the due date of issue). In both cases a tax credit of 20% is available (and should be added to the distribution to give the taxable gross dividend). If your income is too low to pay tax you cannot reclaim the tax credit.

Tax Alert

If you do not pay tax think carefully before you opt for a stock dividend. You may receive less value than if you took cash and recovered the tax credit.

As an incentive to encourage shareholders to take shares instead of a cash dividend some companies enhance the stock alternative so that the shares are more valuable than the cash dividend. Frequently in such a case the enhanced stock dividend is accompanied by an offer to buy the new shares. If the sale offer is accepted you will also have made a disposal for capital gains tax. In order to establish any capital gains tax consequence of the sale the cost of the shares sold must be calculated. To do this you add the net amount of the stock dividend subject to income tax to the cost of your original shareholding. The total cost is prorated over your total shareholding to arrive at the capital gains tax cost attributable to the new shares sold.

Foreign income dividends (FIDs)

These are cash dividends paid by UK companies out of profits which have been taxed abroad. A company must elect for such a dividend to be treated as a FID and the voucher accompanying the payment will clearly show this. The recipient is treated as receiving total income of an amount of the dividend plus the lower rate of tax. The tax is purely notional and no refund of it is made if you are not liable to tax. The benefit to a shareholder of a FID is that the paying company obtains a tax advantage which it may share with its shareholders by paying a higher dividend than it could otherwise afford.

Foreign dividends

Dividends paid by foreign companies form part of your income if you are resident and domiciled (see Chapter 5) in the UK. You must add foreign and UK tax deducted to the amount received to arrive at your gross income. The bank which collects the income for you will normally provide a voucher showing these tax sums. They are then normally credited against your UK liability (see later).

Other distributions

Certain other receipts from companies are taxed similarly to cash dividends even though they are not strictly dividend payments. One example is where a company buys back its own shares. It is also possible for a company to be deemed to have made a distribution to a shareholder. Where, for example, it is a 'close company' (a company controlled by five or fewer shareholders – 'participators') if it has incurred expense in providing a benefit to a participator which is not reimbursed to the company and on which the participator has not paid tax.

Distributions that would not be taxed as income include demerger distributions where a company splits off part of its operations into a separate company, or a purchase of own shares by an unquoted trading company where the Inland Revenue agree that the distribution should be treated as a capital receipt.

Usually the company involved will provide documentation which makes it clear how the distribution should be treated but in case of doubt you should write to the Company Secretary or seek the help of a professional adviser or your Inspector of Taxes.

Personal Equity Plans (PEPs)

Personal Equity Plans are available to investors aged 18 or over who are UK residents. Your money is invested primarily in ordinary shares, unit trusts, or investment trusts or qualifying corporate bonds. The returns are free from income tax and capital gains tax and do not have to be declared on your tax return.

Plans take two forms – general and single-company PEPs – and only one plan of each type may be subscribed to annually. The annual subscription limits are £6,000 to a general PEP and £3,000 to a single company PEP. Income can be paid out or accumulated within the PEP.

Cash held within a PEP earns interest exempt from tax provided it is reinvested within the plan by the end of the following tax year. If cash is withdrawn from the plan without prior investment it is taxed in full on the investor and if it exceeds £180 per annum the plan manager must deduct tax at the basic rate.

Tax Saver

If you are a taxpayer or use your annual capital gains tax exemption each year, maximise your annual subscription into PEPs each year. Lower rate taxpayers should watch that PEP charges don't exceed the tax saving.

Shares acquired under employee savings-related share option schemes or appropriated from approved profit-sharing schemes can be transferred into a single company PEP without incurring capital gains tax. Their value must not exceed the annual subscription limit of £3,000, and the transfer must occur within 90 days of receipt.

Working out tax due on dividends and taxed savings

When you receive a dividend or other distribution you receive a net amount plus a tax credit equivalent to 20% of the gross amount. Your total dividend income comprises these two figures added together.

Example:

Dividend received	£80
Tax credit	£20
Gross dividend income	£100

The tax credit reflects advance corporation tax that has been paid by the company paying the dividend or distribution and you are given the benefit of this tax so that the income from the company is not taxed twice. From 1996/97 tax deducted at source on UK bank or building society interest (savings income) is also restricted to 20% of the gross amount and is treated in a similar manner to dividends. Most savings income is taxed at the 20% rate only, for basic rate taxpayers.

Taxpayers at the lower rate (20%) and basic rate (24%: 1996/97; 23%: 1997/98) have nothing further to pay as both are deemed to have paid their tax in full. If you are liable to tax at the higher rate of 40% however, you only get the 20% tax credit so will pay a further 20% tax to the extent that dividend income exceeds the higher rate income threshold of £25,500 in 1996/97 (£26,100 in 1997/98). This is illustrated in the example which follows under *'Interaction of dividends and capital gains'.*

The effect of this rule is that dividend income and savings income are never subject to tax at the basic rate.

Dividend income and savings income are always treated as the highest part of your income in deciding what tax rates apply to it unless exceptionally you are in receipt of a taxable sum on retirement or loss of office (eg, a golden handshake) or a gain arising from a chargeable event on a life assurance policy. The latter two categories of income are treated as the top slice of income in priority.

Foreign dividends are also subject to income tax at 20%, both when the dividend is collected by a UK paying agent, such as a bank, and when it is paid direct to you as a shareholder. In the case of payment through a UK paying agent, the amount of UK tax deducted will be that which, together with any foreign tax deductions, amounts to 20%. Where payment is made direct to a shareholder who does not pay higher rate tax, tax at 20% less credit for foreign tax deductions will be due. Where tax at a rate higher than 20% has been deducted, a refund may be available on a claim under a tax treaty. The higher rate taxpayer will pay 40% less the credit for foreign taxes.

Interaction of dividends and capital gains

The rate of tax that applies to capital gains is explained in Chapter 2 and will depend on your other income. The requirement that dividend income is treated as the top slice of your income in applying income tax rates creates a difficult interaction between them. The problem only arises if you have taxable non-dividend and non-savings income under £3,900 for 1996/97 (or non-dividend and non-savings income under £4,100 for 1997/98) and you also have capital gains liable to tax. Capital gains are chargeable at the lower rate of 20% in priority to dividends and savings income so that such income is therefore initially disregarded in working out the tax on this lowest rate band.

Example:

		Non-savings income £	Gross savings income £	Capital Gain £
Income		5,400	35,000	15,800
Allowances		(3,765)	–	*(6,300)
Taxable		1,635	35,000	9,500
Income tax at:	£	£	£	£
20% (lower rate)	3,900	1,635	–	2,265
24% (basic rate) (dividends within the basic rate band are only subject to 20% tax)	21,600	–	21,600	–
40% (higher tax)	20,635	-	13,400	7,235
		1,635	35,000	9,500

* See Chapter 2 for explanation of capital gains tax allowance.

If you are a non-taxpayer you can recover the 20% tax credit on dividend and taxed savings income by submitting a tax return to the Inland Revenue. You will need to submit the tax voucher that you receive with the payment to the Inland Revenue in support of this claim so make sure you store this tax voucher safely when you receive it. From 1996/97 you may need to obtain a certificate of tax deducted on your savings, from your bank, building society or other investment source. If you are a basic rate taxpayer you do not have any further tax to pay on dividends or taxed savings income.

Tax Filing Tip

Dividend income and other taxable distributions received from UK companies should be reported on the 'Dividends' section of the question dealing with income from UK savings and investments on page 3.

OTHER INCOME

Income from trusts

You must include on your tax return any income that you receive from a trust. If you are entitled to the income of the trust by right the trustees will give you a certificate (R185E) which will tell you how much income is derived from dividends (from which tax will have been deducted at 20%). If the income you receive has been paid at the trustees' discretion you will also receive a certificate (R185) but tax will have been deducted at the trust rate (34%: 1996/97 and 1997/98) if the trust is a UK resident trust.

If you pay tax at the basic rate or less and receive income from a UK discretionary trust you can recover the excess tax deducted at source. Make sure you file a tax return to recover the tax you have overpaid.

If you have transferred capital to the trust and you or your spouse are entitled to benefit from it or have some other interest in the funds settled, you must show on your tax return all the trust income from the funds you settled, whether it is paid to you or not.

If you are a higher rate taxpayer and pay tax on trust income which you have not received (because you are a settlor of the trust and have some interest in it) you can ask the trustees of the trust to refund to you the tax you have paid. You will need to ask your Inspector of Taxes for a certificate showing the tax paid.

Tax Filing Tip

Income from trusts should be reported on page 2 of the Tax Return and in the schedule Trusts ETC: Page T1.

Income from inheritances

If you have been left an interest in the residue of the estate of someone who has died, there will be a period of administration between death and the handing over of the inheritance. During this period special rules must be followed.

Income which you receive is taxable in the year in which you actually receive it. The executors will provide you with a certificate of income and tax deducted for each tax year. If you are only entitled to the income of the residue, you should report on your tax return the actual amounts paid to you in each year. On completion of the administration the final income paid in the year is treated as the income of that year or if your interest came to an end in an earlier year then the final payment will be treated as the income of that earlier year.

Tax Filing Tip

Income from the estates of deceased persons should be shown on the schedule Trusts ETC: Page T1.

If you are entitled to the capital of the estate as well, any amount paid to you is deemed to be paid as income up to the total amount of the income which has been received by the estate (even if actually paid on account of your capital entitlement) and should be reported as your income. In the year in which the administration is completed any excess income not already distributed is taxed as your income in that year.

Special rules enable the executors to redress deficits and recoup overpayments of income from later years or in the event of an aggregate overpayment, from earlier years' income distributions (on a last in first out basis).

Life assurance policies

The proceeds of UK life assurance policies which are 'qualifying policies' are not subject to income tax. A qualifying policy is usually one on which premiums are payable annually for ten years or more. Non-qualifying policies or single-premium life assurance policies (sometimes called investment bonds) are taxable on the difference between the maturity proceeds and the premiums paid. However, 5% withdrawals can be made each year from bonds without any tax liability and any 5% withdrawal not taken can be carried forward and taken in a later year. The life assurance company will give you a 'chargeable event' certificate showing that a potentially taxable withdrawal has been made. It will also issue a certificate showing how much is taxable when the bond is eventually encashed.

Tax Alert

The manner of taxing such policies is currently under review and if you own any you should watch out for future changes which may affect you.

Tax Filing Tip

This income needs to be reported in the main body of the Tax Return under the question on page 4 dealing with such income.

Investment bonds and non-qualifying life insurance policies

If you have surrendered an investment bond or made a withdrawal in excess of 5% of the premium paid you will have income to report on your tax return (page 4).

The actual gain arising on the surrender of an investment bond or non-qualifying life policy is chargeable to tax. However, no tax is payable at basic rate on this amount (it is deemed to have been paid) so if you are a higher rate taxpayer you simply pay the extra 16% tax for 1996/97 (17% 1997/98) on the amount of the gain. This also means that if you are a basic rate taxpayer you have no further tax to pay but if you are a non-taxpayer or a lower rate taxpayer you will not be able to reclaim any of the basic rate tax deemed to have been paid.

The receipt of a large lump sum in any one year could have the effect of pushing a taxpayer into higher rates of tax when, without the gain, there would only be liability to basic rate or lower rates of tax. If you are in this position, the higher rate tax for which you become liable will be reduced by a special calculation known as top-slicing relief. The amount of this relief is calculated as follows.

First, look to see how many complete years your policy has run before the 'chargeable event' occurred and find the average yearly gain by dividing the gain by that number of years. If there has been a previous 'chargeable event' it is only the complete years since that previous event which can be taken into account.

Now work out your tax on the basis that the average yearly gain on the policy is the top slice of your income and work out how much of the average yearly gain falls into your higher-rate tax band. If none of it falls into your higher-rate band, you have no further tax to pay on the gain.

If some of it does fall into your higher-rate band, multiply that amount by 16% for 1996/97 (or 17% for 1997/98) which represents the difference between the higher and basic rates of tax. Finally, multiply the answer by the complete number of years you first used to establish the average yearly gain. The figure you now have is the higher rate tax due on the gain after allowing for top-slicing relief. You have to claim top-slicing relief within six years of the end of the tax year in which the 'chargeable event' arose.

Tax Saver

Using the 5% withdrawal facility can be a useful way of augmenting your income without increasing your tax liability.

Deep discount and deep gain securities
Gains on these securities are subject to income tax rather than capital gains tax. From 1996/97 such income tax charge is only at the lower 20% rate applicable to savings income, for basic rate taxpayers.

Copyright income
If you are an author or artist and sell copyright for a lump sum, you can choose to spread the income over the current and previous tax year. If the work took more than 24 months to produce you can spread the income to the year before that as well. You must tell the Inland Revenue within six years of the end of the tax year how you want it treated.

Tax Saver

You should elect to spread if it will mean that less of your income is taxed at the higher rate or if you have reliefs that can be used in earlier years.

INCOME OF CHILDREN UNDER AGE 18

Children are taxable individuals in their own right. However, if a child has income of more than £100 in a tax year from funds given to them by a parent, the excess is counted as the parent's income. This does not apply to income which the child has from his own earnings or from gifts made to him by somebody other than parents. It also does not apply if the child is married, although under the age of 18.

Tax Saver

If you give funds to your children invest them in ways that do not give rise to taxable income, eg, in accumulating unit trusts, National Savings Certificates, Children's Bonus Bonds, etc. It is particularly useful if you can invest money on behalf of the child in an investment which will produce capital gains – there is no aggregation of your children's capital gains with yours and they are entitled to a full annual exemption of £6,300 for 1996/97 and £6,500 for 1997/98.

Tax Saver

If you want to put money aside for your children for the future, you can do this by setting up an accumulation and maintenance trust on their behalf (see Chapter 15). Provided the trust is irrevocable and no monies are paid out of the trust to the children while they are under the age of 18, you will not be taxed on the income arising in the trust. The trust will suffer tax but at the trust rate of 34% 1996/97 and 1997/98 compared with your potential income tax rate of 40% if you are a higher rate taxpayer. Once the child reaches the age of 18 distributions can be made. Future income they receive carries a tax credit for the 34% tax paid by the trust, so if they are not taxpayers when they receive the income, they can recover the tax paid from the Inland Revenue. Accumulated income paid out later when the child becomes entitled to capital bears no further tax.

Tax Saver

If someone other than you or your spouse (particularly grandparents), wants to give money to your children, but you are concerned about giving the children control of the capital at a young age, an accumulation and maintenance trust is a practical way of controlling their income. Income can only be paid out to them at the trustees' discretion and the children can use their personal allowances to offset against distributions and recover the 34% tax which has been suffered by the trustees.

Tax Saver

If you want to give money to your child but the sum involved does not warrant the cost of a formal trust, consider using a bare trust. An outright and irrevocable gift of either cash or assets can be invested on behalf of the child by someone acting as their bare trustee, ie, someone who is no more than a nominee for the child. This could even be you or your spouse. Provided the income is not actually paid out but is accumulated within a bank or building society account held in the bare trustee's name for the child, until the child reaches age 18, the income is taxed as the child's, and not yours. A simple document or even a note evidencing the gift would be desirable.

2 Capital gains and losses

Capital gains tax applies to the gains (and losses) you make (or are deemed to make) when you dispose of 'chargeable assets' – for example by selling them or giving them away (but not normally when you die). Most things that you own and hold for personal or investment purposes are chargeable assets, including stocks and shares, antiques, works of art and land. However, chargeable assets do not normally include your own home, private cars, foreign currency for personal use or trading stock. And there are some important exemptions such as chattels (eg, personal possessions) which are each worth £6,000 or less when you dispose of them.

CAPITAL GAINS

Tax Filing Tip

The following paragraphs relate to the completion of the tax return Capital Gains: Page CG1.

Declaring gains on your tax return

Calculating capital gains can be a complex process. You can avoid working out the precise amount of the gain if your total proceeds from chargeable assets you sold and the value of assets you gave away in the 1996/97 tax year does not exceed £12,600 and the gains do not exceed £6,300. (The limits for 1997/98 are £13,000 and £6,500 respectively.)

Tax Filing Tip

If you can meet the above requirements you need only tick the appropriate boxes on page 2 of your tax return, the detailed Capital Gains page CG1 need not be completed.

Tax Saver

Even if it does involve a little extra work it is worth calculating your gains and losses in full. You may be surprised to find that you have a tax loss instead of a gain which you can use to reduce your tax liability on gains in future years.

Calculating chargeable gains

To calculate the gain on an asset you dispose of you deduct the following from the amount for which you sell it (or if you give it away, from its market value at the time):

■ the amount you paid for it (or, if you were given it or you inherited it, its market value at the time)

- incidental costs of acquiring the asset (see below)
- expenditure incurred solely to enhance the value of the asset, eg, restoration costs on a work of art
- expenditure incurred to establish or defend your title to the asset
- costs incurred in making the disposal.

Although not technically a deduction, allowance is made for the effects of inflation by enhancing the value of allowable deductions (see *Allowing for inflation*').

For certain types of assets, if you received the asset as a gift its market value may be treated as reduced if you agreed with the person who made the gift to take over his capital gains tax liability (see later in this chapter under *Holdover relief*').

Incidental acquisition and disposal costs include:

- surveyor's or valuer's fees
- auctioneer's fees
- accountant's, agent's or legal adviser's fees
- costs of transfer or conveyance
- stamp duty
- advertising costs
- reasonable costs incurred in obtaining any valuation required for computing the gain.

You cannot deduct any interest you paid on a loan used to buy the asset. The valuation costs that can be deducted are restricted to the costs of obtaining the valuation. You may incur further costs in negotiating that value with the District Valuer or Shares Valuation Division, which are departments of the Inland Revenue, and you may even have to take the matter to a Land Tribunal or to the courts in order to agree the value. These negotiation and litigation costs are not allowable deductions.

Assets held on 31 March 1982

If you held assets potentially subject to capital gains tax ('chargeable assets') on 31 March 1982, you can elect to substitute their market value on that day instead of their actual cost. This means that appreciation in the value of the asset which arose before that date will not be taxed. You must elect to substitute the March 1982 value within two years of your first relevant disposal of any chargeable asset after 5 April 1988; that is of any such asset which was held at 31 March 1982. Although the Inland Revenue have power to extend this time limit, they will usually not do so. They will, however, disregard disposals of assets on which there is not usually a charge to capital gains tax, eg, your principal private residence where it is wholly exempt. If you have made such an election for March 1982 values to apply, it applies to all assets that you dispose of, including land, investments, etc.

If you have not made such an election but held assets on 31 March 1982 you may still obtain a deduction for the March 1982 value. You must deduct the March

1982 value instead of the original cost if by doing so this causes either a smaller gain or a smaller loss.

For example: use the March 1982 value in the following situations:

	£	Current value £	Gain £	
Original cost	400	1,000	600	
March 1982 value	500	1,000	500	(lower gain)

	£	Current value £	Loss £	
Original cost	1,000	500	500	
March 1982 value	900	500	400	(lower loss)

If there would be a gain by reference to the original cost and a loss by reference to the March 1982 value or vice versa, the disposal is treated as giving rise to neither gain nor loss. Thus no tax is payable but losses are not allowable.

Tax Saver

If you have not made any capital gains taxable disposals since 5 April 1988 you are in time to make a 31 March 1982 election which applies to all of your assets. You should do so if you held any assets on 31 March 1982 where their value at that time was higher than their cost. This is because the election could give you a tax loss (to offset against other gains you make) which is bigger than that which would otherwise be available if you did not elect. However, remember to check that the position on your other assets is not made worse by making an election – for example, if the March 1982 value of certain assets is lower than cost, you will have bigger gains on these assets when you ultimately sell them.

Assets held at 6 April 1965

If you are not calculating your gains by reference to an election for March 1982 value, their 6 April 1965 value is another important date to remember. If you acquired your asset before 6 April 1965, the value of the asset at 6 April 1965 may also be relevant to determine what part of the cost price you can deduct from the gain on disposal.

It will be very rare indeed that these rules apply since the value at 31 March 1982 will almost certainly be greater. If you think these rules apply to you take professional advice.

Allowing for inflation

The indexation allowance is an important capital gains tax deduction designed to ensure that you do not pay tax on gains attributable to inflation. However, its calculation is not for the faint hearted, especially where stocks and shares are concerned!

The indexation allowance effectively enhances the deductible cost of, and expenditure incurred in connection with, the asset. It is calculated by comparing the retail price index for the month in which you dispose of the asset with the retail price index for the month in which you acquired it or 31 March 1982 if this is later.

Example: You acquire a plot of land for £15,000 in June 1990. You sell it in June 1996. The retail price index for June 1996 is 153.0 and in June 1990 it was 126.7. Your indexation factor is calculated as (153.0 – 126.7) ÷ 126.7. You then multiply the cost of the asset (£15,000) by the factor (0.208) to get the indexation allowance (£3,120) which is also available to reduce your gain.

If you have difficulty in working out the indexation allowance, the Inland Revenue publish tables of the correct factors for each month of acquisition and disposal. These are frequently reproduced in the financial press or you can obtain them from your Inspector of Taxes. The table applicable is reproduced on page xxxv.

The indexation allowance on assets acquired prior to 31 March 1982 is worked out on the value of the asset at 31 March 1982. You may have to employ an agent to value the asset for you.

Shares acquired on or after 31 March 1982

The rules for calculating the indexation allowance in relation to stocks and shares are more complex. For shares which were acquired after 31 March 1982, and for shares where you have made the 31 March 1982 election (described above), you add together the cost of all of your shares to get the average cost. Each time you add to your holding or make a disposal, you adjust the total cost of the holding to take account of the indexation allowance. Therefore you work out the inflation adjusted cost which is attributed to all of the shares in your holding. This cost does not need to be adjusted when you receive a bonus issue of shares. You just add in the extra shares, which has the result of reducing the average cost of the holding. You do, however, need to adjust the pooled shares for:

- sales and purchases
- gifts (deemed to be at market value)
- rights issues
- scrip dividends or enhanced scrip dividends.

Shares acquired before 31 March 1982

Shares acquired prior to 31 March 1982 but after 6 April 1965 are recorded separately. You work out your indexation allowance based on actual cost or the 31 March 1982 value, according to whichever gives you the higher allowance. If you acquired some shares before, and some after 31 March 1982, remember that shares which are derived from a pre-1982 holding, such as a rights or bonus issue, are treated as additions to this pool of shares and not to the pool of shares you acquired after 31 March 1982.

Shares acquired before 6 April 1965
Unquoted shares acquired before 6 April 1965 are also noted separately. Again, the indexation factor is based on the value of the shares at 31 March 1982 and on the retail price index at that date.

Identifying the shares sold
The reason why you have to keep three separate pools of shares is that when you sell them, if you have a mixture of shares acquired on different dates, you must work out the cost of what you sold. You are therefore deemed to sell the shares you acquired in the following order of priority:

- If you acquire shares and within the subsequent ten days make a disposal of the same type of shares, the transactions are matched.
- Thereafter you treat disposals as coming from the shares you acquired after 31 March 1982 until that pool is exhausted.
- Then from the pool of shares you acquired before 31 March 1982.
- In the case of unquoted shares, you are deemed to dispose of holdings acquired prior to 6 April 1965 on a 'last-in, first-out' basis.

If you pay for your shares in instalments the indexation allowance will be different for each instalment so working out the cost is more complicated. When you pay instalments due on a purchase you are normally treated as paying on the date the shares are acquired unless you paid the instalment more than 12 months after you acquired the shares. In that case, you need to work out the indexation allowance on the payment from the time payment was actually made. This may be important if you have acquired shares in some of the recent privatisation issues and have paid in instalments.

EMPLOYER SHARE SCHEMES AND TRUSTS
If you receive options to purchase shares in your employer's company under Revenue-approved savings related or profit-sharing schemes, normally neither the grant nor exercise of the option under the scheme rules will be taxable. Sale of the shares acquired will however be subject to capital gains tax. This observation also applies to any options received under approved executive share option schemes to the extent that they have not been subject to income tax on exercise of the rights and to the extent they fall within certain specified limits (see Chapter 1, *Employer share schemes and trusts*).

CAPITAL LOSSES
You work out an allowable loss for capital gains tax purposes in the same way as you work out a capital gain. Any loss you make can be deducted from gains on other assets. However, a special rule applies to the element of the loss that relates to indexation. The general rule is that the indexation allowance on each asset is limited to the amount that reduces the gain on the asset to nil. In other words you cannot create a loss out of the indexation allowance. However, this rule does not apply to losses which were incurred on disposals before 30 November 1993.

If you have not used capital losses against gains on other assets in the same tax year, they can be carried forward and set off against future gains. On disposals of assets after 30 November 1993, there is a transitional relief for losses created by using the indexation allowance. This is limited to a total £10,000 of loss arising on disposals between 30 November 1993 and 5 April 1995 and can only be set against gains made before 5 April 1995. Thereafter these indexation losses lapse and no new ones can be created. Accordingly from 1995/96 the transitional provisions are no longer capable of being used.

Losses which are not attributable to the indexation allowance can be deducted against other gains in the same year of assessment with any balance carried forward and deducted from future gains without time limit providing you notify the Inspector that the loss is available to carry forward.

Tax Filing Tip

Calculation of your losses utilised and carried forward can be made on the tax return Capital Gains: Page CG1.

LOSSES ON UNQUOTED SHARES

If you bought newly-issued shares in a trading company which is unquoted and you dispose of them at a loss, you can offset the loss against your income for income tax purposes rather than treating it as an allowable loss for capital gains tax purposes. To claim the relief, you must make a claim for 1995/96 and 1996/97 by 5 April 1998 and 5 April 1999 respectively.

The loss can be deducted against your total income for the year of disposal or deducted from your income for the preceding year.

Remember that this relief is only available where you have subscribed for new shares. If you bought them from someone else you cannot claim the loss against your income.

EXEMPTIONS

Annual exemption

Once you have worked out your total capital gains less losses for the year, you can deduct your annual exemption of £6,300 for 1996/97 (£6,500 for 1997/98). Husband, wife and children each have an annual exemption available. If you make losses in the same year as gains, you must deduct them before you set your gains against the annual exemption, but if you are using losses brought forward from an earlier year you can use your annual exemption first, and carry unused losses forward again. Annual exemptions cannot be carried forward.

Tax Saver

If you have a portfolio of investments and have not used your annual capital gains tax exemption, then you should consider doing so before 5 April in each tax year. If you do not want to dispose of a particular investment you can use a technique

known as 'bed and breakfasting' to increase your capital gains tax acquisition cost (for offset against future gains).

A bed and breakfast transaction involves selling shares on one day and buying them back on the next day. The sale must precede the purchase. To be effective you must genuinely give up control of your shares by a proper sale, incurring the risk of an adverse price movement overnight. The transaction must be a proper business transaction (ie, with brokers) and at full market value which means that dealing costs will be incurred. Your stockbroker will arrange the transaction for you and give you an estimate of the cost involved, although you must remember that he cannot forecast the price movement which might occur overnight.

Tax Saver

Be extremely careful when bed and breakfasting a holding, part of which has been acquired before 31 March 1982. Refer back to the identification rules described earlier. Remember that you do not average costs over your whole holding but identify the shares sold with those acquired after March 1982 first. If you only dispose of part of your holding and don't take account of these identification rules, you may calculate your gain or loss wrongly.

Chattels

Your tangible movable property (apart from stock exchange investments and currency) – broadly your personal possessions – are called 'chattels'. A special exemption from tax exists where these are sold if the proceeds do not exceed £6,000. If the proceeds exceed £6,000 the taxable gain is limited to the lower of the actual gain or five-thirds of the excess.

For example an asset is acquired for £4,000 and is sold for £8,000:

	£
Excess of proceeds over £6,000	2,000
£2,000 x 5/3	3,333
Actual gain (assuming indexation of say £500)	3,500
Chargeable gain	3,333

Where several separate assets form a set which has a higher aggregate value than the value of the separate assets, special rules prevent parts of the set being sold individually to lower the overall proceeds to enable them to fall within the chattel exemption. Instead they are treated as a single item.

Exempt gilts and corporate bonds

If you sell government securities any gain you realise is not a chargeable gain. Equally you cannot get relief for any loss suffered. The same rule applies to gains and losses on qualifying corporate bonds. A qualifying corporate bond would include most securities issued by a public or local authority or by a company, including permanent interest-bearing shares (PIBS) issued by a building society. However, not all corporate bonds are qualifying corporate bonds and you may have to ask your adviser or the Inland Revenue to confirm the position of your particular holding.

Your home

A gain on the sale or exchange of property is taxable but this does not apply if the property is your principal private residence. The exemption includes a garden area, including the site of the house, of 0.5 of a hectare. If your grounds are larger than this and you can show that, given the size and character of your home, the larger area is required for its reasonable enjoyment as a residence, the Inland Revenue will extend the exemption to include the larger area. A husband and wife can only claim one home as being exempt between them and if you own more than one home you can choose which will be your main residence for exemption purposes by giving notice to the Inspector within two years of acquiring the second house. It does not have to be the same home as the one on which you get tax relief on your mortgage.

Tax Alert

If you do not give notice choosing your main residence the Inspector will determine the matter on the basis of the facts including the time you spend in it.

If the home has not always been your main residence throughout the period of your ownership you will get relief based on the length of time that it has been your main residence but including, in any event, the last 36 months of the period of ownership. In addition, you can treat as exempt the proportion of the gain attributable to:

- any period of absence not exceeding three years, and
- any period of absence throughout which you worked in an employment all the duties of which were performed outside the UK, and
- any period of absence up to four years throughout which you were prevented from living in the house by the geographical location of your job or because your employer required you to live elsewhere.

These periods will only count if:

- both before and afterwards you occupied the home as your main residence
- you did not during those periods have any other home which qualified for the relief (this may be a difficult condition to satisfy).

In addition, if you owned a home on 5 April 1988 which was the sole residence of your own or your spouse's widowed, divorced or separated mother, or any relative who is incapacitated by old age or infirmity and you provide the home to that person rent-free and without any payment 'in kind' then the gain when you sell it will be exempt.

If you have let out your home as residential accommodation and for that reason cannot claim the whole of the gain as exempt as your main residence, then part of the gain, if any, which otherwise would be a chargeable gain because of the letting, is exempt up to £40,000 or the amount which is attributable to the period of, or part used for, residential letting (if less than £40,000).

GAINS ON DEATH

At the date of death, assets in your estate are revalued but appreciation is not generally subject to tax.

GAINS OF SETTLEMENTS

Trustees are liable for tax on the gains of a trust unless the person creating the trust (the settlor) has an interest in the trust or it is not a UK resident trust. The settlor has an interest in a UK trust if he enjoys any benefit from it or any of its property can be applied for his or his spouse's benefit in any circumstance. In such a case the settlor pays the tax attributable to the trustees' disposals. See the end of this chapter for how the tax is calculated.

Offshore trusts

A settlor is also liable to tax on gains of certain trusts he has created where the trustees are not UK resident. If this situation applies to you specialist advice should be sought.

TRANSFERS OF ASSETS

Transfers between husband and wife

These do not give rise to chargeable capital gains. Instead, the spouse acquiring the asset is treated as though they acquired it at a value which gives rise to neither gain nor loss for the spouse making the disposal.

Tax Alert

If you are getting divorced, part of your divorce settlement may involve transferring assets to your spouse. Transfers of assets between spouses are only exempt from capital gains tax if the couple are married and living together. You should therefore make sure that you take account of any potential tax liability in reaching the divorce settlement.

Transfers of assets to others

If you dispose of an asset to another person on favourable terms or make an outright gift, you are treated as if you sold it on open market terms. Market value also applies to transactions between people who are connected – you are connected with any of your own direct line relatives or those of your husband or wife, eg, brother, sister, children, grandchildren, parents or grandparents. You are also connected with persons such as the trustees of any trust you make, and a company of which you have control. You may also be connected with your business partners (and their relatives).

CAPITAL GAINS TAX RELIEFS

Holdover relief

You can avoid paying tax on a gift if you can claim holdover relief. Under this relief the recipient receives the asset at a value which gives you neither a gain nor a loss so that effectively your gain is taken over by the recipient. Assets which qualify for holdover relief are gifts of business assets used for the purposes of a trade, profession or vocation carried on by the person making the gift, or shares or securities in an unquoted trading company (which includes those quoted on the Alternative Investment Market (AIM)). Fully quoted or USM company shares also qualify where the donor can exercise at least 5% of the voting rights in the shares. The relief also applies to disposals of agricultural property and on disposals which are 'chargeable transfers' for inheritance tax purposes such as a gift to a discretionary trust. (See Chapter 15 for details of 'chargeable transfers'.)

As noted, with effect from 6 April 1988, the assumed acquisition cost of assets held on 31 March 1982 is their value at that date. This intended improvement in the position of the taxpayer had an adverse effect for those who had made gifts between the two dates mentioned above, and who had held over (and hence, preserved) the inherent gain. Thus, an arbitrary solution was adopted. In a case where the gain was held over before 6 April 1988, thereby deducting it from the cost basis (the deemed acquisition cost) to the recipient, that deduction is reduced by one-half.

Retirement relief

Despite its name, you do not have to retire to obtain this deduction from your capital gains. However, if you are selling a business or business assets, a distinct part of your business must be shown to have been sold. The relief applies to disposals of the business itself, business assets which you have used for at least a year in a trade which you carry on by yourself or in partnership or on a disposal of shares in a personal trading company (if you are a full-time working director or employee of that company). A personal trading company is one in which you have at least 5% of the voting rights. The relief also applies to disposals of assets you own but which have been used by a company which is your personal company. The asset you dispose of must have been used in the business for at least one full year but to get maximum retirement relief the asset should have been owned as a business asset throughout a period of ten years.

You can obtain relief once you are 50 whether or not you have retired. You can also obtain relief if you are under the qualifying age and have retired on grounds of ill-health, although in these circumstances it is necessary to formally claim the relief. Full tax relief is available for gains of up to £250,000 plus half of any further gains between £250,000 and £1,000,000. However, the actual amount of relief is determined according to a sliding scale which rises arithmetically according to the length of the period for which you have owned the business asset. If you have owned the asset for the minimum period of one year, the percentage of the £250,000 exemption is 10%, (ie, you can deduct £25,000 from your gains on the asset, plus up to 10% of one-half of £750,000, ie, £37,500). If you have owned the asset for five years the percentage would be 50% and so on. Husband and wife are each eligible for the relief if they each satisfy the conditions.

Tax Saver

If you are planning to dispose of your business, consider the timing carefully and try to arrange your affairs so that you will qualify for retirement relief. For example, if you and your wife own 5% of the company's shares between you but neither of you owns 5% individually, consider whether one of you should transfer their shares to the other so that the whole gain is exempt. You can also elect to treat a business interest you received from your spouse as having been owned by you during the prior period of ownership of your spouse. You should take advice on this matter.

Reinvestment relief

If, after taking into account all other deductions in calculating your capital gains, you still have a high tax bill, you could consider reinvestment relief. Reinvestment relief applies to an investment in an unquoted trading company. Provided you reinvest some or all of the chargeable gain element of the proceeds of disposal of other chargeable assets, in shares of a qualifying company, you can deduct the gain from the cost of the company shares you buy, effectively deferring payment of capital gains tax until such time, if ever, as you dispose of those new shares.

Example: You sell some land for £200,000 making a capital gain of £50,000. You apply £30,000 in acquiring shares in an unquoted trading company. You can claim reinvestment relief and reduce your chargeable gain to £20,000.

There is no limit on the amount you may invest, enabling you to eliminate all your capital gains if you are so inclined. There are some restrictions on the companies which qualify as an investment for reinvestment relief purposes and certain trades are ineligible, eg, dealing in land, commodities, futures, shares or securities; providing financial, legal or accountancy services. Investments made before 29 November 1994 also excluded property development and farming companies. However, such businesses are acceptable investments from that date.

It should be noted that investments in such unquoted trading companies will involve an element of risk.

Reinvestment relief can also be available where the proceeds of a disposal are wholly or partly invested in a company which qualifies under the Enterprise Investment Scheme (see Chapter 3). This is in addition to the existing income tax relief making a possible tax deduction of up to 60%. If you are seeking both reliefs, take professional advice as to whether your chosen investment is appropriate for this purpose.

Tax Saver

You could use reinvestment relief to eliminate your capital gains altogether in some circumstances. For example, you could hold your new investment until you reached age 50 when you may meet the retirement relief conditions in relation to it.

Tax Saver

Remember you do not have to reinvest the whole proceeds of your asset sale – you need only invest sufficient to eliminate your tax liability (ie, the gain element).

Rollover relief

In addition to the above, if you carry on a trade and assets used in that trade are disposed of, any gain arising may be deferred if the proceeds of sale are reinvested into new business assets used for trading purposes. (See Chapter 12.)

Assets of negligible value

If you own an asset which has been lost or destroyed or become of negligible value, you can claim a capital loss. For example, if you own shares in a company that has gone into liquidation, you can claim a loss on the cost of your asset. You will need to make a claim and your Inspector of Taxes will have to be satisfied that the value of the asset is negligible.

Tax Saver

If you own shares in a company that has gone into liquidation you should make a claim before 31 January 1998 on your tax return. That way you can set off the loss against other gains realised in 1996/97.

WORKING OUT CAPITAL GAINS TAX DUE

Under the new self assessment provisions, effective for 1996/97 and later years, the capital gains tax arising is due on 31 January following the end of the tax year, thus tax due on capital gains of 1996/97 will be due for payment on 31 January 1998. Any delay in submitting your tax return could result in interest and penalties being charged. (See Chapter 4.)

Tax Filing Tip

To calculate your capital gains/loss position the tax return Capital Gains (page CG1) should be used.

You may find when you have carried out all your computations on disposals of assets in the year that you have some assets which have resulted in gains and some which have resulted in losses.

You may also have available capital losses from earlier years which you did not utilise and which you have carried forward. Your first step is therefore to work out the total amount of chargeable gains taxable in the year.

Subtract this year's losses from this year's gains. If the overall result is a loss, it is available to carry forward against future gains. If the overall result is a gain, you then deduct your annual exemption of £6,300 for 1996/97 (£6,500 for 1997/98). If you have not used your annual exemption in full, the balance is lost. If your net gains exceed your annual exemption you should then look to see if you have any losses brought forward from an earlier year. These must be set against the remaining gain until it is exhausted. Any balance of losses brought forward which remain after the gain has been reduced to nil, will be carried forward to be used in a future year. If you have no losses to bring forward or they are insufficient to reduce the remaining gain to zero, what remains is chargeable to tax.

The tax rate applicable to your net taxable gains depends on your income tax position. If you have no income at all, then the income tax rate bands are applied against your net taxable gains, ie, for 1996/97 the first £3,900 (£4,100: 1997/98) of gains is taxed at 20%, the next £21,600 is taxed at 24% (£22,000 taxed at 23%: 1997/98), and any excess is taxed at 40%.

In the more likely situation where you do have other income, the net taxable gains are taxed at the rate applicable as though they were the top slice of your income. This means that if you pay income tax at 40% the whole of your net taxable gains will be taxed at 40%. If you pay income tax at 24% (23%: 1997/98) your net taxable gains will be taxed at 24% (23%: 1997/98). However, if when added to your taxable income, they take you through the basic rate threshold of £25,500, for 1996/97 (or £26,100 for 1997/98) part of your gains will be taxed at 24% (23%: 1997/98) and part at 40%.

Tax Saver

If you have large capital gains you may be able to reduce your tax liability on them by increasing your income tax deductions or by investing in assets providing tax-free income. Income tax deductions cannot be set off against capital gains but by reducing your rate of income tax from a higher band to a lower band the rate of tax applicable to your capital gains will reduce.

Tax Saver

Only deductions from total income reduce your liability to capital gains tax in this way – deductions which are an income tax reduction, such as the married couple's allowance or the enterprise investment scheme relief, will have no impact on your rate of tax or your capital gains tax liability.

Settlor-interested trust gains

Where a trust makes capital gains and it is treated as one in which you have an interest as settlor, tax on the gains is calculated by reference to your tax position and charged and assessed on you. The trust will work out its capital gains in the usual way and will deduct any losses in the year of assessment or losses from earlier years but the trust cannot deduct any annual exemption to which it is entitled (ie, normally £3,150 for 1996/97 and £3,250 for 1997/98). The resultant gains are treated as though they were your gains.

3 Tax reliefs

PERSONAL ALLOWANCES

Personal allowances (also called 'personal reliefs') are the final deductions you make to arrive at your taxable income. Everyone, including children, is entitled to a basic personal income tax allowance which for 1996/97 is £3,765 and for 1997/98 will be £4,045. However, people aged 65 or over may get higher allowances – see *'Age allowance'* overleaf.

Tax Filing Tip

Basic personal allowances will be available automatically but additional allowances as noted below must be claimed on the Tax Return: Page 6.

Tax Saver

Personal allowances are not normally transferable between husband and wife. A special rule applies if a husband's income in 1991/92 was less than £3,295 and has continued in subsequent years to be less than the level of the personal allowance. If you think you might qualify for this relief you should speak to your local tax office.

Tax Saver

To reduce your tax bill ensure that all of the members of your family use their reliefs. If your spouse's income is less than their personal allowances but you have taxable investment income consider transferring investments to them so that their personal allowances can be used. This is worthwhile even if your spouse does have taxable income if their tax rate is lower than yours.

Married couple's allowance

A married man whose wife is living with him can claim the married couple's allowance in addition to the basic personal allowance. The amount of the allowance is £1,790 for 1996/97 but you get tax relief on this at only 15% (saving you up to £268.50 tax). The allowance is given by reducing your tax bill by the appropriate amount (but cannot reduce it below zero). The allowance for 1997/98 is £1,830 and the tax saving is £274.50. The allowance is given in the first instance to the husband but the wife has the right to claim one-half of the allowance without her husband's consent. In addition, husband and wife can jointly elect to transfer the whole of the allowance to the wife. In either case, ask your Tax Inspector for Inland Revenue Form 18. Only the married couple's allowance can be transferred in this way, not the husband's or wife's personal allowances.

Tax Filing Tip

Complete section A of Form 18 if you wish to transfer the whole married couple's allowance, or section B to claim one-half of the allowance.

You must give notice that you intend to make an election before 6 April at the start of the tax year for which it is to operate. Ideally you should return the form by that date but provided you have notified your Tax Inspector in writing that you intend to make the election, you can return the completed form by 5 May.

Tax Filing Tip

Whether the whole of the married couple's allowance is transferred, or husband and wife each claim one-half, the relevant boxes of the tax return should only be ticked if you have previously received acknowledgement of the allocation from your Tax Inspector. Refer to Tax Return: Page 6.

An election made in the year of your marriage operates straight away. However, the allowance will be reduced by one-twelfth for each complete month in the tax year before the date of marriage. Once you have made an election it continues to operate either until you withdraw it or until you make a different election. There is a tax saving in electing if you know that the husband will not have enough taxable income to set against the allowance but the wife will. There can also be a cash flow advantage in making the election if the husband is self-employed. If you do not elect and there is an unused amount of the relief, the balance can be transferred to your spouse provided you give notice to the Revenue (on Form 575) not later than six years after the end of the relevant tax year. If a couple separates or divorces in the year, relief is given in full for the year of separation but not in any subsequent year.

The personal allowance and the married couple's allowance are given in full for a person who dies during the tax year.

Age allowance

People aged 65 or over at the end of the tax year get higher amounts of personal allowance, known as age allowance. In 1996/97 their allowance is £4,910 or, for those aged 75 or over, £5,090. In 1997/98 these allowances are £5,220 and £5,400. Where figures are shown in brackets in the following paragraphs they represent the 1997/98 figures. To qualify for the full amount of these allowances, your 'total income' (see below) must not exceed £15,200 (£15,600). If your 'total income' is higher than this, the allowance is scaled down by one-half of the excess until it reaches the normal personal allowance of £3,765 (£4,045). The annual income above which there is no increase is therefore £17,490 (£17,950) for someone aged 65 or over, and £17,850 (£18,310) for someone aged 75 or over.

Total income: Your 'total income' is your gross income from all sources, less your outgoings. These are defined as follows:

■ Your 'gross income' includes your earnings, pensions, income from investments and all the types of income described in Chapter 1 except for tax-free income. Include the gross amount of income which was paid to you with tax deducted (ie, add back in the amount of that tax). With share dividends and unit trust distributions add the tax credit or amount on the tax voucher to the amount you actually received. You must also include any taxable gain arising as a result of making withdrawals from or surrendering an investment bond or non-qualifying life insurance policy.

■ Your 'outgoings' are all the deductions and reliefs described in this chapter and in Chapter 1 which qualify for relief and can be deducted from your income in working out your tax, except personal allowances.

Married couple's allowance for over-65s

The married couple's allowance is also increased if either of the couple is aged 65 or over at the end of the tax year. The tax reduction is 15% of £3,115 (£3,185 for 1997/98), but if either or both are 75 or over at the end of the tax year it is 15% of £3,155 (£3,225 for 1997/98).

In this case, the husband's 'total income' must not exceed £15,200 (£15,600 for 1997/98) in order to qualify for the higher allowance in full. If his 'total income' exceeds this figure the allowance is reduced by one-half of the income over that figure, down to the normal married couple's allowance of £1,790 (£1,830 for 1997/98). However, this 'excess income' is first taken into account to reduce his personal age allowance to the level of the normal personal allowance. Only the remaining 'excess income' if any, goes to reduce the married couple's allowance.

Example (1996/97): Husband aged 65

Maximum personal age allowance 1996/97:		£4,910
Total income:	£17,600	
Threshold for full allowance:	£15,200	
Excess income:	£2,400	
His allowance is reduced by half this excess, ie by	£1,200	
But the maximum reduction is:		£1,145
So he gets the normal personal allowance of:		£3,765
Maximum married couple's allowance:		£3,115
This is reduced by (£1,200 – £1,145), ie by:		£55
So his married couple's allowance is:		£3,060

Tax Saver

Married couples over 65 should consider organising their affairs so that they qualify for the higher relief. You will benefit most if the 'total income' of each of you is kept below £15,600 (1997/98). Next best would be for the husband to restrict his income to that level without causing the wife's income to be subject to higher rate tax. You may be able to do this by exchanging taxable investments for tax-free ones, such as National Savings Certificates, TESSAs, etc. (see Chapter 1 and Chapter 13).

Additional personal allowance for children

Additional relief is available to single parent families or where a man is married to and living with a wife who is totally incapacitated by physical or mental infirmity throughout the year.

The tax relief is given by reducing your tax liability by £268.50 (15% of £1,790) for 1996/97, but it cannot reduce it below zero. For 1997/98 the reduction is £274.50 (15% of £1,830).

To qualify a child must be living with you for the whole or part of the tax year. If the child is over 16 at the start of the tax year they must be in full-time education or training at university, college, school or other educational establishment. If the child is not your own child or your adopted or step-child, he or she must be under 18 at the start of the year and you must maintain them for the whole or part of the year at your own expense. You cannot claim this allowance as well as the married couple's allowance and you only get one allowance even if you have more than one qualifying child living with you. An unmarried couple who live together can only get one allowance which must be claimed for the youngest child of either of them. Where two or more people are entitled to relief for the same child, the relief can be apportioned between them either as they agree or in proportion to the length of the periods during which the child resides with each of them.

Tax Saver

If you are entitled to this relief in the year of marriage you can elect to keep it instead of claiming the married couple's allowance for the year. This will be advantageous since the married couple's allowance will be proportionately reduced if you marry part way through the year, while this additional relief will not be.

Widow's bereavement allowance

A woman gets this allowance in the tax year in which her husband dies and in the following tax year (unless she has remarried before that tax year begins). The tax relief is given by reducing your tax liability by £268.50 (15% of £1,790), but it cannot reduce it below zero. For 1997/98 the reduction is £274.50 (15% of £1,830).

Blind person's allowance

A registered blind person (or a person who becomes so during the year) can claim a deduction of £1,250 (£1,280) from their total income. A married person without sufficient total income to deduct the whole of the £1,250 (£1,280), can pass the balance of the deduction to their spouse.

PENSION CONTRIBUTIONS

Employers' pension schemes

Approved schemes have to comply with Inland Revenue and other regulations, and in return get generous tax concessions. Unapproved schemes have far fewer controls but no tax concessions. There is more information about pension planning in Chapter 14.

Approved schemes

An approved scheme can provide you with a pension at the scheme's normal retirement date of up to two-thirds of your final salary. If you joined the scheme after 1 June 1989 there is an 'earnings cap' on your final salary which for 1996/97 is £82,200 and for 1997/98 is £84,000. The scheme can also provide other benefits, including a tax-free lump sum and widow's and dependants' pensions up to two-thirds of your pension. You are not taxed on the contributions your employer pays into the scheme and investments in the pension fund can grow free of tax, but you are taxed on your pension when it is paid.

You can contribute up to 15% of your earnings from your job to your employer's pension scheme and get tax relief at your highest rate on what you pay. However, unless the scheme came into existence before 14 March 1989 and you joined it before 1 June 1989, you cannot pay contributions on earnings of more than the 'earnings cap' (see above).

If your employer's scheme is non-contributory or your contribution is less than the maximum of 15% of your earnings, you can choose to make voluntary contributions (as long as these would not make your eventual benefits more than the maximum allowed). These can be either additional voluntary contributions (AVCs) to your employer's occupational scheme or free-standing additional voluntary contributions (FSAVCs) to a personal free-standing AVC scheme of your choice.

Tax relief on pension contributions and AVCs into your employer's scheme is given by deducting them from your pay before working out the tax on it. You get tax relief on FSAVCs at the basic rate by paying a reduced amount to the pension provider. Any relief from higher rate tax which is due will be given either through adjustment to your PAYE code during the year or by deduction on your self assessment after the end of the tax year.

Tax Filing Tip

Deduction for employee contributions may be claimed on the Tax Return: Page 5.

Unlike personal pension plans and retirement annuity contracts (referred to later in this chapter), there is no opportunity within employers' pension schemes either to carry forward or to carry back any voluntary contributions paid into a different tax year.

Lump sum benefits

Most employers' pension schemes permit members to exchange part of their pension for a tax-free cash lump sum. The maximum lump sum you can draw under Inland Revenue rules is one and a half times your final salary.

Life insurance benefits

An employer's pension scheme can also provide life insurance benefits which will pay out a tax-free lump sum of up to four times your current annual salary (plus a return of the value of any personal contributions) if you die before retirement.

You can nominate the people you would like the trustees to pay it to on your death. The scheme may also pay pensions to your widowed spouse and dependent children.

Tax Saver

Generally, contributing to an approved pension scheme is a tax-efficient way of saving for the future as you get tax relief at your highest rate on contributions you make and the pension fund does not pay tax on its investment income or gains. These factors mean the long-term returns can be much greater than if you made a direct investment yourself.

Tax Alert

Deciding whether or not to pay additional voluntary contributions and whether they should be made to your employer's scheme or to a separate scheme depends on a number of factors:

- *If your employer's contributions are enough to provide you with the maximum benefits permitted under Inland Revenue rules, you will not gain anything by paying either kind of AVCs.*
- *If the rules of your employer's scheme would give lower benefits than the maximum permitted by the Inland Revenue rules, you might do better by taking out a FSAVC so that you top up the benefits you get under your employer's scheme.*
- *If you will get less than full pension benefits at retirement age, because you joined the scheme late in your working life, AVCs and FSAVCs can be an effective way of topping up your entitlement.*

You should take professional advice in this area before making any decision.

Unapproved retirement benefit schemes

In addition to an approved scheme an employer may provide benefits under an unapproved retirement benefits scheme or funded unapproved retirement benefits scheme (FURB). These schemes are generally used to top up benefits available under approved pension schemes, particularly where the 'earnings cap' applies. An unapproved unfunded arrangement is simply a promise to provide retirement benefits. A FURB, on the other hand, is safer from the employee's point of view, because the employer sets up a trust to hold and administer funds to which he contributes to provide benefits.

Generally the contributions your employer pays into the FURB towards your pension count as a benefit in kind and you have to pay tax on them, but they are usually not subject to National Insurance. Because the scheme is unapproved the benefits can be more flexible. At retirement the fund built up can be used to purchase an annuity or simply provide you with a cash lump sum. If the lump sum is funded solely from contributions on which you were originally subject to tax, then it is wholly tax-free when paid over.

Personal pensions

If you are self-employed or you are not a member of an occupational scheme provided by your employer, you can provide your own pension by making contributions to a personal pension plan. If you took out a pension contract before 1 July 1988 it will be a retirement annuity contract (the predecessor of a personal pension plan) and you can continue to make contributions to it as well as to personal pension plans. The limits on the contributions you can pay to each type of contract are described in detail below.

If your employer operates a Group Personal Pension or contributes to your personal pension (unfortunately only a few employers are willing to do so) you do not have to pay any tax on the contributions he makes.

Personal pension plan contributions

Tax Filing Tip

Relief for premiums paid into a personal pension plan should be claimed on the Tax Return: Page 5.

You get tax relief at your highest rate on contributions which you make to your own personal pension plan. However, there are limits on the contributions you can pay for each tax year. You cannot pay more than a set percentage of your *'net relevant earnings'* (see below). Nor can you pay contributions on an income higher than the 'earnings cap' (£82,200 in 1996/97 and £84,000 in 1997/98).

'Relevant earnings' means income from self-employment, a partnership, freelance earnings or from your employment (unless approved pension arrangements have already been provided by your employer). They also include income from such sources as an inventor's patent rights from his inventions.

Your 'net' relevant earnings are found by making all the allowable deductions to arrive at your taxable business profits, any allowable expenses in respect of your employment income, any payroll donations you make to charity, as well as any losses and capital allowances to which you are entitled.

The maximum contribution to your personal pension plan is a percentage of your net relevant earnings, depending on your age at the beginning of the tax year, as shown below.

Age	Percentage of 'net relevant earnings'
Under 36	17.5%
36 - 45	20%
46 - 50	25%
51 - 55	30%
56 - 60	35%
61 or more	40%

Up to 5% of the permitted contributions can be used to provide life assurance cover on death before age 75. You can thus get full tax relief on such life assurance premiums.

Premiums do not necessarily have to be paid in the tax year for which they qualify for tax relief:

- *Unused relief* If you have net relevant earnings in any year but do not pay the maximum permitted contribution, the difference between what you pay and what you could have paid is known as unused relief. Unused relief can be carried forward and contributions made in any of the next six tax years up to the maximum relief for that year plus the unused relief brought forward. Unused relief is given on a first-in, first-out basis – you have to use up relief from an earlier year before relief from a later year.

- *Carrying back contributions* You can elect to carry a premium back to the preceding tax year or, if you had no net relevant earnings in that year, to the one before that. This is particularly useful in letting you maximise contributions if you do not know what your net relevant earnings are for a year until after it has finished. An election to carry back contributions must be made by 31 January after the end of the tax year in which the contributions are paid. (See also *'Carry back of premiums'* under *'Retirement annuity contracts'*.)

You can combine the ability to carry premiums back and to carry unused relief forward to maximise your tax relief in each year.

Tax Saver

If your earnings fluctuate so that you are a higher rate taxpayer in some years but not in others, try to carry forward relief and carry back contributions so that you get the biggest deduction in the years in which your tax rate is highest.

Tax Alert

If you overpay contributions to a personal pension plan, the plan provider is obliged to repay the contribution in full and you will get no tax relief.

Benefits from personal pensions

At some time between the ages of 50 (though it can be earlier if you are too ill to work again) and 75 you must use your accumulated pension fund to buy an annuity which will pay you a pension for life. However, you can take up to 25% of the value of the fund (less the value of protected rights under the Social Security Act 1986) as a tax-free lump sum. In the past you had to buy the annuity at the same time as you took the lump sum; as annuity rates vary over time, this meant that you could be obliged to buy the annuity at a time when it was relatively expensive. However, you can now defer buying the annuity (whether or not you take the lump sum) until annuity rates are more favourable (but not beyond your 75th birthday). Meanwhile, you will be able to take an income withdrawal every 12 months of not less than 35% nor more than 100% of the annuity which your pension fund could otherwise buy for you at specified 'relevant dates'. These are broadly every three years at which time the scheme is reviewed to ensure withdrawals are not depleting the fund too rapidly.

The plan can also provide for a pension to be paid after your death to your surviving spouse or dependants, and for a lump sum to be paid if you die before drawing your pension. The lump sum cannot be more than the value of your contributions plus a reasonable amount of interest (or the actual value of a unit-linked contract).

Both types of lump sum benefit (on retirement and on death) are free of tax but the pensions are taxable as earned income. If there is a refund of the pension fund (a return of contributions) made on death in a case where advantage has been taken of the new rules for deferring the purchase of an annuity, the payment will suffer a tax charge of 35% deducted by the pension scheme administrator.

Retirement annuity contracts

Tax Filing Tip

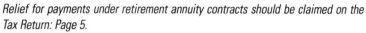
Relief for payments under retirement annuity contracts should be claimed on the Tax Return: Page 5.

The benefits provided by a retirement annuity contract are similar to those from a personal pension plan except that the pension cannot commence before age 60. The annuity can be partly exchanged for a lump sum which must not exceed three times the remaining annual pension. On contracts taken out between 17 March 1987 and 1 July 1988, the maximum lump sum is £150,000 per contract. The annuity is taxable as earned income but the lump sum is tax-free. As well as providing for a widow's, widower's or dependant's pension, a separate contract could also be taken out to provide life assurance up to age 75. The premiums you pay for this qualify for tax relief and the insurance proceeds are tax-free.

You cannot now take out a new retirement annuity contract, but if you have existing contracts you can continue to pay premiums into them (up to certain limits) and claim full tax relief. The contribution limits for retirement annuities differ from those for personal pensions but are still linked to a percentage of 'net relevant earnings' (see page 61).

Age	Percentage of 'net relevant earnings'
Under 51	17.5%
51 - 55	20.0%
56 - 60	22.5%
61 or more	27.5%

There is no 'earnings cap' in relation to a retirement annuity contract so if your earnings are above the earnings cap you may be able to contribute more to an existing retirement annuity than you could to a personal pension – though the higher percentage contribution levels for personal pensions may reverse this position.

A tax deduction is given for premiums paid in the year but as with personal pensions, you can elect to carry a premium back to the preceding tax year or, if you had no net relevant earnings in that year, to the one before that. Again, as with personal pensions, if you do not pay the maximum permitted premium in any year, the unused relief can be carried forward and used in any of the next six tax years. See above for how this can help your planning.

Carry back of premiums

Relief for carried back premiums under retirement annuity contracts and personal pension plans is calculated by reference to the tax rates for the previous year, but, unlike the arrangements prior to self assessment, this is no longer given by reducing the tax of the previous year but by reducing the tax due for the year in which the premiums are paid.

Tax Saver

Due to the above change in the mechanics of giving relief if you normally carry back your premiums you will have a gap year in 1996/97 when your tax liability will have no relief for such premiums. This can be avoided if you can afford a double premium in 1996/97 part to relate back to 1995/96 and part to obtain relief in 1996/97.

Tax Alert

Unlike personal pensions, if you overpay contributions into a retirement annuity contract, the contract provider is not obliged to refund your contribution – you simply do not get tax relief on the excess paid.

Tax Saver

If you have a retirement annuity contract but want to draw pension before age 60, it is usually possible to transfer your fund into a personal pension plan so you can take advantage of the earlier retirement date. However, you should find out what penalties might be imposed.

If it is customary in your line of work to retire earlier than the specified retirement date, both types of contract permit this. The Inland Revenue have a list of occupations with agreed retirement dates of which your pension adviser will be aware.

Trade union schemes

Some trade unions or bodies representing a substantial number of people engaged in a particular occupation operate their own trust schemes approved by the Inland Revenue. The provisions relating to retirement annuities also apply to such schemes.

Interaction of personal pensions and retirement annuities

You are not confined to paying either retirement annuity premiums or personal pension premiums in any one year of assessment – you can pay a combination of both. The overall limit, however, is that set for personal pensions and if you pay retirement annuity premiums as well you must deduct these from the maximum permitted personal pension contributions. The effect is that if your limit of personal pension contributions is smaller than your retirement annuity limit, by paying a mixture of premiums you are restricting the total relief available to the smaller figure.

By paying a mixture you may also restrict the amount of unused retirement annuity relief available for carrying forward to a later year. In working out the unused relief you must deduct from the maximum annual relief available not only the retirement annuities paid in the year, but also the personal pension contributions paid in the year or carried back from a later year.

Tax Alert

If you earn in excess of the earnings cap, paying a mixture of retirement annuities and personal pension contributions will restrict your total deductible contributions. By paying only retirement annuity premiums you may be able to pay a higher level of contributions into your pension plan, giving you more tax relief, and hence a higher tax saving.

Comparing personal pensions with retirement annuities

If you have a choice (ie, you already have an existing retirement annuity contract), which type of contribution should you pay? This depends on a variety of factors. Retirement annuities offer different benefits at a different age from personal pension schemes so you may want to consider when you are most likely to retire and draw your pension. On the other hand, if you decide to retire early most retirement annuity contracts can be converted into personal pension schemes before they are drawn, though there will be costs involved. If you have only one or two retirement annuity contracts and you want a wider range of investments, then you may decide to use personal pensions instead. If you just want to maximise the tax deduction for the premium, then you will need to do your calculations very carefully.

If you are below the earnings cap, personal pensions will usually offer the biggest deduction. As you get older the percentage deduction under personal pension schemes increases more rapidly than that for retirement annuities and personal pensions may still offer a better option for those only slightly above the earnings cap. If you earn significantly above the earnings cap, however, you are likely to find that paying retirement annuities only, is your best option.

Payments into pension schemes are one of the most tax advantageous investments you can make. You are entitled to full tax relief on your contributions. If you pay tax at basic rate this means that £1,000 worth of pension investment will only cost you £760 (£770 1997/98) whereas if you are a higher rate taxpayer the same £1,000 investment only costs you £600. Your premiums are then invested and accumulate, free of income and capital gains tax, until you draw your retirement benefits. So the fund grows faster than it would if funded by taxed savings. To get the best out of the tax-free roll-up within the pension plan, always pay your pension contributions as early as possible so that funds accumulate tax-free for the longest period of time.

RELIEF FOR INTEREST YOU PAY

If you pay interest on a loan you may be entitled to tax relief on the interest paid, depending on the purpose of the loan. Interest relief is available on:

- loans to purchase property to be let
- loans to buy your main home
- loans to buy machinery or plant for use in a partnership of which you are a partner
- loans to buy an interest in or to lend money to certain companies (close companies)
- loans to buy an interest in a co-operative or employee-controlled company
- loans used in contributing capital to a partnership
- loans to pay inheritance tax
- loans on certain home income plans where the loan is used to buy a life annuity by a person who has attained age 65.

Whatever the purpose of the loan, you cannot get any relief for simple overdraft interest unless the overdraft was incurred wholly and exclusively for the purpose of a business and the interest is an allowable expense.

How tax relief is given

Normally interest you pay which qualifies for tax relief may be subtracted from your income before the tax is calculated, so that you get relief at your highest rate of tax. However, with loans to buy your main home and loans taken out by the elderly to buy annuities the amount of relief is restricted, both in amount and percentage relief. In each case qualifying loans are limited to £30,000 and the relief in the former case to 15% and in the latter case to 24% for 1996/97 (23% for 1997/98). In addition, most borrowers get their relief by making lower payments to the lender; others can deduct a fixed percentage of their qualifying interest from their tax bill.

Loans to purchase property to be let

You can get tax relief on the interest you pay on a loan used to buy land and the buildings on it or to improve or develop it, or alternatively to repay an existing loan taken out for this purpose. This relief for interest applies equally to UK properties and loans to purchase properties overseas and is secured by deduction in the first instance from the letting income.

Loans to buy your main residence

Most people who buy their own home take out a loan or mortgage to help fund the cost. Interest relief is available on such borrowings but is more restrictive than on property which you buy to let commercially. Relief is available on only one property which is your only, or main, residence. In addition, relief is available only on loans you take out to acquire the property, not on loans for improving it (unless the improvement loan was made before 6 April 1988).

There is a limit to the amount of the loan on which you can get interest relief. This limit is £30,000 and applies per residence, not per borrower (unless the loan was made before 1 August 1988).

For unmarried owners jointly owning a home who have each taken out a loan to buy their share, the £30,000 limit is divided equally among those paying the interest. If anyone cannot use all their share of the limit because their loan is less, the excess is distributed amongst those owners who can use it.

A married couple can jointly elect that qualifying interest payable by either of them is allocated between them in whatever proportions they choose. It does not matter which of you actually pays the interest or owns the home. An 'allocation of interest' election must be made on Form 15-1 obtainable from your Inspector of Taxes. The election must be made by both of you within twelve months of the end of the tax year to which it applies. Once made, it applies for all subsequent years until you change it by jointly lodging a new election. Although the election must be made jointly, it can be withdrawn in subsequent years by either spouse.

Tax relief is given in one of two ways. In most cases the mortgage interest relief at source (MIRAS) arrangement applies, and the amount the lender asks you to pay each month will have been reduced by tax relief at the appropriate rate on the first £30,000 you borrowed. (You get this 'tax relief' even if your income is too low to pay tax.) Where MIRAS does not apply you get relief by claiming a deduction against your overall tax liability. In either case, the rate at which tax relief is given is 15% for 1996/97 and 1997/98.

Tax Filing Tip

Claim for relief for interest paid other than in MIRAS must be made on the Tax Return: Page 5.

To qualify for the MIRAS scheme, the interest must be payable in the UK to a qualifying lender (which includes most UK banks and building societies) and the property must be situated in the UK and at least two-thirds of it must be used as your main residence. The question of whether a property is used as a main residence or not will be determined in the first instance by your Inspector of Taxes. This may be important where you live in rented accommodation during the working week but live in your own property at weekends – or alternatively if you own two properties and have a loan on one but not on the other. Usually it is possible to settle this question quickly with the Inland Revenue based on the facts of the situation. If a husband and wife each own a property which each uses as their main residence, only one property qualifies for tax relief: the home bought first is treated as the main residence of both and the other does not qualify for relief.

If you are temporarily absent from your home you will not lose the mortgage interest relief provided that the absence does not exceed one year. If you are required to live away from home because of your job (either in the UK or abroad) you can still get mortgage interest relief for up to four years of absence provided you expect to live in the home again when you return.

Tax Saver

Married couples should consider making an allocation of interest election if they do not get tax relief under MIRAS and the spouse paying the interest does not pay tax while the other does.

Moving home

When you move home there may be a period of time when you have two loans, one to buy the new home and one on the old home which has not yet been sold. These may be either mortgages or bridging loans. If interest on each loan would qualify for tax relief on the criteria given above, you will get relief:

- on the new loan, provided you are using the new home as your main residence when the interest is paid or within twelve months of paying the interest, and
- on the old loan, provided you intend to take steps to sell it within 12 months of moving out.

If you are having difficulty selling your home the Inland Revenue have discretion to extend the twelve-month periods which they will do in appropriate circumstances. You should write to your Inspector of Taxes to explain why you have two homes and what steps you are taking to sell one.

Loan to buy an interest in a 'close company' or a partnership

In order for a loan to buy an interest in a company to qualify for tax relief:

- The company must be a 'close company' – ie, more than 50% of the ownership must be in the hands of five or fewer 'participators' (people who own the share capital or voting rights in the company).
- The company must exist for the purpose of carrying on a trade on a commercial basis or for making investments in land let to people not connected with the company.
- The loan must be used to buy ordinary shares, or to make a loan to the company.
- Broadly you must own or be able to control more than 5% of the ordinary share capital or have an entitlement to receive more than 5% of the assets available for distribution on winding up.

Interest will also qualify for relief if the loan is used to replace another loan which was eligible for relief.

In the case of a loan used to buy into or to lend to a partnership, you must have been a member of the partnership (though not a limited partner) throughout the period from when the loan was taken out until the interest was paid. Additionally, you must be able to show that you have not received any capital payment from the partnership. Salaried partners in professional firms may also claim this relief.

Tax Saver

Interest relief on partnership loans is now more tax advantageous than mortgage interest relief because you get relief at your highest rate of tax rather than it being restricted to 15%. If you have a number of loans it may be beneficial to restructure your borrowing so that you increase your partnership loans and reduce your mortgage. You may be able to do this by withdrawing capital from the partnership and using it to repay other borrowings, and then at a later date taking out further partnership borrowings. You must be extremely careful about the order in which you restructure borrowings as otherwise you could lose interest relief altogether. You should take advice from your accountant or tax adviser on whether this may be feasible for you.

Loan to pay inheritance tax

When someone dies their executor must pay inheritance tax before they are able to obtain authority to administer the estate. If a personal representative takes out a loan to pay inheritance tax, he can get tax relief on the interest he pays for up to one year by deducting the interest from the income of the estate.

Loan to buy a life annuity

If you are 65 or over, you can get tax relief on the interest you pay on up to £30,000 of loans secured on your home if you use at least 90% of the loans to buy a life annuity. This is in addition to tax relief you get on up to £30,000 of loans used to buy your home. The property on which the loan is secured must be in the UK or Republic of Ireland and must be your only or main residence at the time the interest is paid.

You get tax relief at the basic rate of 24% (23%: 1997/98) on the interest you pay, whatever your top tax rate and even if you pay no tax. The relief is normally given to you by the lender reducing your monthly payment. If not, you can deduct 24% (23%) of the interest you pay in the tax year from your tax liability for that year.

MAINTENANCE PAYMENTS

Tax Filing Tip

Claims for maintenance payments should be made on the Tax Return: Page 5.

Maintenance payments are amounts paid to a spouse or former spouse or child following divorce or under a separation agreement. You get tax relief on payments which qualify either because you make them under 'existing obligations' or because they count as 'qualifying maintenance payments'.

What is an existing obligation?

An existing obligation is:

■ a Court order made before 15 March 1988, or

■ a Court order made by 30 June 1988 which was applied for on or before 15 March 1988, or

■ a written agreement or deed made before 15 March 1988, or written particulars of which were submitted to your Inspector of Taxes by 30 June 1988.

For those whose divorce or maintenance agreement is governed by Scots law a maintenance agreement registered for preservation and execution in the Books of Council in Session is treated as equivalent to a Court order.

What is a qualifying maintenance payment?

A qualifying maintenance payment is one which is:

- paid under an order made by a Court in the European Economic Area or under a written agreement which is subject to the law of such a country or under a maintenance assessment made under the Child Support Act 1991

- made to your divorced or separated spouse for their benefit and maintenance or for the maintenance of a child of the family

- made when you are not living together and when the party to whom they are paid has not re-married.

How much tax relief?

If you make payments to a separated or divorced spouse under an existing obligation, compare the amount you paid in the current tax year with the amount on which you received tax relief in 1988/89. Then deduct the married couple's allowance (£1,790 in 1996/97 and £1,830 in 1997/98) from the smaller figure. The answer is the amount you can deduct from your total income and on which you therefore get tax relief at your highest rates of tax. The amount of the married couple's allowance deducted is treated as a qualifying maintenance payment and tax relief is given only at 15%, that is £268.50 for 1996/97 (1997/98: £274.50).

If you make qualifying maintenance payments you can claim an income tax reduction on the amount you pay up to a maximum of the married couple's allowance, ie, £1,790 in 1996/97 (£1,830 for 1997/98). The amount of the income tax reduction is 15% for 1996/97, ie, £268.50 (£274.50 for 1997/98).

Whichever type of payment you make, you pay the maintenance gross without any deduction for tax.

Child Support

If you make payments to a child under an existing obligation, and you received tax relief for a payment under the same obligation in the 1988/89 tax year you can continue to receive relief in later years up to the amount of relief given in 1988/89.

If the child was 21 before 6 April 1994, you deduct basic rate tax from each payment; otherwise you make the payments gross. The child is liable to pay tax on the payments, up to the amount you paid in 1988/89.

Apart from this, you cannot get tax relief on payments which are ordered to be made direct to a child, nor is the child taxed on any other such payments. However, if the money can be paid to your separated or divorced spouse for the children, then the payments may count as qualifying maintenance payments within the limits given above.

Tax Saver

If you get relief for maintenance payments under the old rules for existing obligations, you may be able to obtain a larger tax benefit by electing to switch to the new rules. This will apply if the income tax reduction under the new rules is higher than the amount you paid in 1988/89 multiplied by your highest tax rate. Your former spouse may also be better off as amounts paid under the new rules are not liable to tax. To switch to the new rules, obtain Form 142 from your Tax Office and send it to your Tax Office within twelve months of the end of the tax year in which you want the new rules to apply. The election takes effect from the beginning of that tax year and applies to all maintenance payments made in that year and later years. Once you have made the switch you cannot withdraw the election or change back to the old rules, so check carefully before you act.

Tax Alert

You cannot claim tax relief on:

- *voluntary payments which are not made under a legal obligation*
- *payments under a Court order or agreement made outside the European Economic Area*
- *capital payments or lump sums*
- *payments on which you already get relief, such as mortgage interest.*

CHARITABLE GIFTS

Tax Filing Tip

Tax relief for charitable gifts may be claimed on the Tax Return: Page 5.

Although gifts to charitable organisations are made for charitable reasons, the potential tax benefits of such contributions should not be ignored. In many cases the tax benefit can lower the cost of making a gift, either enabling you to make an even more generous gift, or enabling the charity to reclaim tax you have paid.

Qualifying organisations

Only gifts to charities recognised by the Inland Revenue as charitable are deductible from your taxable income. In England and Wales that applies to charities which are registered by the Charity Commissioners. In Scotland it applies to recognised bodies whose charitable status has been approved by the Inland Revenue. Foreign charities are not eligible. There are three ways of making tax-deductible charitable donations:

- Give As You Earn (GAYE)
- Gift Aid
- Deed of covenant.

GAYE

GAYE is sometimes known as the 'payroll giving' scheme. Only those in employment can donate under the scheme, and only if their employer is prepared to operate it. Under the scheme the employer withholds donations from the employee's earnings and pays them over to an agent who pays them in turn to a charity. The most you can donate in this way is £1,200 for the tax year 1996/97 (and 1997/98). Since the donation is deducted from your pay before PAYE (ie, the tax deducted by your employer) is worked out, you obtain immediate tax relief for the donation.

Gift Aid

Gift Aid payments may be made by any taxpayer. Donations must be at least £250 and made in cash. Tax relief on the donation is obtained in two parts. You get basic rate tax relief simply by making a lower payment to the charity. For example, you can give the charity a gift of £1,000 by making a Gift Aid donation of £760 (£770: 1997/98) as the charity can then recover from the Inland Revenue the £240 (£230: 1997/98) basic rate tax you have effectively deducted.

If you are a higher rate taxpayer, the balance of the tax relief is obtained on your self assessment. As you have already had basic rate tax relief, you get relief at the difference between the higher and basic rates (16%) (17%: 1997/98) of the gross amount of the payment. In the example above your higher rate tax would be reduced by 16% of £1,000 = £160 (17% of £1,000 = £170: 1997/98). Your total tax relief on the gift is £400 (£240 by retention and £160 by reduction in tax liability for 1996/97 and £230 by retention and £170 by reduction in tax liability for 1997/98).

Benefits received

You cannot get tax relief on a Gift Aid donation if you receive a benefit from it worth more than 2.5% of the amount of your gift, nor if the benefits you receive from that charity are worth more than £250 in the tax year. Nor will your gift qualify if you donate money to a charity in order to let it purchase an asset from you. There is no upper limit to the value of Gift Aid donations and you can make as many gifts as you wish in the year provided the recipients are qualifying charities. Relief can only be claimed by people who are resident in the UK for tax purposes. Even if you are liable to UK taxation, if you are not UK resident you cannot get tax relief.

Deeds of covenant

A deed of covenant is a legally binding written promise to pay a fixed sum of money each year for a number of years. In order to qualify for tax relief the covenant must be capable of lasting for more than three years and for that reason most charitable deeds of covenant are based on payments for a four-year period. You obtain basic rate tax relief by handing over to the charity the amount you have promised to pay less income tax at the basic rate. If you are a higher rate taxpayer you obtain the balance of the tax relief by deduction in your self assessment to income tax, in much the same way as Gift Aid.

Example: You covenant to pay a charity for four years, or during your lifetime if shorter, such a sum as after deduction of income tax at the basic rate amounts to £76 per year (ie, £100). You pay the charity £76. If you are a basic rate taxpayer you need do nothing more. The charity will recover £24 from the Inland Revenue, making its total income £100. If you are a higher rate taxpayer you can deduct £100 from your total income. As you have already received tax relief of £24 by retention, you will receive another £16 reduction in your tax liability when completing your self assessment. For 1997/98 when the basic rate of tax is 23%, to make a gross gift of £100 the net payment would be £77 and the additional tax reduction for a higher rate taxpayer £17.

This route is less flexible than the Gift Aid route as you have to commit to payments over a number of years. It is therefore most suitable for gifts which are less than £250 and hence fall below the minimum Gift Aid limits.

As in the case of Gift Aid donations, the Inland Revenue do not like anything to be given by the charity in return. But if you receive membership benefits of the charity in exchange for covenanted payments, the Inland Revenue will ignore them if they are worth less than 2.5% of the subscription. They will also ignore rights of entry to view the charity's property in the case of national heritage or wildlife charities.

Non-deductible contributions

Some organisations which you might expect to be charities will not be and you cannot deduct contributions to them. They include:

■ Chambers of Commerce and other business organisations

■ Political organisations

■ Housing associations (unless the housing association itself has charitable status).

Direct contributions to needy or worthy individuals are not deductible. If you want to benefit a needy individual you should find a charity which is prepared to help and make your donation to that organisation instead.

Tax Alert

If you do not pay tax or pay at the lower rate of 20%, you will not get the above tax benefits from making a Gift Aid or a deed of covenant donation. If you do make such a gift, the tax which you are deemed to have deducted from the donation, currently 24% (23%: 1997/98), will be recovered by the Inland Revenue through the completion of your self assessment.

Tax Saver

If you want to make a single lump sum donation of, say, £100 which is too small to qualify for Gift Aid, you can still obtain tax relief by making it a loan covenant. If you make out a deed of covenant under which you promise to pay the charity £25 per year net and then make the balance of your donation an interest-free loan to the charity which is to be repaid in instalments as your annual covenant is due, you will obtain tax relief spread over a four-year period. The charity benefits from the immediate use of the money and can recover the basic rate tax each year as each covenanted payment falls due.

Tax Saver

If you like to make ad hoc charitable donations, perhaps in response to fund-raising appeals, consider schemes run by the Charities Aid Foundation. You can make larger payments to this charitable organisation which will direct smaller payments to other qualifying charities in accordance with your wishes.

Capital gains tax

You can obtain relief from capital gains tax if you give to a charity an asset which has appreciated in value and which would normally be subject to capital gains tax on disposal. The disposal to the charity creates neither a gain nor loss.

Tax Saver

Giving assets containing otherwise taxable gains can be a cheaper way of donating to a charity than selling the asset and giving cash. For example, if you sold shares containing gains of £10,000, and gave the cash to a charity, you may have to pay capital gains tax. By giving the shares you have no capital gains tax to pay and the charity can then sell the shares without incurring any tax liability.

Tax Saver

For most people the simplest approach to charitable giving is to make an outright gift. Even then proper planning can pay surprising dividends for you. A £1,000 gift reduces taxes by £240 for a basic rate taxpayer and £400 if you pay tax at 40%. Thus if you can control the timing of your charitable contributions, you should consider making larger contributions in years in which you are subject to higher rate tax.

Consider also at what time of year your gift is made. For higher rate taxpayers a Gift Aid donation made on 6 April reduces your tax payable on 31 January of the second year following the donation. A gift made on 5 April will qualify for tax relief against the payments you are due to make on 31 January in the year immediately following. While it is not always practical to defer your giving until the last day of the tax year, when planning substantial gifts the time value of money should be considered.

Inheritance tax

Inheritance tax considerations are important when deciding whether to make a gift in your lifetime or in your will (see Chapter 15 for details). Making gifts to charities can reduce the inheritance tax liability on your death. You can make a transfer to a charity either in cash or in assets, and the gift will be fully exempt from inheritance tax. There is no upper limit to the amount you may donate. Bearing in mind that on death your estate in excess of £200,000 (£215,000 from 1997/98) is liable to inheritance tax at the rate of 40%, this is a very valuable way of ensuring that the charity of your choice, rather than the Government, benefits from your assets after death.

Lifetime gifts v bequests on death

If you are philanthropically minded, you may wonder whether it is more advantageous to make gifts to charity during your lifetime or to leave a bequest to charity in your will. This depends on your tax position and whether or not you can afford to give cash to the charity. If you donate cash during your lifetime and provided your income is large enough, the charity will benefit from the tax refund it can obtain from a Gift Aid donation. In addition, the charity will benefit from the earlier application or investment of the cash you donate. If you make a gift on death, then the tax saving accrues to your estate but if you want to donate an asset which you enjoy owning during your lifetime, such as a work of art, bear in mind that you cannot retain any benefit in the asset which you give to the charity, so it would be better to make the gift in your will (see *'Gifts with reservation'* in Chapter 15).

You don't have to be inordinately rich to consider setting up your own private foundation or charitable trust, though your gifts will have to be substantial to make it worthwhile. A private charitable trust affords you flexibility in determining how your charitable gifts will be spent and the funds can be controlled by a single person or your family if they are appointed as trustees. Once the trust has charitable status, you can use it to receive your Gift Aid donations, deeds of covenant or donations of assets at times and in amounts that suit you. Then you can decide later which benevolent objects should receive distributions.

RELIEF FOR INVESTMENTS YOU MAKE
Enterprise Investment Scheme (EIS) relief

Tax Filing Tip

Claims for relief for EIS investments should be made on the Tax Return: Page 5 and Page CG1.

If you subscribe for new shares in a company which qualifies under the Revenue rules you can obtain a reduction in your income tax self assessment based on the amount subscribed. The maximum subscription is £100,000 per annum and the tax credit is given at 20% making the maximum income tax reduction £20,000. In addition, it is possible to defer the chargeable gains on any assets which you have disposed of, if you re-invest the proceeds in a qualifying EIS – see *'Reinvestment relief'* in Chapter 2. This enables up to 60% tax deduction to be obtained for this type of investment in appropriate cases.

Various conditions apply to the granting of tax concessions and some of these are described below. If you are interested in such investments you should take advice.

The shares must be new ordinary shares in an unquoted trading company but not one whose trade involves dealing in land, commodities, futures, shares, wholesale or retail distribution, banking, insurance or money lending, oil extraction, leasing, providing legal or accountancy services, etc.

Shares in qualifying EIS companies are usually marketed as 'tax shelters' and you can find details of shares on offer by scanning the financial press or by asking your professional adviser.

To obtain the relief you must hold the shares for a minimum period of five years but you can transfer them to your spouse without the relief being withdrawn. You must not be 'connected with' the company within two years before and five years after the issue of your shares – that means you cannot be in partnership with the company or be an employee of the company or a director (unless you became a director after making the investment and you are paid no more than a reasonable fee for your services). You are disqualified from relief if you possess or are entitled to acquire more than 30% of the share capital in the EIS company. After five years, if you sell your EIS shares at a gain, the gain is tax-free. If you have 'rolled over' a gain and deferred paying tax on it after 29 November 1994 by investing in an EIS company the deferred gain is not tax-free and the gain will crystallise. Any gain attributable to a rise in value of the EIS shares will however be tax-free. If you sell your shares at a loss, the capital gains tax loss is allowable for offset against other gains but you are required to limit your loss by the amount of any EIS tax relief you previously obtained. You do this by reducing your acquisition cost by the amount of tax relief you were given. The following example illustrates this.

Example: You subscribe £100,000 for shares in 1996/97 on which tax relief of £20,000 is obtained. You sell the shares in 2002 for £50,000. Your capital gains tax cost is £100,000 – £20,000 = £80,000 and your capital gains tax loss is £30,000 (ie, £80,000 – £50,000).

You could instead claim this capital loss as a deduction from your income in the tax year in which you disposed of the shares or the prior year provided you make a claim within 22 months (ie, 31 January) after the end of the year of disposal. Thus your income tax liability is reduced rather than a capital gains tax loss arising.

A deferred gain also becomes chargeable if the EIS investor leaves the UK to take up residence abroad within five years of the EIS shares being issued. An exception exists for persons working abroad who return home within three years without having disposed of the shares.

Relief for part of the investment may be claimed in the previous year if this is beneficial. To qualify for such relief, the relevant shares must be issued before 6 October in the current tax year and no more than the lower of £15,000 or 50% of the subscription may be related back to the previous year.

If you pay a lot of tax and have spare capital to invest, the Enterprise Investment Scheme is potentially an excellent tax shelter. However, you must remember that you will tie up your capital for a five-year period at least and, by definition, investing in a new trading company is a high-risk investment.

Venture Capital Trusts (VCTs)

Tax Filing Tip

Claims for relief for VCT investments should be made on the Tax Return: Page 5 and Page CG1

These investments have now been available to those over 18 years since 6 April 1995 and take the broad form of a quoted investment trust company (exempt from tax on its gains) which holds a spread of unquoted investments. A VCT must invest 70% of its assets in unquoted companies with no more than 15% in any single company at the time it makes investment. 50% of its income must be received from shares or securities, of which 85% must be distributed. These distributions are tax-free to investors. As with the EIS, both income tax relief at

20% and the reinvestment relief (enabling capital gains tax deferral) are available on making the investment, but in the case of reinvestment relief, the investment must have been made either one year before or no later than two years after the transaction giving rise to the gain. The maximum investment is £100,000 in any tax year and income tax and capital gains tax reliefs depend on the investment being held for five years. Capital gains, previously deferred, are crystallised in broadly the same circumstances as under the EIS. Again, specialist advice should be sought if you consider making a VCT investment.

Enterprise zone investments

Tax Filing Tip

Claim for relief for enterprise zone investments should be made with the Tax Return: full details must be given as a separate note appended to the return.

The Government encourages economic development in certain areas within the UK by designating 'enterprise zones'. The construction costs of industrial buildings in such areas qualify for tax allowances equal to 100% of the expenditure.

You can invest directly in your own enterprise zone property but as this is a large expense smaller investors find it easier to do so through a property enterprise trust. You can deduct the amount of your expenditure which qualifies for relief from your total income.

There are some points you should watch. You will not get tax relief until your property or share of the property is occupied by a tenant who carries on a trade. Not all of your expenditure in a property enterprise trust will qualify for tax relief – some expenditure relates to the cost of the land and to management fees. Because of the tax relief you may pay more for your property than its actual market value. When you dispose of your property interest the allowance you have received is clawed back and is charged to tax – you can avoid this charge if you hold your investment for twenty-five years. Usually, the company operating the property enterprise trust will try to arrange a way out before 25 years have elapsed that does not result in the tax clawback. However, there are no guarantees and you may find yourself locked into a very illiquid investment. Although you should obtain an income in the form of rent from your investment you will be dependent upon the financial position of your tenant.

Although enterprise zone investments are an effective way of reducing your tax bill, the points mentioned above make them both an inflexible and a high-risk investment.

VOCATIONAL TRAINING

Tax Filing Tip

Relief for your expenditure on vocational training may be claimed on the Tax Return: Page 5.

You can obtain a tax deduction for the costs of attending certain vocational training courses and related examination fees. Courses must lead to a qualification accredited by the National Council of Vocational Qualifications or by the Scottish Vocational Educational Council. To qualify you must have attained school leaving age and must not be undergoing full-time education at school. You must not undertake the course as a leisure activity or for recreational purposes, nor must you be in receipt of any grants.

If you are UK-resident and you pay the costs of your training yourself, you get basic rate tax relief immediately by paying the course or examination fees net of income tax at the basic rate. If you pay tax at higher rates you can obtain a further reduction in your higher rate tax liability by making a claim to your Inspector of Taxes. The costs can be set against any of your income (not just income from employment).

MEDICAL EXPENSES

Generally you cannot claim a deduction for private medical and dental expenses but there are two circumstances when you can get tax relief. The first is if your employer pays for the cost of medical treatment or medical insurance outside the UK while you are working abroad. In these circumstances you are not taxed on the value of this payment.

The second circumstance relates to people aged 60 and over who pay for private medical insurance. They can pay premiums on eligible contracts net of a 24% deduction for income tax at the basic rate (23%: 1997/98). You get this relief whether or not you pay tax. You cannot get relief from higher-rate tax on these payments. The insurance company will be able to tell you whether or not the policy qualifies for tax relief.

If you have existing medical insurance and reach the age of 60 it pays to check with your insurance company whether or not you should switch to a contract eligible for tax relief. While you may lose some benefits under the contract, you may find that the reduction in cost due to the tax relief more than outweighs the benefits that you give up.

DOUBLE TAX RELIEF

If you have income or gains earned abroad you may suffer tax in a foreign country. You can obtain relief for foreign tax paid in one of two ways. If the foreign tax is paid to a government of a country with which the UK has a double tax agreement, the agreement may specify that the income will be taxable in only one country. Therefore the income will either be taxable in the UK or subject to tax in the other country. Alternatively, you will be entitled to a credit for the foreign tax paid or for UK tax as a credit against the liability in the foreign country.

If you cannot get relief under a double tax agreement, then the UK will give unilateral relief. This usually works in much the same way as treaty relief.

If you think you may be entitled to double tax relief consult your professional adviser.

4

You and the Inland Revenue

REPORTING YOUR INCOME AND PAYING YOUR TAX

The process of reporting your income and working out your tax for 1996/97 will be a significant change from earlier years.

Tax returns

The time limits for the submission of tax returns have changed significantly. Previously, you would have been expected to make the return within 30 days of the date of issue although, in practice, the Revenue took no action against an individual who filed his return by 31 October for returns issued on or soon after 6 April. For 1996/97 and subsequent years the return will have to be submitted by the later of the following two dates:

- 31 January following the end of the tax year to which the return relates; and
- three months after the date of issue.

Also, for 1996/97 onwards you will be required to include an assessment in your return showing the tax due for the year to which the return relates. This self assessment will be based on the information contained in the return and will create the legal charge to tax. You can, however, be excused from this requirement if you submit the information section of the return by the later of:

- 30 September following the end of the tax year to which the return relates; and
- two months after the date of issue.

Self assessment

As noted above, all tax returns must include an assessment of the tax due for the year to which the return relates – a self assessment – unless the information section of the return is filed in sufficient time for the Revenue to calculate the tax due. A self assessment is required even though the tax due may be 'nil' or where you are entitled to a net repayment of tax.

If you file your return without a self assessment and within the latter two of the above noted time limits the Revenue is automatically required to calculate the tax due and send you a copy of the calculation. However, it is important to note that such calculations will simply be based on the information that you have provided in the return and does not mean that the Revenue has satisfied itself as to the completeness and accuracy of the return.

Strictly, if a return is filed outside the specified time limits for Revenue calculations and without a self assessment, it will be incomplete and could result in a penalty being charged. In practice, the Revenue is likely to calculate the tax due, again based simply on the information contained in the return. However, the Revenue will not guarantee that it will notify you of any tax due before the due date for payment. Interest and surcharges will therefore be payable on any tax which is paid late. (See 'Automatic Interest and Surcharges' on page 88.)

Information to be included in the return

Under self assessment, all income and gains must be shown in specific amounts. A return containing a blank entry, or an entry such as 'to be agreed', 'per accounts' or 'per P11D' will be incomplete and could result in a penalty for late filing. Therefore, where necessary, a numerical 'best estimate' should be included and, where appropriate, a corresponding 'best estimate' of the tax due. The estimate should be clearly identified as such and, where appropriate, accompanied by a note explaining how the estimate was calculated and when the final figure is expected to be available.

Once the correct figure is available, it should be notified to the Revenue without delay together with any amended self assessment. If there is unreasonable delay in submitting the correct information and there is additional tax to pay, the Revenue could charge a penalty up to the amount of the additional tax due, on the basis that the original estimate was insufficient. This penalty could be sought even if the original return had not been submitted negligently.

With the exception of partnerships whose annual turnover exceeds £15 million, separate accounts and computations are not required to be submitted with the return. Instead, specific details including standard accounts information (SAI) are required within the return. Nevertheless, it is recommended that accounts and computations are submitted in all cases. Partnerships with an annual turnover in excess of £15 million are required to submit accounts and computations instead of completing the SAI.

If you are in partnership with others in a trade, profession or business you will be required to include details of your share of the partnership profits on your own personal tax return. The partnership return will be separate from and in addition to any personal tax returns issued to the individual partners.

Corrections and amendments following submission of a return

The Revenue may amend a self assessment to correct ('repair') any obvious errors or mistakes in a return at any time during the nine months following the date on which the completed return is filed with the Revenue. This process of repair does not require the Revenue to make a judgement as to the accuracy of the figures contained in the information section of the return. It is simply a question of replacing an incorrect calculation based on the information you have provided with a correct calculation based on the same information. If the Revenue regard the information itself to be incorrect, it must make a formal enquiry into the return.

A repair may increase or decrease the tax due. If there is an increase, penalties could arise if the return is shown to have been submitted fraudulently or negligently. (See 'Penalties' on page 84.)

However, if you disagree with the Revenue's repair, you may amend the return back to its original state. The Revenue would then be able to pursue the matter only by means of a formal enquiry.

You may amend the information entered in your return and make a corresponding amendment to your self assessment at any time during the 12 months following the filing date. However, you may not formally amend a self assessment during any period in which the corresponding return is under enquiry. Your right to make amendments will be restored once the enquiry is complete.

Where an error is discovered after the time limit for repairs or an amendment has passed, action may still be taken to correct it:

■ where the error has resulted in an overpayment of tax, it may be recovered by an *error or mistake* claim

■ where the error has resulted in an underpayment of tax then, depending on the time when the error is discovered, the Revenue may be able to either

  – open an enquiry; or

  – make a *discovery* assessment.

If you become aware of an error after the time limit for making an amendment has passed, you should notify the Revenue so that they can take the appropriate corrective action. If you do not do so and the Revenue becomes aware of the error and makes a discovery assessment, you expose yourself to increased interest, surcharge and penalties.

Sanctions against failure to file a return

If you do not file a tax return on time:

■ fixed penalties will automatically apply;

■ additional penalties may be sought;

■ tax related penalties may be imposed;

■ the Revenue may make a *determination* of the tax due.

See 'Penalties' below.

Where a tax return has not been filed, the Revenue may make a *determination* of the tax due. There are several things to note:

■ A determination will be treated as a self assessment until such time as you file an actual return and self assessment for the relevant year.

■ There is no right of appeal against a determination but once the actual self assessment has been filed it will automatically replace the determination.

■ The tax charged by a determination is payable and enforceable until it is replaced by a self assessment at which point any tax overpaid will be repaid.

- The due date for payment of the tax charged by the determination is the due date that would have applied if the self assessment had been filed on time.

- The tax charged by the determination also sets the level of the payments on account required for the following year.

- No determination can be made after the normal time limit for making a self assessment – normally five years ten months from the end of the relevant tax year.

- An actual self assessment can only replace a determination if made within the normal time limit for making a self assessment or, if later, within twelve months of the date of the determination.

- All determinations must be served on the taxpayer and state the date of issue.

Your obligations if no tax return is issued to you

If you do not receive a tax return but have income or chargeable gains on which tax is due you are required to notify the Revenue that you are chargeable to tax.

Previously, in this situation you would have had twelve months from the end of the relevant tax year to notify the Revenue that you are chargeable to tax. This time limit has been reduced to six months.

Penalties may be imposed if notification is not made within the six-month time limit. This penalty will be calculated by reference to the net tax due but unpaid at 31 January following the end of the tax year in which the tax liability arose.

Tax Alert

Even if notification is not given within the six-month time limit, the penalty can be eliminated by ensuring that any tax due is paid in full by 31 January following the end of the relevant tax year.

Records

If you are required to file a self assessment tax return you are also required to keep sufficient records to enable you to make a correct and complete return for the year concerned. Strictly, this requirement applies even if you do not normally receive an annual tax return to complete but may be sent one at some time in the future. The Revenue has stated, however, that it will not seek a penalty if you have not previously received a return.

Records to be kept

In the case of a business, the records that must be kept include records of:

- all receipts and expenses;

- all matters in respect of which receipts and expenditure take place;

- for dealers, all sales and purchases of goods made in the course of the trade;

- all supporting documents relating to the transactions of the business which specifically includes accounts, books, deeds, contracts, vouchers and receipts.

There are no specific rules for other sources of income apart from the general requirement to make a complete and correct return. It is important to note if you let property that you are required to keep the same kinds of records as a person who is self-employed, since a letting activity is in many ways treated as a trade.

The Revenue has indicated that you will need to keep records to support any claim to reduce your liability to UK tax on the basis that you are not resident, not ordinarily resident or not domiciled within the UK. The sorts of records mentioned are:

- records of living overseas and travel to and from the UK;
- employment documents such as employment contracts or letters of assignment;
- evidence that show which country is your 'permanent home'.

As far as business income is concerned (including letting income) all expenditure should be supported by bills or other evidence. If you do not get a receipt for small items of cash expenditure you should make a note as soon as possible of the amount spent and what it was for.

In general, you do not need to keep the original documents provided you preserve the information contained in them. The Revenue take this to mean that photocopies will normally be acceptable.

Nevertheless, certain original documents must be kept, and photocopies or copies held on microfilm will not be acceptable. This applies to:

- Dividend vouchers and other certificates of tax deducted.
- Certificates or other records relating to payments to subcontractors in the construction industry.
- Records relating to a claim to foreign tax relief.

The legislation relating to the retention of records was first introduced in Finance Act 1994. This stated that it would take effect for 1996/97 and all subsequent years of assessment. Therefore, as 1996/97 is the transitional year from the preceding year to the current year basis of assessment, if you are self-employed you should, strictly, have been keeping records from some time prior to 6 April 1996 ie, from the start of any accounting period which will be used to establish the taxable profits for 1996/97. Nevertheless, the Revenue has stated that no penalty will be charged for any failure to keep records relating to events which occurred before 6 April 1996 (see below).

Period for which records must be kept

Where a return is issued at the normal time, the relevant records must be kept until the latest of the following:

- The date on which a formal enquiry into the return is treated as complete.
- The date on which it becomes impossible for any such formal enquiry to be started.

- In the case of a taxpayer with a business (including a letting business) the fifth anniversary of the annual filing date for the period covered by the return.
- In any other case, the first anniversary of the annual filing date.

It is important to note that if you carry on a business venture, whether as a partner or sole trader, or you let property, the five-year time limit noted above applies to all records and not just those directly related to the business.

Penalties

A penalty of up to £3,000 may be charged for each year of assessment for which there has been a failure to keep adequate records to back up a tax return or a claim. A penalty will not be charged automatically.

The Revenue has stated that where a failure to keep adequate records comes to light during the course of any enquiry, it is likely to be one of the factors taken into account in determining the extent to which any penalties are to be mitigated in respect of other offences, for example, where a return has been made fraudulently or negligently. Where a record-keeping failure is taken into account in this way, a separate penalty specifically in respect of the record-keeping failure will not normally be made.

PAYMENT OF TAX

For all types of income tax payments for 1996/97 (eg, higher rate tax, tax on income from land and property) the due dates of payment for any year have been changed to the following:

- 31 January in the tax year (payment on account);
- 31 July following the tax year (payment on account);
- 31 January following the tax year (final and balancing payment).

So only a maximum of three payments are required for any given tax year, however many sources of income there are. Each payment will cover tax due on all sources of income.

Therefore, the dates of payment for 1996/97 and following years will be:

	First POA*	Second POA*	Final Payment
1996/97	31 Jan 1997	31 July 1997	31 Jan 1998
1997/98	31 Jan 1998	31 July 1998	31 Jan 1999
1998/99	31 Jan 1999	31 July 1999	31 Jan 2000

* POA – Payment on account

Hence on any given 31 January, you will be paying tax for two years of assessment – a final balancing payment for the previous year plus the first payment on account for the current year.

Payments on account 1997/98 onwards

Payments on account or *'interim payments'* are required for each year in respect of income tax due. Capital gains tax (CGT) payable will not be paid on account and any CGT due for any year will not be payable until the final balancing payment for the year is due, which will be 31 January, ten months after the end of the tax year.

Payments on account will only be required if you have a liability to income tax for the immediately preceding year.

The payments, due on 31 January in the tax year and 31 July immediately following the tax year, will normally each be 50% of the assessed income tax liability (less any tax deducted at source) of the previous year.

This 50% method should be used as a rule of thumb for calculating payments on account, and by using it, you will not go far wrong. However, the Inland Revenue has stated that:

> "The payments on account will not be calculated simply by reference to the total income tax assessed in the preceding year, but by reference to a 'relevant amount' of income tax assessed. The relevant amount is the amount by which the total income tax assessed exceeded the credits for tax deducted at source."

Each payment on account will be 50% of the *'relevant amount'.*

'Tax deducted at source' will include:

- any tax already deducted (or treated as deducted) from any income, or tax treated as paid;
- any PAYE tax deducted – including any amount relating to one year but deducted in a subsequent year under PAYE;
- any tax credit on dividends, etc;
- any foreign tax credit relief.

However, any amounts deducted at source under PAYE in a tax year in respect of a previous year should be excluded.

The actual amount of the payments on account will be calculated by you when you self assess for the previous year. The Revenue will calculate the payments on account only where a Revenue calculation of the previous year's tax liability is requested (the return having been submitted by 30 September following the year end).

De minimis limits

Where the relevant amount of tax due is below a de minimis limit then payments on account will not be required. The de minimis limits apply as follows:

- if the total additional tax due (ie, the 'relevant amount') for the previous year was less than £500; or
- if the tax deducted at source, for the previous year, accounted for more than 80% of the total tax due.

You should note, however, that for 1996/97, only the fixed £500 de minimis limit applies. The additional test, the 80% proportion test, applies for 1997/98 onwards.

There will be other occasions where payments on account will not be required. The Revenue have power to give a direction that payments need not be made on account. This would normally apply when an employee who pays his tax under PAYE has an exceptional receipt that triggers the payment on account rules for the following year. If it is clear that payments on account are not needed, then the Revenue can direct that no such payments be made.

Tax Alert

Coding notices issued by the Inland Revenue now take on a renewed significance because you will need to retain such notices to enable you to calculate payments on account. To calculate these payments, tax deducted under PAYE that relates to a previous year is excluded from the calculation.

Payments on account: 1996/97 only

There are transitional rules which last for one year only, to facilitate the changeover to payment by self assessment. The 1996/97 payments on account are due on 31 January 1997 and 31 July 1997 but the calculation of the payments is different from the calculation of the on account payments for 1997/98 onwards.

The transitional rules for 1996/97 continue the 1995/96 one instalment/two instalment treatment of tax payments for one final year. The payments on account are based on the 1995/96 tax paid, and will be made up as follows:

	31 Jan 1997	*31 July 1997*
Income from trade or profession	50% of 95/96 tax	50% of 95/96 tax
Investment income and miscellaneous income	100% of 95/96 tax	nil
Property income	100% of 95/96 tax	nil
Higher rate tax	nil	nil

Capital gains tax does not form part of the payment on account calculations. Also, for 1996/97 only, higher rate tax on investments is excluded from the calculation. Both of these tax liabilities will be paid as part of the final balancing payment on 31 January 1998. Additionally, tax on employment income is not included in the payment on account calculations for 1996/97. This applies even for taxpayers who habitually have income tax underpayments on employment income. The only exception relates to a small number of taxpayers who pay tax on employment income quarterly under Direct Collection arrangements. Direct collection will be no longer available as from April 1996. Payments on account of this tax will be required by these taxpayers for 1996/97.

Amendments to payments on account

It is possible that the 'relevant amount' on which payments on account are based is either unknown or incorrect when the payments on account are made. This may occur where:

- a self assessment for the previous year is amended as a result of a repair or enquiry, or
- a self assessment for the previous year is not made in time.

In these instances, it would not be possible to calculate the correct 'relevant amount' on which to base payments on account for the current year.

When the 'relevant amount' is established it will be treated as having been established in a self assessment made on the normal filing date. If the revisions mean additional tax is payable, then it must be paid along with any interest running from the original due date.

For example, if a self assessment for 1997/98 is made by 31 January 1999, but is then 'repaired' on 25 March 1999, the amended relevant amount, as calculated on the amended self assessment, will be treated as having been established on 31 January (the normal filing date).

Tax Alert

Any revisions to a self assessment will have a knock-on effect on payments on account for the following year. As interest will run on increased payments on account from the original due dates (31 January and 31 July) it is essential that these knock-on effects are examined and any additional tax due paid quickly to minimise any interest charges.

Reductions in payments on account

Payments on account are made based upon the previous year's tax liability. It therefore follows that if income is falling then the payments on account will total more than the actual liability for the year. Accordingly, there is scope for reducing or even cancelling the payment on account.

A claim can be made to cancel a payment on account if there will be no income tax liability for the year or if the liability will be covered by tax deducted at source. A claim can also be made to reduce a payment on account if the amount due will be less than the amount due based on the preceding year's figures.

The claim must be made at any time before 31 January following the relevant tax year and can be made either:

- on the new style self assessment tax return; or
- on a claim form; or
- in writing.

If the payments on account have already been made, any overpayment will be refunded. So, for example, adjustments can be made to 1997/98 payments on account at any time up to 31 January 1999. The payments on account would have been due on 31 January 1998 and 31 July 1998, so if an adjustment after these dates results in an overpayment, a refund will be made by the Revenue.

A claim to reduce or cancel a payment on account should be as accurate as possible because if it subsequently transpires that the payments *should* have been higher, then interest will be charged based on what the payments should have been, from the original due date. This contrasts sharply with the previous system where tax postponed but subsequently found to be payable did not generally begin to attract interest until 30 days after an amended assessment was issued. Under the payment on account system, any part of a payment that is 'postponed' (ie, reduced) but subsequently found to be payable will carry an interest charge from the date it was originally due (31 January or 31 July).

There is provision for the Revenue to charge a penalty for an incorrect claim to reduce or cancel a payment on account. This occurs where you may have acted fraudulently or negligently. The penalty provisions are to prevent 'gross or persistent abuse' by someone who persistently claims excessively reduced payments on account. Care should therefore be taken to ensure that you can justify any claimed reduction on enquiry by the Revenue.

Balancing payments

Payments on account of the income tax liability for any year are precisely that, payments on account. Any balancing adjustments will be made on 31 January following the end of the year, the same date that the tax return is due to be filed. On this date any additional tax will be payable (or a repayment claimed) – having assessed the liability, accounted for tax deducted at source and payments on account previously made. (Of course, the first payment on account for the following tax year is due on the same date and any repayment can be set against the first payment on account due.)

The final balancing payment due is the difference between:

■ the amount shown on the self assessment included in the tax return, and

■ any amounts deducted at source (eg, PAYE), together with amounts already paid on account the previous January and July.

The tax credits allowable in the calculation of the balancing payment due will include tax to be coded out in a future year but it will exclude any amounts deducted at source during the year of return in respect of previous years.

AUTOMATIC INTEREST AND SURCHARGES

Interest

Interest will automatically be charged on any tax which is paid late. 'Tax' includes income tax, capital gains tax and Class IV National Insurance contributions. Interest will be charged on tax paid after the due payment date even if the tax is not actually payable until some time later.

Tax payable	Date from which interest will run
Payments made on account	Due dates – 31 January and 31 July
Balancing payments	Due date – 31 January or three months from issue of return
Additional tax on an amended self assessment and tax on discovery assessments	Due date for the balancing payment regardless of the date the tax itself becomes payable

However, in the case of Revenue calculations, provided you have filed the information sections of your tax return on time (see the beginning of this chapter 'Tax Returns'), interest will not arise until 30 days after the date of issue of the assessment if this is later than the date noted above.

Where a tax return is issued late but you notified chargeability on time (ie, by 5 October following the end of the tax year) interest will not start to run until three months from the date of issue of the return.

Interest will be paid on any overpayment of tax, calculated by reference to the date on which the tax was actually paid. Interest will also be paid on any repayments treated as tax, such as a penalty or surcharge. But interest will not be paid on any amounts of tax (surcharge or penalties) over and above the statutory maximum due. Therefore if, for any reason, you deliberately overpay tax, you will not receive interest on that part of the resulting repayment.

The rate of interest will be calculated using a specific formula and will be changed automatically when there is a change in bank base rates. It is intended that the rate charged on late tax will be in line with the average rate for borrowing. The rate paid on overpaid tax will be in line with the average paid on deposits.

Tax Alert

There will therefore be a difference in the Revenue's favour between the amount of interest it charges and the amount it pays. It is important that you should be aware of this because this is new and runs contrary to the original proposals.

Surcharges

In addition to any interest that may arise on late paid tax, surcharges will be imposed as follows:

- an initial surcharge of 5% of a balancing payment unpaid more than 28 days after the due date;
- a further surcharge of an additional 5% of any tax still unpaid more than six months after the due date.

However, no surcharge will be payable on late payments on account nor will it be payable on any tax in respect of which a penalty is being sought because:

- you have failed to notify the Revenue of your chargeability to tax; or
- the return issued to you is more than 12 months late; or
- you have fraudulently or negligently filed an incorrect return, etc.

Surcharges are payable 30 days after the Inspector has issued a written notice to you. You may appeal against the notice within 30 days. The Commissioners may set aside the surcharge if it appears to them that you have a reasonable excuse throughout the period of default for not paying the tax. Alternatively, the Revenue may mitigate or remit the surcharge at its discretion.

Interest will be charged on any surcharge not paid within 30 days of the date the surcharge notice is issued.

ENQUIRIES

It is important to distinguish between formal enquiries and the right of the Revenue (or you) to correct, or 'repair', a return. The Revenue may correct any obvious errors or mistakes in a return at any time during the nine months following the date the completed return was filed without starting a formal enquiry.

Starting enquiries

The Revenue has the right to make enquiries into any return forming the basis of a self assessment including those where the Revenue has calculated the tax due. This right applies to both the original return and to any subsequent amendment made by you. The only pre-condition which has to be fulfilled before the Revenue can start enquiries is that you must be notified in writing that the Revenue intend to enquire into the return.

A certain proportion of enquiry cases will be chosen by random selection although the Revenue has stated that most will continue to be selected by reference to the information contained in the return and other information in the Revenue's possession. Whether the enquiry is 'focused' or random, the Revenue does not have to give reasons for making enquiries and has stated that it will not do so although it may identify particular areas in which the enquiries will focus.

Only one notice of enquiry may be issued in respect of any return or amendment. This means that when an enquiry is completed, that return cannot be subject to 'enquiry' again although the normal right to make 'discovery assessments' will, in most cases, still give the Revenue right of access into a particular year of assessment.

There are specified time limits within which enquiries may be started:

- Where a return is filed or an amendment is made on or before the fixed filing date for the year (31 January following the end of the tax year), enquiries can only be started during the 12 months ending on the following 30 January ie, the day before the fixed filing date for the next return.
- Where a return is filed or an amendment is made after the fixed filing date for the year, enquiries may be started at any time during the period ending on the quarter date (31 January, 30 April, 31 July and 31 October) following the anniversary of the actual date the return was filed or the amendment made.

Note: correcting an estimate to a final figure counts as an amendment for this purpose.

Once the time limit for starting enquiries has passed, the return and its associated self assessment will be treated as final unless the Revenue have grounds for making a discovery assessment. Where an amendment to the liability for an earlier year is required because of an event which happens in a later year, for example because of a claim to carry back personal pension contributions, the amendments will not re-open the earlier year for enquiry.

Enquiry procedures

The Revenue's right to make enquiries is supported by a new information power which is in addition to its existing powers which will continue to apply. Under the new rules, a formal written notice requiring the production of the information relevant to the Revenue's enquiries may be made either at the same time as the notice of enquiry or at any subsequent time. It must specify a time limit within which you are expected to comply which must not be less than 30 days. The Revenue can only ask for *written* information (ie, documents or other particulars) that it can show to be reasonably relevant to an entry in your personal tax return.

You may appeal against the formal notice on the grounds that:

(i) the information requested is not 'reasonably relevant' to the Revenue's enquiries, and/or

(ii) you have been given insufficient time to comply with the notice.

Any such appeal must be made within 30 days of the date on which the notice was issued to you.

If the Commissioners confirm the notice, or part of it, you have 30 days from the date your appeal is determined to produce the relevant information.

If you fail to produce the relevant information, you will be liable to an initial penalty of £50 and, if the failure continues, an additional penalty of up to £150 per day.

Settling enquiries

The Revenue's enquiries will be treated as completed once you have been sent a written notice informing you that the Revenue has completed its enquiries and stating its conclusions regarding any adjustments which may be needed to your self assessment.

Penalties

A penalty may be due if a return is incorrect and is shown to have been made fraudulently or negligently. This extends to:

(i) incorrect statements or declarations made in a claim; and

(ii) submission of incorrect accounts.

The penalty is up to 100% of the difference between the correct tax and the tax shown as due according to the return. The penalty may be reduced for disclosure and co-operation and according to the size and gravity of the offence.

Discovery assessments
The only assessments which will be issued by the Revenue are discovery assessments and may only be made if there has been fraud, neglect or incomplete disclosure which has resulted in a loss of tax because:

(i) profits have not been assessed which should have been; or

(ii) an assessment is insufficient; or

(iii) excessive relief has been given.

There are specified time limits for making discovery assessments:

■ In the case of incomplete disclosure without fraudulent or negligent conduct, the time limit is five years ten months from the end of the tax year to which it relates.

■ In the case of fraudulent or negligent conduct, the time limit is 20 years ten months from the end of the year of assessment to which it relates.

The due date for tax charged by a discovery assessment is 30 days after the date of issue. However, interest will be due from the due date for the relevant tax year. Either surcharge or penalties may be sought in respect of the tax charged by a discovery assessment.

CLAIMS, ELECTIONS AND NOTICES
Under self assessment there is a comprehensive set of new procedures for making claims and elections and giving notice. The general rule is that, wherever possible, a claim, election or notice (generally abbreviated simply to 'claims') should be included in a tax return or an amendment to it.

SETTLEMENTS AND TRUSTS
Trustees of trusts have to file a tax return in their own right.

If you are the trustee of a trust in which someone is entitled to the income as of right, you will complete tax return form SA 100. You must give details of the trust's taxed and untaxed income and capital gains. You will also have to include details of trustees' expenses to calculate the beneficiaries' income details for the tax year. Trustees will be taxed on untaxed income and capital gains in the normal way under self assessment, at the tax rate of 24% (23% 1997/98). You do not pay tax at the higher rate of 40% or at the lower rate of 20%, except in relation to trust dividends and savings income where the tax credit of 20% satisfies your full liability.

If you are the trustee of a discretionary or an accumulation and maintenance trust (see Chapter 15), you also have to file a tax return, form SA 100. This includes details of all the trust's income, deductions and capital gains and includes a computation for working out the trustees' liability to tax at the rate applicable to trusts. A discretionary trust pays tax at 'the rate applicable to trusts' which is currently 34% (for 1996/97 and 1997/98), on all its income. Thus you pay an extra 14% tax on dividend income and savings income and 10% (11% for 1997/98) on other income. Trustees will be taxed in the normal way under self assessment on untaxed income and capital gains with the rate applicable to trusts due on the usual due payment dates. In addition a further payment of 14% will be due on 31 January 1998 in respect of dividend income and savings income received in 1996/97 carrying a tax credit of 20%.

Where income distributions are made by trustees to beneficiaries they will carry a credit for tax paid by the trustees. The amount of the distribution and tax credit needs to be inserted on a certificate (form R185E for life interest trusts and form R185 for discretionary trusts) and given to the beneficiary. This must be done in time for the beneficiary to submit his return to the Revenue within the appropriate filing deadline to avoid any penalty.

Capital gains and trusts

Trustees are entitled to an annual exemption but this is less than the amount which is available to an individual. The maximum is one-half of the normal exemption, ie, £3,150 for 1996/97 (£3,250: 1997/98) and the minimum is one-tenth of the normal exemption, ie, £630 (£650: 1997/98). The appropriate amount for each trust depends on how many other settlements have been made by the same settlor since 6 June 1978. If there are two such settlements you halve the trust exemption, ie, £1,575 to each settlement for 1996/97 (£1,625: 1997/98). You repeat this exercise until you reach the minimum exemption of £630 1996/97 (£650: 1997/98). The rate of capital gains tax applicable to trust gains in excess of the annual exemption is 24% (23%: 1997/98) where a beneficiary is entitled to the income of the trust as of right, or 34% in the case of discretionary or accumulation and maintenance trusts.

TABLE 1: Are payments on account required for 1996/97?

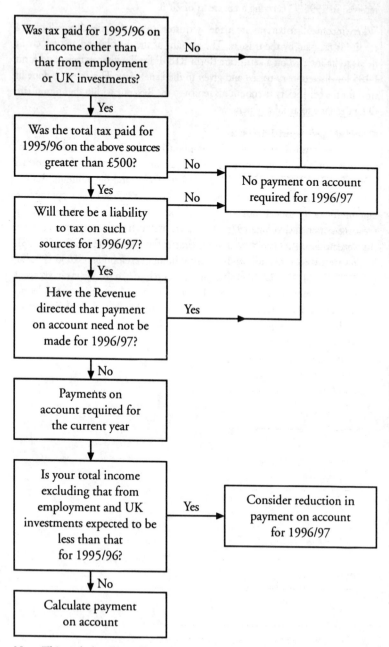

Note: This excludes the small number of cases where tax on employment income is paid under the Direct Collection arrangements. For taxpayers to whom this applies, the Inland Revenue will calculate any payments on account required.

TABLE 2: Are payments on account required (1997/98 and following years)?

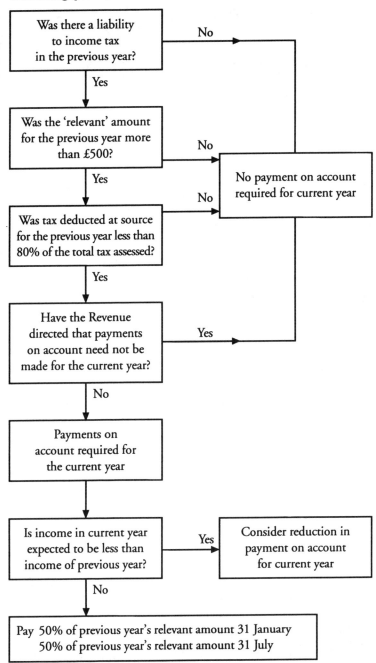

Note: 'Relevant amount' – refer to page 85 of this book.

5 An individual's residence and domicile position

If you are coming to, or leaving, the UK to take up a job, or if you are a foreign national living in the UK, there are two important concepts which have to be considered before your UK tax liabilities can be established. These are the concepts of:

- residence and
- domicile.

Not only are these concepts important to work out your tax liability, but they can give rise to many planning and tax-saving opportunities in the UK.

Equally when you move to another country you will need to take account of the local tax and other laws (such as entitlement to your estate after your death) which might affect you or your family.

RESIDENCE

Residence is not a general legal concept, but a specific tax status determined by criteria which sometimes seem to have scant connection with our everyday use of the term.

The reason it is difficult to determine if a person is considered resident in the UK is that there is no definition of residence in the Taxes Acts. Over a number of years, the Revenue have built up a code of practice to determine residence and this is embodied in their booklet IR20.

General rule

Wherever you normally live, the Inland Revenue will regard you as resident in the UK for a tax year if you are physically present in the UK for 183 or more days in that tax year. If you are in the UK for less than 183 days, residence depends on whether you are:

- someone whose home is overseas but who visits the UK, or
- someone whose usual home is the UK, but who may live abroad temporarily.

Visitors to the UK

Visitors to the UK are subject to the general rule that a taxpayer must normally be physically present in the UK for at least part of the year to be considered UK resident.

You will not normally be regarded as resident unless you visit the UK for periods which amount to an average of 91 days or more per tax year over a four-year period.

Example:

Total days spent in the UK over 4 years

Year 1	=	78
Year 2	=	102
Year 3	=	91
Year 4	=	121
		392
Divide by 4 (years)	=	98 days average

Residence commences from 6 April in year 5.

Where you visit the UK without intending to stay for any length of time but you are detained here through exceptional circumstances beyond your control, for example illness, that period will not normally count in calculating the 91-day average. However, the whole period is counted when applying the general rule given above.

If you decide to make visits in excess of the 91-day average from the outset, or at a later date, you will be regarded as resident for the beginning of the tax year in which this decision is made (provided that you actually make such visits).

Longer-term residents

Strictly, each tax year should be viewed as a whole. However, in practice, under certain circumstances the Revenue will normally allow the year to be split between resident and non-resident periods while giving you full annual personal allowances, etc for the period of UK residence. Thus, the day of arrival in, and departure from, the UK will usually mark the parameters of your UK residence status, and hence your UK tax exposure.

This treatment is applied if:

- you intend to live in the UK for more than two years, or
- you own, or lease for three years or more, accommodation in the UK in the year of arrival.

ORDINARY RESIDENCE

Ordinary residence is a different concept which is important for some tax purposes. You need to consider your usual residence position and must therefore look at your movements in more than one year.

Visitors

A visitor to the UK will usually establish ordinary residence in the tax year after his visits to the UK have averaged 91 days or more over four years. However, if it is clear that he intends to meet the 91-day average at the outset, or before the end of the four-year period, he will be regarded as ordinarily resident in the UK either from the beginning of the first tax year or the tax year in which his intentions change.

Longer-term residents

For longer-term residents leaving or arriving in the UK, Revenue practice is again to split the tax year of arrival and departure. However, as ordinary residence status is determined by reference to more than one tax year, a provisional ruling at the start of an individual's stay in the UK will depend upon his intentions at the outset.

Arriving in the UK

You will normally become ordinarily resident from the day of your arrival where the following criteria are met:

- you intend to stay in the UK for three years or more
- you either own or lease accommodation in the UK for three years or more in the year of arrival.

Otherwise, you will become ordinarily resident at the beginning of the tax year:

- during which such accommodation is acquired
- during which you decide to stay in the UK for three years or more
- following the third anniversary of your arrival in the UK.

Leaving the UK

Certain long-term UK residents (including Commonwealth citizens and citizens of the Republic of Ireland) will continue to be regarded as UK resident (and assessable to UK tax) despite having left the UK for 'occasional residence abroad'. It is therefore necessary to prove to the Revenue that your departure from the UK is more than temporary in nature if non-UK residence status is to be granted.

If you have already been living in the UK for some years you need to prove to the Inland Revenue that your departure is for a substantial period – generally for three years or more. Temporary absences from the UK are ignored in determining your residence position. In particular, any absence from the UK is regarded as temporary unless you spend at least a complete tax year overseas.

In order to obtain a provisional ruling of non-UK residence you need to show your intentions by severing UK ties – for example, selling your UK home and establishing a home overseas.

If you qualify as a non-UK resident on the basis that you are leaving the UK permanently, you will be regarded as non-resident and not ordinarily resident in the UK from the day following your departure.

Once you have emigrated permanently from the UK you are not generally regarded as UK resident provided your visits to the UK do not amount to 91 days or more per tax year on average over a four-year period.

Overseas employment

If you take up a full-time job abroad you will not be regarded as UK resident if:

- your absence from the UK and the employment itself both extend over a period covering a complete tax year, and
- your visits to the UK do not amount to:

– 183 days or more in any one tax year; nor

– an average of 91 days or more per tax year.

If you qualify for non-UK resident status under these rules, you will be regarded as not resident from the day following your departure until the day immediately preceding your return. Note, however, that if you perform substantial duties in the UK on your return visits, a UK tax charge can arise on the earnings attributable to those duties.

DOMICILE

There is no totally satisfactory definition of domicile. Domicile essentially denotes the country or state you consider to be your permanent home. It is said to be the place to which one would wish to retire after one's travels and return to die. If you do not live in your 'homeland' for many years this does not preclude you from being domiciled there, provided you have an intention to return to live in that country.

Domicile is not necessarily defined by reference to a country but by reference to a place which has a separate legal system. Thus, it is not strictly correct to speak of having a 'UK domicile' because an individual would have to be domiciled in England and Wales, Scotland or Northern Ireland (our references to UK domicile are shorthand for a person having a domicile in any of those countries). For the same reason, an American or Australian domicile would be defined by reference to a particular state, a Canadian domicile by reference to a province and a Swiss domicile by reference to a canton.

Types of domicile

Under the present law there are three types of domicile:

■ *Domicile of origin* Everyone has a domicile of origin which will normally be the domicile of their father at the time of their birth. You never lose your domicile of origin. Even if your domicile is changed because you acquire a domicile of choice or domicile of dependency elsewhere, if either of these is lost for any reason then you automatically revert to your domicile of origin.

■ *Domicile of choice* You can surrender your domicile of origin by acquiring a domicile of choice in another jurisdiction. To do this, you must show that you wish to make your 'adopted' country your permanent home and have no intention of returning to live in your domicile of origin. If you wished to relinquish your domicile of origin you would normally be advised to remove all property from that country and to sever as many ties as possible there.

■ *Domicile of dependency* Where someone (eg, a minor under the age of 16) is legally dependent on another person, their domicile will normally follow the domicile of that other person. For example, a child will take a father's domicile of origin at birth but if the father were to subsequently acquire a domicile of choice during the child's minority, the child would also acquire that domicile.

Domicile of dependency used to be important for a married woman. A woman who married before 1 January 1974 automatically acquired her husband's domicile. The position changed in January 1974 so that a wife can now have a domicile independent of her husband. However, you need to take care if you married a foreign husband before 1974.

Importance of domicile of origin

Of the three categories, the domicile of origin is undoubtedly the most important because of its resilience. The fact that you merely have an intention to return to the jurisdiction of your domicile of origin is sufficient for that domicile to be retained under UK legal principles.

In practice this makes the retention of a domicile of origin outside the UK an extremely valuable commodity in tax terms. If the taxpayer has retained some connection with his 'home' country, it is difficult for the UK Inland Revenue to prove that his domicile of origin has been forsaken. UK tax advice should be taken at the outset by a foreigner coming to live in the UK, and his non-UK domicile status agreed with the UK Inland Revenue. A domicile questionnaire will need to be completed and submitted to the Revenue, although the Revenue may not give a ruling until some event occurs which has a tax consequence. If you are in this situation you should seek professional advice.

Domicile status for inheritance tax

There are two circumstances in which you may be regarded as domiciled in the UK for inheritance tax (IHT) purposes, even though you are not regarded as domiciled in the UK for general purposes (in particular, income tax and capital gains tax). These are:

- If you emigrate permanently from the UK, you will be regarded as domiciled in the UK for IHT purposes for three tax years after your general UK domicile ceases.

- You will be regarded as domiciled in the UK for IHT purposes if you have been resident in the UK for tax purposes in (any part of) 17 or more of the 20 previous tax years.

The second rule works by reference to the number of 'tax years' you have been resident in the UK and it is possible to be regarded as domiciled in the UK after being present here for only 15 years and two days. For example:

Date of arrival	First tax year of residence
5 April 1982	1981/82
Date of deemed domicile	Seventeenth tax year of residence
6 April 1997	1997/98

If you are likely to infringe this rule you should consider the relevant tax planning opportunities (which are beyond the scope of this book) at the very latest after 13 calendar years of residence in the UK.

Reform of the law of domicile

The General Election will take place no later than May 1997. A Labour administration would be likely to seek to restrict some of the tax advantages which non-UK domiciliaries currently enjoy. It is possible that individuals with significant connections with the UK, who are currently taxed favourably as non-UK domiciliaries, could be subjected to a new domicile test for example based on years of residence.

Non-UK domiciliaries who have relaxed their links with the jurisdiction of their present domicile should in any event endeavour to rebuild those connections.

PLANNING MEASURES FOR NON-UK RESIDENTS

The UK income and capital gains tax system is residence-based. Therefore if you spend time abroad and the Revenue agree you are not UK resident, you can limit your UK tax liability.

Income tax

As a general rule non-UK residents are liable to UK tax on income which arises in the UK, but various concessions apply to certain types of income which exempt the non-resident from tax. Even if income from UK sources remains subject to UK tax, if it is also taxable in your new country of residence it may be exempt from UK tax under an agreement between the two countries – a Double Tax Treaty (see '*Double tax relief*' in Chapter 3).

UK source income which is tax-exempt to non-residents includes:

- UK bank interest (but this is exempt only in tax years when you are non-resident for the whole tax year)
- income from certain government securities (designated by the Revenue).

Tax Saver

If you are not resident in the UK, you should review your UK investments, or consider transferring assets overseas (to a country with a favourable tax system eg, Jersey) so that income can arise free of UK tax throughout your period of non-UK residence. You will also need to consider the tax regime in your new country of residence to ensure there is no tax exposure there.

Tax Saver

For UK income which remains subject to UK tax (for example income from shares), it may be possible to apply for double tax treaty relief limiting the UK tax withheld at source, commonly to 15%.

The following non-UK residents can continue to claim unrestricted UK personal allowances against any income which is subject to UK tax:

- Commonwealth citizens and citizens of the Republic of Ireland
- Crown servants, past or present
- Nationals of the European Economic Area
- servants of British Protectorates
- residents of the Isle of Man or Channel Islands

- people abroad for health reasons after a period of residence in the UK
- widows or widowers of Crown servants.

If you are not resident but have income from doing a job in the UK, it is subject to UK tax, though again it may be possible to claim exemption under a Double Tax Treaty.

Tax Saver

If you contemplate returning to the UK after a period abroad, consider closing down overseas income sources (eg, foreign bank accounts) in the tax year before you return so as to limit the UK tax on income arising whilst not resident.

Capital gains tax

Capital gains tax is chargeable on gains realised by an individual while he is either resident or ordinarily resident in the UK.

Tax Saver

When possible, realise gains in a period when you are regarded neither as resident nor as ordinarily resident in the UK – preferably in a tax year when you have not been resident in the UK at all. If you have assets which stand at a loss, however, you should consider deferring sales until you are again resident in the UK so that you can use the losses to reduce future taxable gains.

Tax Saver

If you have shares or securities, foreign currency, etc, it should be possible to realise gains tax-free before returning to the UK by selling assets (and repurchasing them if desired the following day – 'bed and breakfasting') or converting currency. Specialist advice should be taken in this respect.

To take advantage of the concession on part-year residence mentioned earlier, you must have spent at least 36 months abroad during which you were regarded neither as resident nor as ordinarily resident. However, tax planning should preferably take place during a tax year for the whole of which you are regarded neither resident nor ordinarily resident. This is in case the Revenue should decide to withdraw the concession.

The opportunity to realise tax-free capital gains by becoming non-UK resident/not ordinarily resident does not extend to gains on UK business assets.

PLANNING MEASURES FOR NON-UK DOMICILIARIES
Income tax

If you are domiciled, resident and ordinarily resident in the UK, you are liable to tax on your worldwide income. However, if you are not domiciled in the UK, whilst your income from UK sources will be fully chargeable to UK income tax, your income arising overseas is liable to UK income tax only if it is actually remitted to (or in some cases enjoyed in) the UK.

The term 'remitted' has a wide definition. It not only applies to income actually brought to the UK but can also apply where foreign income is used to repay foreign loans brought into the UK.

Tax Saver

If you are resident but not domiciled in the UK, gifts of income you make to a third party who subsequently remits the funds to the UK will not be liable to UK income tax. The gifted sum ceases to be yours when you make the gift. However, care is needed to ensure that the gift is legally completed overseas.

A charge to income tax can only arise on income remitted if the source of income is in existence in the particular tax year of remittance.

Tax Saver

If you are resident but not domiciled in the UK and you earn interest in, say, an offshore bank account, no liability to UK tax will arise if you close the account in one tax year and the interest which has been earned on it is remitted to the UK in a subsequent tax year. Careful organisation of such accounts is necessary.

Capital gains tax

As with income tax, if you are resident but not domiciled in the UK, capital gains you make when you dispose of foreign assets are only liable to capital gains tax if the proceeds are remitted to (or enjoyed directly or indirectly in) the UK. If the proceeds are retained abroad there is no capital gains tax liability.

Trusts which are not resident in the UK (a detailed discussion of which is beyond the scope of this book) are not subject to capital gains tax if created by someone not domiciled in the UK, who remains non-UK domiciled thereafter.

Tax Saver

If you have substantial assets and are not UK domiciled you should take advice on this subject. Tax-saving opportunities exist.

Inheritance tax

This subject is discussed in detail in Chapter 15.

If you are not domiciled in the UK, you are only liable to inheritance tax on assets located in the UK. Rules of international law determine where an asset is located. You should, if possible, retain assets outside the UK or reduce the value of assets in the UK by securing loans against them.

Tax Alert

If you emigrate from the UK it can pay to wait three full tax years before giving away any non-UK assets so that inheritance tax does not apply to the transfers.

Tax Saver

If you have been living in the UK for many years and may soon be deemed to be domiciled in the UK, consider setting up trusts to hold your assets. Provided you are not UK domiciled at the time the trusts are set up and the assets are located outside the UK, you can avoid inheritance tax in the future. Take professional advice on this.

Tax Filing Tip

Remember when declaring remittances of overseas income and/or gains to the UK to disclose not only the amount received here but also any foreign tax suffered on this amount.

For example, if you remit £80 from overseas income which has borne foreign tax of £20, you will be regarded as remitting £100 with a £20 tax credit. Leaving you with a possible further £20 UK income tax to pay (if you are taxable at the UK top rate of 40%).

Tax Filing Tip

If you are not UK domiciled and need to report a foreign income source from which you have remitted funds to the UK you need to complete supplemental tax return forms 'Non-residence etc.' and 'Foreign etc.'

6 Year-end planning for individuals

If you are reading this in March 1997, there are still ways you can cut your 1996/97 tax bill. Even if the tax year has already ended, there are steps you can take to minimise your taxes for the past and for the future. Tax planning is difficult however because of the uncertain course of tax law changes. Nevertheless, it is often possible to discern future trends – and some tax legislation changes are announced in advance.

The General Election will take place no later than May 1997. There is no certainty to the political outcome of the election or of the tax reforms that a new Government might introduce. The main aim of any pre-election tax planning should be to exploit current reliefs and exemptions which might be removed by a new Government.

Generally the tax environment in the UK is favourable for those who earn over £29,265 (£30,145 for 1997/98) given the 40% flat rate.

REDUCING YOUR TAX BILL
The first step in your year-end planning should be to estimate your 1996/97 and 1997/98 taxable income. The worksheet provided in Table 2 at the end of this chapter will help you do this.

We have headed this chapter 'year-end planning'. That is because 5 April is often (though not always) the last day in the tax year by which you can take action that reduces your taxes in that year. For practical reasons, however, the most effective tax or investment planning takes place early in the tax year. For example, if you are taking advantage of an investment such as a personal equity plan (PEP), or TESSA where income on a capital sum rolls up tax-free (see Chapter 13), you will get the benefit of a whole year's tax-free return if you make the investment at the start of the year rather than at the end.

Married couples transferring income
If you are a married couple, accurately forecasting your income will open up a number of opportunities for saving tax. You will be able to decide whether to make elections which, for example, attribute interest on a joint bank account to one or other spouse. This may enable you to obtain greater tax savings than would otherwise be the case.

You will also be able to see whether each of you is making the best use of the lower and basic rate tax bands. Ideally, each spouse should have enough income to absorb their personal allowance of £3,765 for 1996/97 (£4,045 for 1997/98) and the lower rate tax band of £ 3,900 in 1996/97 (£4,100 for 1997/98). Also if one of you pays tax at higher rates and the other does not, it makes sense to look at ways of transferring income-producing assets to the spouse with less income to avoid or reduce the higher rate tax charge.

The tax savings may be further enhanced as tax on investment income is restricted to 20% for those paying tax at the basic rate. If you pay tax at the higher rate, you will continue to pay 40% tax on your investment income, so you should consider ways in which such income can be restricted to a minimum or otherwise consider transferring cash to tax-exempt investments.

The main element of your income may well be earnings or pension and there is little you can do to transfer this. However, if you run your own business either as a sole trader or in partnership or as a limited company, consider whether your spouse makes enough contribution to the business to justify payment of a salary. If you are self-employed you are allowed a deduction for any salary paid to an employee, so your income will be reduced and your spouse's increased. This will reduce your joint tax bill if your spouse pays tax at a lower rate than you (but remember to take the cost of National Insurance contributions into account). If your business is a limited company and you are in this situation, you could consider reducing your salary in favour of paying a salary to your spouse, giving rise to the same deduction to the company, but a lower tax bill spread between you.

For many couples the only way of transferring income will be to look at investment income. But saving tax is not the only consideration. If you decide that transferring income might be a good idea, you will have to transfer the assets which produce that income. So you should also consider points such as security (is one spouse more exposed to potential claims from third parties?), strength of the marriage (is separation a possibility?) and who will inherit the money if one of you dies. If you are comfortable with these considerations, an outright transfer of assets producing investment income is the easiest way to transfer income.

As an alternative you could consider opening joint bank accounts or transferring investments into joint ownership. Unless you make an election to the contrary, income from sources which are in the joint names of husband and wife is treated as if you are entitled to it in equal shares, even if one of you contributed all the capital. Thus if you have a joint bank account you will each be taxed on one-half of the income you receive.

However, if you do not in fact own the cash in the account in equal shares, you can make a declaration that you wish the income to correspond proportionately to your ownership. The declaration must match the facts. A declaration can only affect income arising on or after the date of the declaration.

Other than using a joint account, if one spouse wishes to transfer funds to another they must do so by means of an outright gift, otherwise they will not have achieved an effective transfer of the income for tax purposes. If you do not make an outright gift of the asset to your spouse or if all you are transferring is a right to income in itself (eg, an annuity or income rights in a trust), the income arising will continue to be treated as your income and not that of your spouse.

Tax Saver

Making transfers to your spouse not only enables you to take advantage of both sets of personal allowances and lower rate tax bands, but also further tax savings in view of the restriction to 20% tax on investment income. Remember, however, that the restricted 20% rate on investment income will not apply if the income from assets transferred takes your spouse into the 40% tax band. Making transfers to your spouse may also enable you to double up on some deductions and amounts invested in tax-efficient investments such as PEPs, TESSAs, etc.

Tax allowances and reliefs of your children

You can also use a child's personal allowances and reliefs by creating a simple form of trust – a bare trust. The use of trusts is discussed in Chapter 15. Income of £3,765 for 1996/97 (£4,045 for 1997/98) earned on assets held for the benefit of a child under 18 can be accumulated tax-free. Assets put in the trust by the child's parent cannot be used while the child is under 18 without the income being taxed as the parent's income. However, gifts placed in the trust by other friends and relatives can be used for the benefit of the child whilst under 18, and the child's allowances and reliefs can be set against any income they produce. If a bare trust could be useful for you, you should speak with your tax adviser.

Special issues for the elderly: maximising age allowance

If you or your spouse are aged 65 or over, look at your income forecasts carefully. Consider whether there is an opportunity to organise your income level so that you qualify for the enhanced personal allowances and tax reduction for married couples. This will be a consideration in any arrangements you make to transfer income-producing assets between you. The object is to ensure that at least one spouse will have a total income not exceeding £15,200 for 1996/97 (£15,600 for 1997/98) so that they qualify for the full age allowance.

Whether you are single or married you can consider buying investments which will produce a return that is disregarded for income tax purposes. Income that you receive from a PEP or a TESSA is ignored. So too is a 5% per annum withdrawal from an investment bond, but see '*Changes in the Tax Law you should know about when planning in 1997*'.

Although National Savings Certificates are intended as a five-year investment, you can make regular encashments to produce an annual income which is tax-free. The example below is based on the 43rd Issue but you can adapt this for any later issues using the same principle.

Example: National Savings Certificates income encashment plan – 43rd Issue. Investment of £10,000. National Savings Certificates (43rd issue) Encashment Scheme

Year	No. of £25 units at start of year	No. encashed at end of year	Value of units encashed (income)	Maturity value
1	400	20	£519	
2	380	19	£513	
3	361	18	£511	
4	343	17	£512	
5	326	17	£552	
6	309			£10,025
Total receipts			£12,632	

Tax Saver

If your income for the current tax year looks as though it is going to be too high to get the full amount of age allowance, consider if there is any income tax deduction you can claim (for example charitable donations under 'Gift Aid' or 'Deed of covenant' – see Chapter 3) which will reduce your income.

CAPITAL GAINS

There are a number of steps you can take prior to any 5 April to reduce your capital gains tax liability. If you are about to sell an asset on which there is a large capital gain, consider whether you can defer the sale until after 6 April in the following tax year. This will defer the payment date of the tax by a full twelve months. If you can sell part of the asset in one year and part in the next tax year you will get the benefit of two annual exemptions against the capital gain (see Chapter 2). Remember, however, that tax rates may increase following a change of Government.

If you are married, consider gifting part of the asset to your spouse before a sale is made. Gifts between husband and wife do not attract capital gains tax and this would enable each of you to take advantage of your individual annual capital gains tax exemption and possibly lower tax rates.

Combining these strategies could enable a married couple to make tax-free gains of up to £25,600 using the 1996/97 and 1997/98 exemptions.

If you are selling shares in a company that has been taken over, it could be to your advantage to accept loan stock or shares in the new company instead of cash, if they have been offered. It is usually the case that by accepting the loan stock or shares you will not incur a capital gains tax liability when you dispose of your existing shares. Instead, the new stock will be regarded as if you had acquired it at the same time and price as your original stock. You should check the takeover documentation carefully to confirm that tax approval has been received for this option. By accepting new stock you may be able to defer the gain, perhaps to a tax year when your tax liability is lower. You may be able to spread sales over a number of years and set your annual exemption against each of them. Alternatively you may be able to defer the capital gain until a time when you are neither resident nor ordinarily resident in the UK (see Chapter 5) and hence not liable to tax on the gain. You will need to consider how secure your investment will be. Ideally loan stock should be guaranteed by a reputable bank if the purchaser is not a quoted company on a stock exchange.

Bed and breakfasting

Towards the end of the tax year you should have a good idea of what your total capital gains for the year will be. Look closely at your portfolio of stocks and shares. If you have not used your annual exemption in full, consider bed and breakfasting some shares standing at a gain (ie, selling and repurchasing the next day) to take advantage of that part of the annual exemption you have not used. Any gain within the exemption will be tax-free and you will have increased the base cost of your shares, reducing the gain (or increasing the loss) when you ultimately dispose of them.

If your gains presently exceed the annual exemption you may be able to bed and breakfast other stocks and shares which stand at a loss before the end of the tax year. The loss will then be available to offset your capital gains. You need to remember in this case you will have reduced your tax cost for the future (deductible against proceeds) in computing future gains/losses. However, you may be able to dispose of these shares at a time when your annual exemption will cover the gain.

If you have no gains or losses, it may still be worth bed and breakfasting shares to use the indexation allowance (see Chapter 2). If the stock were to fall in value in future, by bed and breakfasting you effectively convert the indexation allowance into a loss which can be set against your gains.

Example: You hold an investment which cost £3,000 and on which your indexation allowance amounts to £1,800. You bed and breakfast the investment at a value of £5,000, making a gain of £200 which is covered by your annual exemption. The tax cost of the investment will have increased to £5,000. If the investment subsequently falls in value to £1,500 and you then sell it, you will have made a tax-allowable loss of £3,500. If you had not bed and breakfasted your loss would have been limited to £1,500 (original cost less sale proceeds) as the indexation allowance cannot be used to create or increase a loss.

Accrued income

As was explained in Chapter 1, if you buy or sell a security which carries interest at a fixed rate, you may cause an accrued income charge to arise, ie, part of the sale proceeds is deemed to constitute income rather than capital. You do not suffer an accrued income charge if the face value of the securities you hold does not, on any day in the tax year, exceed £5,000. You can use this rule to obtain tax-free income.

Example: You purchase £4,500 worth of 10% Treasury Stock 2001, at a time when the seller will be entitled to the next interest payment. The price you pay is reduced to take account of the fact that you will not be entitled to any part of the next interest payment.

You sell the holding at a particular time so as to ensure the purchaser receives the entire next interest payment and you receive none. The proceeds you receive when you sell are increased to take account of the interest you have forgone. Thus in effect you receive the interest through augmentation of the price you are paid.

However, because you have not held more than £5,000 worth of nominal value of stock in the year, there is no accrued income charge, nor are you liable to any capital gains tax on selling a government stock.

You should remember that the price at which you can deal in the stock is subject to movements on the stock market and may go up or down as well as reflecting the interest rate movement. For example, if interest rates rise, the price of gilts may fall.

ANNUAL ALLOWANCES

Before the end of the tax year always check you have fully used any allowance for the year. Refer to the following checklist.

Checklist for 1996/97 and 1997/98

Personal Equity Plan maximum investment	-	General PEP £6,000 Single company PEP £3,000
TESSA maximum investment	- - -	£3,000 in year one, £1,800 in years two to four, £600 in year five (or up to £1,800 if less than £3,000 has been contributed in year one) reinvested TESSAs - £9,000 in year one.
Enterprise Investment Scheme allowance	-	Maximum subscription £100,000 in any tax year. Minimum £500. Note that if you subscribe for shares between 6 April and 5 October you can elect for one-half of the subscription to be carried back to the previous tax year up to a maximum of £15,000.

Venture Capital Trusts	-	Maximum subscription £100,000 in any tax year.
Annual capital gains tax exemption	- -	£6,300 for 1996/97. £6,500 for 1997/98.
Inheritance tax annual exemption on lifetime gifts	-	£3,000 per annum. To the extent that you have not utilised this exemption in full in any one tax year, you can carry it forward and add to the exemption for the next tax year only, increasing that year's exemption to £6,000.
Inheritance tax small gifts exemption	-	£250 per person. Note that this allowance is a maximum gift to each person but it covers all gifts in the year such as birthday and Christmas presents as well as specific amounts to take advantage of the exemption.

TIMING PERSONAL INCOME

One way of moving income between tax years to take advantage of better tax rates or deductions available is to alter the timing of receipt of the income.

Employment income is taxed in the year in which you receive it or in which you become entitled to receive it, if that is earlier. So if you receive a payment on account of future earnings it is taxed on receipt. These facts can enable you to trigger your tax exposure at a particular time.

If you are a director of a company and your fees are not actually paid to you but are credited to an account you have with the company, your fee is treated as paid when the account is credited in the company books. If you are entitled to a bonus paid in respect of the company's year end, the date you are treated as receiving it is very broadly speaking the date when the bonus is agreed rather than the date on which it is actually paid to you. Note that if more than one date is capable of applying to your payment, you take the earliest of them.

The self-employed and those owning companies also need to consider the timing of income and deductions but for them the scope is greater and they should refer to *Part II Tax Strategies for Businesses* which covers this in detail.

You can accelerate the payment of bank or building society interest by closing your account prior to a year end. If you are in receipt of untaxed interest on an account opened before 6 April 1994 you should consider whether closing the account in 1996/97 may be beneficial.

Under the transitional rules applying to self assessment (see '*An overview of Self Assessment*' at the beginning of the book) remember that on an existing account the interest that will be taxed in 1996/97 will be one-half of the interest arising in 1995/96 and 1996/97. By closing the account, the interest that will be taxed in 1996/97 will be the whole amount arising in 1996/97. This could be beneficial if the interest is generally decreasing. You need to take into account, however, that the Inland Revenue can choose to revise the assessment for 1995/96 to the interest arising in 1995/96 (rather than interest arising in 1994/95) if greater tax would result. You should check the figures carefully.

Tax Saver

If you already have a sum of money earning untaxed interest from an account that was opened before 6 April 1994, it may be tax-efficient not to reduce it in 1996/97. You will only pay tax under the transitional rules on one-half of the interest arising. If you increase the sum on deposit the Inland Revenue can treat each addition or withdrawal as new sources of income to prevent the use of the account for tax avoidance, so you are better leaving the account intact.

CLAIMING RELIEFS

As noted elsewhere, the Inland Revenue apply strict time limits for claiming certain reliefs. Table 1 at the end of this chapter lists the deadlines for the most common claims and reliefs and before 5 April you should check very carefully that you have lodged any election or claim for which you are eligible. Don't forget that some claims are not linked to the end of the tax year but to the date on which a particular event occurred. Keep a careful diary note during the year of any such deadlines approaching.

REVIEWING EXISTING INVESTMENTS

If you have invested in a tax 'shelter' in the past, review it at least once a year to make sure it is still beneficial.

If Business Expansion Scheme investments made in the past have reached the end of their five-year minimum ownership period, you could consider selling them as the original tax relief is now secure.

If National Savings Certificates have reached the end of their five-year holding period, re-invest the proceeds rather than leave them earning interest at the low general extension rate.

If an SAYE scheme is reaching its fifth or seventh anniversary, you should consider what to do with the proceeds.

Review your alternatives under any share option plans or profit-sharing schemes operated by your employer. Should you exercise the options this year? Have any profit-sharing scheme shares been transferred to you? If so, should you transfer them into your single-company PEP?

By setting time aside each year to review such matters, you will make sure you do not lose out because the tax benefit changes with the passage of time.

PENSION CONTRIBUTIONS

Always review your pension position each year (see Chapters 3 and 14). Should you pay AVCs to your employer's scheme or FSAVCs to your own contract? If you do not pay these contributions by the end of the tax year, you will not get a tax deduction for them against your income of the current year.

If you pay personal pension or retirement annuity premiums, you should carry out a thorough review at least once every tax year. Try to allocate premiums paid to the years in which you pay the highest tax rates.

TABLE 1
Personal tax time limits
Income tax elections and claims

Election/claim	Description	Time limit
Married couples	Married couple's allowance may be transferred to the other spouse in whole or in part.	Make 1997/98 election by 5 April 1997.
Interest paid	Election for qualifying interest paid by one spouse may be treated as paid by the other.	Make 1995/96 election by 5 April 1997.
Maintenance payments	Pre-14 March 1988 obligations may be brought within the new rules (ie, no tax relief for payer but no tax liability for the recipient).	Make 1995/96 election by 5 April 1997.
Enterprise Investment Scheme	Relief in respect of EIS investments made 1995/96 and earlier.	Make election within 12 months of issue of EIS 3.
Capital allowances	Various claims in respect of capital allowances (eg, set off against other income; short life assets; equipment leasing, etc).	Review all allowances due for 1994/95 which may need action by 5 April 1997.
Trading losses	Trading losses relieved against other same year income or (for a new business) income of earlier years.	Claim for 1994/95 losses by 5 April 1997.
Losses on unquoted shares	Losses on unquoted trading company shares relieved against income tax, rather than capital gains tax.	Claim 1994/95 losses by 5 April 1997.
Retirement annuity or personal pension contributions	Premiums paid in 1996/97 related back to 1995/96.	Claim by 31 January 1998 (applies to retirement annuities by concession).

Capital gains tax elections and claims

Election/claim	Description	Time limit
Rebasing	All assets acquired before 31 March 1982 to be deemed to have been acquired on that date.	If first disposal after 5 April 1988 falls in 1994/95 claim by 5 April 1997.
Deferred charges	Relief for one-half of gain held over when gift acquired between 31 March 1982 and 6 April 1988 disposed of during 1994/95.	Make 1994/95 claim by 5 April 1997.
Retirement relief	Claim by reason of ill-health.	Make 1994/95 claim by 5 April 1997.
Trading losses	Such losses can be set against capital gains for year of loss or subsequent year.	Make 1994/95 claim by 5 April 1997.
Rollover relief	Deferral of tax by reinvesting proceeds of qualifying asset in another such asset.	Make 1990/91 claim by 5 April 1997.
Hold over relief	Deferral of tax on gifts of business assets or transfer to discretionary trusts.	Make claim for 1990/91 by 5 April 1997.

TABLE 2
Worksheet to estimate 1996/97 income tax

	Income £	Tax deducted at source £
Employment earnings		
Add: Benefits in kind (value)		
Deduct: Expenses	( )	
Gross pension contributions	( )	
Self-employed earnings		
Deduct: Gross pension contributions	( )	
Rental income		
Deduct: Allowable expenses	( )	–
Other taxed income from savings (grossed)		
Dividend income and unit trusts		
Stock dividends		
Foreign dividends		
Bank/Building society interest		
Other		
Other untaxed income from savings		–
Untaxed interest		–
Other		–
TOTAL INCOME		
Deduct		
Loss relief	( )	–
Charitable covenants (grossed)	( )	–
Gift Aid donations (grossed)	( )	–
Allowable interest	( )	–
Other	( )	–
Deduct		
Personal allowance	( )	–
Other allowances	( )	–
TAXABLE INCOME		

TAXABLE INCOME

If taxable income is less than £25,500 use (A), otherwise use (B)

(A)   Taxed at   Tax

    (i)   first £3,900   x 20%   =

    (ii)   income from savings (grossed)   x 20%   =

    (iii) balance   x 24%   =

Less income tax reductions:

Married couple's allowance (if applicable = £268)   ( )

Enterprise investment scheme   x 20%   =   ( )

Mortgage interest
(not in MIRAS and on first £30,000)   x 15%   =   ( )

Other

Add:

Basic rate tax withheld on pension
contributions and charitable covenants, etc.

TOTAL TAX LIABILITY
Less tax deducted at source   ( )

TAX PAYABLE

(B) Taxed at

    (i)   first £3,900   x 20%   =

    (ii)   income from savings (grossed)
           [max £21,600]   x 20%   =

    (iii) £21,600 [less (ii)]   x 24%   =

    (iv) balance   x 40%   =

Tax strategies for businesses

This part of the book has been designed to answer both general questions on business activities and specific points that may be of concern now. Throughout this section we focus on the way in which the tax system has changed in 1996/97, the first full year of self assessment.

In Chapter 7 we look at how you might choose to structure your business if you are just starting out.

In Chapter 8 we look in detail at how each type of structure determines its taxable income and what business tax deductions are available.

In Chapter 9 we look at the special issues which partnerships and sole traders face in linking their taxable income to income tax years ending on 5 April.

In Chapter 10 we explain how to work out the tax due on business income. In Chapter 11 we look at some business tax planning opportunities not considered elsewhere, and finally in Chapter 12 we look at some tax issues when you dispose of your business.

7 Setting up a business

Starting a business can seem a daunting task, and one of the first decisions you will need to make is the form your business will take. This chapter describes some of the main legal and tax issues to be considered in choosing between setting up as a sole trader, partnership or company. This choice exists primarily at time of set-up but as a business grows the same issues can arise in seeking to move from one structure to another.

CHOOSING THE RIGHT BUSINESS STRUCTURE

Tax is an important consideration in deciding the form in which you will do business but by no means the only one. In subsequent paragraphs we will discuss the various types of structure you can use in carrying on a business. However, you must consider the following in making that decision:

1 Are there any legal or professional requirements governing your choice of a particular business entity? For example, certain professions prohibit their members from trading as a limited company.

2 Do you need to protect your personal assets from the liabilities of the business?

3 Do you intend to pass on an interest in the business to your children or grandchildren or other relatives?

Your answers to these questions can affect your choice of business structure.

SOLE TRADER

A sole trade is not a legal entity separate from its owner. Accordingly a sole proprietor has unlimited personal liability for the debts of the business. In other words, your liability is not limited to the business assets: your personal assets are also at risk.

Tax

One-tier taxation
Because the sole trade is not a separate legal entity, any profit from your business is simply added to your other income and taxed in the same way and at the same rates. The income of a sole trade is taxed at whatever income tax rates apply to your total income. The profit after tax can be spent without further tax charges. National Insurance costs on a sole trader are generally lower than they are on an employee of a limited company.

Preparing accounts
Usually you will need to prepare business accounts to determine your profit or loss. Lenders such as your bank, as well as the tax authorities will require such information.

Your business income includes all sales you make in carrying on your business, while your tax allowable deductions are any expenses wholly and exclusively incurred in connection with the business. If the business is involved in selling goods, the primary expense is the cost of goods sold including materials, labour and overheads. You will have to adjust the cost of goods sold for the stock which you own at the year end. You should add the stock to purchases made at the start of your accounts year and deduct the stock which you held at the end of the year in arriving at the cost of sales. Other expenses include salary, wages, business interest, rent, bad debts, travel, insurance, fees for accounting and tax advice, etc (see Chapter 8).

Expenditure on certain types of assets, such as plant and machinery, cannot be deducted from your profit but instead qualify for capital allowances. Normal depreciation (ie, the allowance for wear and tear) in accounts is not tax-deductible. Instead the capital allowances regime sets out tax-allowable depreciation. These allowances can reduce taxable profits (see Chapter 8).

Sale of the business

As a sole trade is not a separate entity, a sale of the business will be treated as if each asset in the business had been sold separately. You will have to distinguish whether each asset is a chargeable asset for capital gains tax purposes or not. The gain or loss on such a sale is the total of the gains or losses separately computed for each individual asset. One asset that is chargeable to capital gains tax and may not feature in your balance sheet is goodwill. If you receive a payment for goodwill then this will be liable to capital gains tax. Two capital gains tax reliefs are particularly important if you sell your business – retirement relief (see Chapter 2) and rollover relief (see Chapter 12).

Employed v self-employed

Most people who start in business will be clear as to whether they are employed or self-employed. A director of a limited company is always classed as employed. For some people, especially those who provide their own services for hire, the position may be more difficult. Most people prefer to claim they are self-employed for tax purposes because:

1 There are more expenses which are tax-deductible. The expenses need only be incurred wholly and exclusively for the purpose of the business whereas an employee must also show they are necessarily incurred.

2 Tax is payable later – employees pay tax sooner under PAYE.

3 National Insurance costs are lower for the self-employed.

The Inland Revenue and Contributions Agency (for Class I National Insurance contribution purposes) will examine claims to be self-employed quite critically. The main distinction applied is that to be self-employed you must show that you act under a contract for services whereas an employee acts in a 'master/servant' relationship under a contract of service. Specific indicators examined are:

■ Do you work for only one customer? If you work for several people this is indicative of self-employment.

- Can you pick the hours you work and the time you work?
- Do you provide your own tools and equipment? Again this suggests self-employment.
- Do you operate a business structure, eg, office, invoices, business bank account? The more trappings of a business that exist, the more it points to self-employment.
- Are you registered for VAT? This also suggests self-employment.
- How much freedom do you have in determining how the work should be carried out, including hiring others to work for you? If you work under direction this may suggest employment.
- Do you take financial risk by investment of your own funds in the business or responsibility for losses or correction of unsatisfactory work? If yes, this suggests self-employment.
- Do any written agreements indicate the nature of the contract?

Tax Alert

None of the criteria listed are by themselves conclusive – you will have to consider the position as a whole and if in doubt you can seek the Inland Revenue's or Contribution Agency's views. You may find that without such confirmation customers will withhold tax under PAYE.

PARTNERSHIPS

A partnership has a different legal status depending on the law of the country in which it is set up. For example in Scotland it is a separate legal entity while in England and Wales each partner is regarded as having an interest in every partnership asset.

Tax

Profit shares

Despite the difference in legal status either side of the Scottish border, the tax system imposes a uniform treatment on all partnerships throughout the UK. However, with the imposition of self assessment, that treatment has undergone a change. Previously (and this regime applied, up to and including 1996/97, for all UK partnerships in business before 6 April 1994), they were treated as separate taxable entities. This meant a tax assessment would be issued and tax and National Insurance collected on the partnership profits, just as they were on sole traders. From 1997/98 onwards the partnership taxable profit is split between the individual partners in accordance with the partnership sharing ratios operative in the accounts period concerned, and then included in the individual partner's own tax return. Each partner accounts for his own tax on his share of the partnership profit.

All partnerships set up and starting to trade after 5 April 1994 effectively went on to the new basis straightaway. But since there was no 'self assessment' system in place, individual assessments were raised on each partner on his share of the profit.

The rules for calculating a partnership's taxable profit and relating it to tax years are the same as apply to sole traders and are described in Chapter 9 which deals with particular tax issues facing partnerships.

Sale of a business or business assets

When a partnership disposes of an asset or sells its business, the gain is allocated to all the partners in proportion to the way in which they share capital profits. But capital gains can arise in partnerships even if there is no disposal of assets to a third party. A gain may arise if there are chargeable business assets in the partnership and the partners' interest in each asset changes, perhaps because their profit sharing ratio changes. In these circumstances, capital gains tax may be due if the balance sheet of the partnership reflects a revaluation of assets. If the assets are shown at their cost no capital gain arises on a change of profit sharing ratio unless actual payment (whether in cash or in kind) changes hands between the partners, or the parties are 'connected' (eg, are relatives).

LIMITED COMPANIES

A limited company is a corporate body governed by the Companies Acts. The main features are:

1 It is a separate legal entity, distinct from its shareholders and it remains in being until it is wound up.

2 What the company can do is set out in its Memorandum and Articles of Association. The Memorandum sets out those activities which the company is authorised to carry out. The Articles of Association regulate the relationship between the company and its members (ie, the shareholders), including the appointment of directors, the issue and transfer of shares and the rights of shareholders.

3 In general a shareholder in a limited company is liable for the debts of the company only to the extent of the nominal share capital he holds. Thus a subscriber for shares in a limited company will not lose more than the capital he subscribed in the event of failure of the business unless he has given personal guarantees for transactions the company has entered into. One exception to this general rule is that the Contributions Agency does have the right, in certain circumstances, to collect outstanding NIC due from an illiquid company from the directors.

4 The company's annual accounts must be prepared and audited in accordance with the provisions of the Companies Acts and approved by its shareholders. The audit may involve a more extensive examination of the books and records of the company by the auditor than is needed for the preparation of accounts for an unincorporated body. Consequently, it may be more time consuming and expensive. Limited companies with a turnover below £90,000 do not need an audit. Those with turnovers between £90,000 and £350,000 require more limited review and are not subject to full audit procedures.

5 A limited company is under the jurisdiction of the Registrar of Companies. The company must maintain a register of members and must keep proper books of account. Each year it must make an annual return to the Registrar of Companies giving details of its shareholders and officers.

6   The audited accounts of the company, together with a report by the directors, must be filed annually with the Registrar of Companies. The accounts, directors' report and other documents held by the Registrar may be inspected for a very modest fee by members of the general public. Thus the company's suppliers, clients, bankers and employees have access to the information in them. Small companies can, however, preserve a degree of privacy by filing only an abridged balance sheet if they wish.

7   Companies governed by the Companies Acts are not allowed to make general loans to directors, although there are certain exceptions for expenses.

8   A company pays corporation tax on its income and gains instead of income tax or capital gains tax.

In considering setting up a company you should consider the following points:

■ Limited liability.

■ Flexibility in terms of the ability to transfer shares, and generally a greater ability to raise capital finance.

■ Compare likely corporate tax rates with the income tax rates you will bear if you trade in unincorporated form.

■ The tax system treats companies as taxpayers separate from their owners, unlike sole traders or partners.

■ You should remember that you may need to withdraw funds from the company in order to live and that means you may sacrifice lower corporation tax rates in exchange for higher personal income tax rates and a significantly greater National Insurance contribution cost. The tax advantage of lower corporation tax rates may not be significant if profits are not retained in the company.

■ There are certain minimum costs incurred in running a limited company which don't apply to unincorporated businesses – eg, costs of setting up the company; annual running costs such as the annual return filing fee; and audit fees (although not for smaller companies). There are also more stringent statutory regulations governing limited companies.

■ A limited company must file its accounts which then become a public document. An unincorporated business can keep its financial affairs private.

■ As it is possible to transfer a business into a company without incurring significant tax charges, a business could start as a sole trade and then incorporate once a 'critical mass' had been achieved to justify the extra administrative costs, etc.

Forming a company

Forming a limited company requires you to incur some costs. You can buy 'shelf' companies (ie, ready made) fairly reasonably but there are usually additional legal fees required to adjust the Memorandum and Articles of Association to suit the business that you intend to carry on. You may also wish to change the name of the company.

Raising finance

A limited company has a considerable advantage over an unincorporated business with regard to the raising of finance. It has the ability to give a floating charge over all its assets as opposed to an unincorporated business which can only raise finance on the security of specific fixed assets. The ability to take security over varying current assets as well as fixed assets may well make lending more attractive to a banker in a marginal case. In addition, because a limited company has an aura of greater reliability and permanence, suppliers and sources of finance are often more ready to grant credit than they would be if they were dealing with an unincorporated business. It should be borne in mind that the benefit of limited liability may not afford individual shareholders full protection as bankers and other lenders will often require personal guarantees in respect of borrowings made. You should consider carefully before agreeing to give any personal guarantees.

Directors' duties

The directors, as officers of the company, are responsible for ensuring that the company complies with all the regulations laid down in the Companies Acts. Failure by the company to comply with the Companies Acts can result in penalties being imposed on the individual directors of the company. Being a director is an onerous responsibility. Their duties include the exercise of skill, care and honesty in conducting the affairs of a company.

Senior recruitment

A corporate structure enables the owners of a family company to bring in as directors or senior management, people to whom they might hesitate to grant an equity interest in the business. This is useful when the company has grown to such a size that it requires further management personnel. It is easy to make a salesman or manager a director and it gives that person status.

Spreading wealth

Within a corporate structure, the ownership and management can be clearly divided in that the shareholders are the owners of the business but the management is in the hands of the directors. This means that shares can be passed to other members of the family whilst the original owners retain the control and management of the business. A company can be advantageous for someone who wishes to transfer wealth now and in the future among members of their family. Shares with future rights, and with little present value, can be set aside for future generations.

8 Running a business

ARE YOU TRADING OR INVESTING?

This question is important, because on it will depend how the Inland Revenue treats the profits or losses that you make and the deductions they will allow. If the Revenue is to treat your activities as a business, they must agree that you are trading. Most taxpayers will be clear when they are carrying on a trade or profession but occasionally an individual will engage in an isolated transaction or series of transactions where it is less obvious whether or not the activity constitutes a trade for tax purposes. In marginal cases each must be decided on its own facts and circumstances but there are a series of recognised considerations to help make the decision which are known as the 'badges of trade'. These are as follows:

- *The subject matter of the sale* Although you can trade in almost anything, some items are more obviously investments because they produce income or some other benefit. Property which does not provide any income or personal enjoyment by virtue of its ownership is more likely to have been acquired with the object of resale at a profit.

- *The length of the period of ownership* If you acquire something and re-sell it within a very short time, this is more indicative of trading than if you hold it for a longer period.

- *The frequency or number of similar transactions by the same person* If you buy and sell the same type of goods or property over successive years, this is more likely to indicate that you are trading.

- *Supplementary work on or in connection with the property sold* If you acquire an asset and spend time working on it so as to make it more saleable or expend effort in advertising to find purchasers, or open an office to help you run the business, such organised effort is indicative of trading.

- *The circumstances which were responsible for the sale* If you acquired an asset with the intention of keeping it but an emergency prompted you to sell it within a short time, that unforeseen circumstance may indicate that you were not trading.

- *Motive* Your motive for buying an asset is clearly important. For example, if you bought an asset with the express intention of selling it to realise a profit, then you were probably trading. The motive will not just be taken from evidence which you give, but must be inferred from all the circumstances surrounding each case.

As well as these recognised badges of trade, other factors may be relevant, eg, the method of financing the transaction. The remainder of this part of the book covers the treatment of income which is accepted as coming from trading.

CHOOSING AN ACCOUNTING DATE

Generally speaking if you are in an unincorporated business you should consider both tax reasons and non-tax reasons for deciding on your accounting date. Non-tax reasons will include considering whether your business is seasonal. If it is, you will wish to choose a date that finishes at a time when your busy period is over – you do not want to be counting stock or preparing accounts when you are also busy serving your customers. There may be a traditional date in your industry to which accounts are made up – you will want to stick to this if you wish to compare your results with those of competitors.

Tax Saver

If you have a quiet season and a busy season it may be tax-effective to draw up accounts to the end of the quiet season. That way the profits of the busy season will fall into the next tax year and you will obtain the benefit of a delay in paying tax due.

You may also wish to pick a time when your stocks for re-sale are low. Not only will it be easier for you physically to count the stocks but there will be less impact on your profit for the year of unsold stocks. For tax purposes remember that the higher your stock is at the end of your accounting period the greater is the reduction in your cost of sales and hence the higher your taxable profit. The tax reasons include *'Overlap relief'* (see Chapter 9), *'Cashflow'* (see Chapter 10) and filing deadlines (see below).

Accounting periods

Taxable income is returned to the Inland Revenue and taxed on the basis of an accounting period which with few exceptions will generally be an annual twelve-month period for both companies and unincorporated bodies. Any date in the year may be adopted as an accounting period end.

Companies

There are legal requirements for the preparation of company accounts and normally these will be drawn up for a twelve-month period but they can be for shorter periods or for longer periods not exceeding 18 months. Companies pay corporation tax for 'accounting periods' which need not coincide with the period of account.

An accounting period for corporation tax begins when the company first comes within the charge to UK tax, acquires a source of income, or when an earlier accounting period ends. An accounting period generally ends after 12 months or on the next legal accounting date or when the company begins or ceases to trade, if earlier.

If a company's accounts cover a period longer than 12 months there will be two accounting periods for tax purposes, the first for 12 months and the second from the end of the first period up to your chosen accounting date. The profits of the whole period of account will be apportioned to these two tax accounting periods to determine your corporation tax liability.

Unincorporated businesses

The choice of accounting period for an unincorporated body is very important because of special tax rules for a new business. When a business starts up the choice of accounting date can determine which profits are assessed more than once to tax. For new businesses starting after 5 April 1994 the choice of accounting date determines the period on which the 'overlap profits' are based. See Chapter 9 for an explanation of *'Overlap profits'*.

Another particularly important tax reason to consider relates to the timing of payment of tax on the profits reflected in the accounts for that accounting period. This is particularly important with the advent of self assessment. An accounting date early in the tax year maximises the time you have both to prepare accounts and file a tax return and also before you are due to pay tax on these profits.

Example: If you draw up accounts for the accounting period ended 30 April 1998 the profits will be taxed in the tax year 1998/99. You will need to file these accounts and your tax return with the Inland Revenue by 31 January 2000. You will therefore have 21 months to prepare your accounts and before you need to pay tax on any increase in your profits. If, on the other hand, you had drawn up accounts to 31 March 1998 just one month earlier, you would have to file accounts by 31 January 1999, only ten months after your accounting period ends and you would have to pay any increased tax due on these profits at the same time. By delaying your accounting date just one month you have doubled the amount of time you have to pay your tax.

PREPARING ACCOUNTS FOR THE SELF-EMPLOYED

Taxable business income

You must include as turnover all the money you receive for selling goods or services. See *'Earnings or cash basis'* on page 133 for how you might need to adjust this. Other business income such as bank interest or investment income is not included in business profits. See *Part I* for how to include this in your tax return and if you include it in your accounts make sure you take it out again in working out your taxable profit.

Deductible business expenses

The general rule is that expenses are only tax-deductible if they are incurred wholly and exclusively for the purpose of the trade, profession or vocation to which they relate. Note that the expense does not need to be 'necessary', unlike the position for employees. This makes it easier for the self-employed to justify tax deductions. You cannot deduct personal or domestic expenses. Capital expenditure includes items which are of a permanent nature such as equipment, motor cars, or business premises. It may also include expenditure in connection with such items, for example, legal expenses in acquiring property. A statutory rate of depreciation known as capital allowances is allowable for such expenditure (see *'Calculating Capital Allowances'*).

Most revenue expenditure which forms part of your day-to-day running costs in carrying on your business will be deductible. You can deduct the cost of goods you buy for resale and the cost of materials you use in manufacturing goods.

Wages

You can deduct wages you pay your employees, including related costs such as National Insurance, PAYE and costs of providing pensions. If you are self-employed any money that you draw from the business on your own behalf is not wages but is classed as 'drawings'. You cannot deduct drawings from your income as an allowable deduction.

Tax Saver

If your spouse helps you in the business there may be a tax advantage in paying him or her a wage. You will be able to deduct this if it is reasonable payment for the work they do. Bear in mind that if you pay your spouse more than £61.99 per week in 1997/98 you will incur National Insurance charges as well. You may therefore wish to ensure his or her earnings are less than this. Depending on whether or not your spouse has other income, these earnings may be less than their personal tax allowance (£4,045 for 1997/98) so although you obtain a full tax deduction for wages paid, no tax is due on the receipt.

Borrowings

If you have borrowed money or taken out an overdraft to use in your business, you can obtain a deduction for the interest on such business loans.

Overheads

You can also deduct overheads and indirect costs of your business, eg:

- rent of business premises
- business rates
- heating and lighting
- cleaning
- telephone charges
- consulting and professional fees
- stationery and postage
- repairs and maintenance
- insurance
- electricity
- administration expenses
- accountancy and tax fees.

Business travel

If you have a regular place of work you cannot deduct the cost of travel between your home and your business. You can, however, deduct the cost of any travelling that you do in connection with your business. If you use a car you can deduct motoring costs such as road tax, insurance, petrol, repairs, oil, motor organisation subscription, etc. However, you will have to split these between the part relating to the business use of your car and any part relating to your private use. You should keep a record of your total mileage and your private and business mileage to justify any split expenditure to your Inspector of Taxes.

Leasing assets

Normally the full costs of leasing any plant or equipment are allowed as a deduction from the profits or gains of your trade. If, however, you lease a car which costs more than £12,000 when new, the allowable trading expense is calculated using the following formula:

$$\text{Total rental charges paid} \times \frac{£12,000 + (\text{excess of original cost over } £12,000)}{\text{original cost}}$$

Entertainment expenses

Entertainment expenses fall into two types – entertainment of customers and business contacts, and entertainment of staff. Generally you cannot deduct expenses of business entertainment. If, however, you give your employees a 'round sum allowance' (ie, an agreed fixed sum) to cover entertaining, you can deduct the 'round sum allowance' from your taxable profits but your employee will be required to pay tax on it. If you entertain staff, the cost of the entertainment is deductible. However, remember that your employee will be liable to tax on the cost. There is an exception where the expenditure is modest. For example, if you hold an annual dinner dance or Christmas party for your staff, your employees will not be charged to tax on expenditure of up to £75 per head per tax year.

Business gifts

The cost of providing business gifts or giving customers the use of an asset which belongs to you is treated as business entertainment. If, however, the business gift contains a conspicuous advertisement for your business, eg, a pen with your business name on it, you can deduct the cost provided it does not exceed £10. The gift must not consist of food, drink, tobacco or any voucher which is exchangeable for goods.

You are not allowed to deduct any expenditure, the payment of which is a criminal offence. That would include bribes or extortion payments, etc.

You can deduct the cost of making a gift to charity. Gifts to certain trade benevolent associations are deductible provided the charity or association is in the locality of your business and provided it does not only benefit persons who are connected with you. The gift must be small in relation to the scale of your business.

Using your home as an office

Many self-employed people work from home. Although you are not as a rule allowed to deduct domestic expenditure, you may be able to deduct a proportion of the expenses you incur in running your home if you can show that you use part of your home for business purposes. If you use one room exclusively as an office, an appropriate proportion of expenditure to deduct would be to take that room divided by the total number of rooms in your home, excluding bathrooms and kitchens. For example, if you have a six-roomed house, you could claim one-sixth of your expenditure. Expenditure that can be claimed will include gas, electricity, oil and other heating costs and your house insurance. If you do not use one room exclusively as an office, you will have to estimate what business use you make of your home and claim only that percentage of your domestic expenditure.

Tax Alert

If you use one room exclusively for business purposes and claim expenses as an income tax deduction, you may prejudice part of your principal private residence exemption for capital gains tax purposes. Any gain you make on sale of your house would have to be apportioned between the part used for residential purposes and the part used for business purposes. If, however, you make general use of your home, and that used for business purposes is not confined to one room, the Inland Revenue do not normally seek to restrict the capital gains tax relief (see Chapter 2).

Depreciation
You cannot deduct any depreciation on assets charged in your accounts.

Bad debts
Taxpayers are allowed a deduction for specific bad debts owed to them which have become irrecoverable during the tax year. Where the bad debt has not yet become totally irrecoverable but you have made a specific provision against it the provision may be deducted but a general provision to cover non-specific bad debts cannot be deducted. The Inland Revenue will not allow a deduction for a provision against a specific debt just because the debtor is a slow payer – there must be reason to believe the debt will not be paid.

Keeping records
You should keep careful records of expenditure which you incur and which you wish to deduct for tax purposes. The Inland Revenue may ask you to provide supporting information such as copy invoices or other evidence that you incurred the expense. From 1996/97, if you carry on a trade you will need to keep records of your income and expenditure until the fifth anniversary of the 31 January following the end of the tax year of assessment. If you don't keep the appropriate records you could be charged a penalty of up to £3,000. The records you need to keep include your accounts, books, deeds, contracts, vouchers and receipts.

Small businesses
If your business turnover is £15,000 per annum or less you do not need to prepare detailed accounts. Turnover is the gross amount your business earns before deducting any expenses. Instead of accounts, you can prepare a summary of your turnover and allowable business expenses. You still need to keep detailed records in case the Inland Revenue ask you for more information but it is not necessary to include that detail with your tax return.

Tax Filing Tip

Enter these details on Self Employment: Page SE1.

PREPARING ACCOUNTS FOR COMPANIES

Taxable income

A company must generally report any income it receives unless such income is specifically excluded by a provision of the tax legislation. The reportable income may be cash, property or services received and it includes interest, dividends, rents, royalties, payments for services, and gains from dealings in property and in investments. Some cash or property received by a limited company is in certain circumstances not taxable. For example, where its shareholders subscribe for new shares or where it receives money for the issue of loan stock this is not subject to tax.

Deductible expenses

Like unincorporated businesses, limited companies are entitled to deduct expenditure wholly and exclusively incurred for the purposes of their trade. Extra deductible expenses include:

- directors' remuneration
- capital allowances
- charitable contributions
- audit and accountancy fees.

Non-deductible expenses include:

- dividends
- transfers to reserves.

Charitable contributions

Donations to charity by a limited company can be relieved as 'charges on income'. Qualifying donations that may be deducted in this way include donations by means of a deed of covenant and gift aid donations. The company must deduct basic rate income tax from any payment it wishes to claim as a deduction. It accounts for the income tax so deducted to the Inland Revenue on form CT61. Form CT61 is completed by companies quarterly and reflects income tax on charges paid which is offset against income tax on income received deducted at source and advance corporation tax on dividends paid which are offset against the tax credit on dividends received.

EARNINGS OR CASH BASIS

A business, whether an incorporated company or an unincorporated business, must compute its taxable profits based on a method of accounting which reflects generally accepted accounting practice (unless this is specifically overruled by the tax legislation). The accountancy bodies publish extensive guidance notes as to what is acceptable accounting practice and this is known as generally accepted accounting principles (GAAP). Generally speaking these principles require that your profit must be calculated on an 'earnings basis', ie, you must accrue in your accounts any unpaid bills due by your debtors and you must adjust for stocks on hand or work in progress at the beginning and at the end of your accounting period. Any other accruals and prepayments of expenditure or income must also be made in computing your profits or gains for tax purposes.

The Inland Revenue will accept accounts prepared on a 'cash' basis from an individual or partnership which carries on a profession or vocation. It might apply to a barrister or to a partnership of lawyers for example. In these circumstances the business would only account for work on a cash received basis or a work completed basis and would disregard debtors and stock. This is often also described as the 'conventional' basis. A company cannot prepare its accounts on a cash basis.

Before this basis can be accepted the profits of the first three years from the date of the setting up of the business must be computed on a full earnings basis. You can then ask to change to the cash basis and the change will be accepted if the Revenue agree it will probably provide a reasonable measure of your taxable profits, ie, that taking one year with another profits will not differ materially from profits computed on an earnings basis.

When the change is made, receipts for work done prior to the change must be brought into the computation of profits on the cash basis, even though they may already have been brought into account in the computation for the previous year on an earnings basis. On the other hand, expenses which were accrued in the previous year under the earnings basis may again be debited in the next year's accounts on a cash basis.

Before a sole trader or partnership is permitted to operate the cash basis he must give a written undertaking that he will issue bills for work done at regular and frequent intervals. These should be at least quarterly and the taxpayer must specify in his undertaking what the periods will be.

If you compute profits on a cash basis and your business ends you will be charged to tax under Schedule D Case VI with any profits or gains that are received after the date of the cessation.

You are always permitted to change back from a cash basis to an earnings basis but once you have made this change you are not allowed to revert to cash basis again.

STOCK VALUATION

When you are valuing stock and work in progress for accounts prepared on an earnings basis, the accepted accounting practice is that stock should be valued at the lower of cost or 'net realisable value' (ie, broadly market value). In the case of long-term work in progress the valuation principles to be adopted are set out in a professional guidance note known as SSAP 9. This statement provides that where a loss on a long-term contract is foreseen the loss must be anticipated by accounting for it at the time when it is first predicted. The Inland Revenue will allow expenditure already incurred on such a contract or where the long-term contract has been substantially completed so that it is possible to assess its financial outcome with reasonable certainty. However, the Inland Revenue will not allow a provision for an expected future loss on long-term work in progress to be deducted for tax purposes.

TAX ADJUSTMENTS TO NET PROFIT OR LOSS

Generally with sole traders, partnerships or companies' accounts are produced in accordance with normal accounting criteria. As tax law has special rules regarding deductibility, as described in the preceding paragraphs, then it is necessary to adjust the profit shown in the accounts. You must add back to your accounting profit any expenses you have deducted but which are not deductible for tax purposes. Similarly you may deduct from your accounting profit any income which is not taxed as trading profits and any tax-deductible expenses not already deducted.

Tax Filing Tips

Enter these details on Self Employment: Page SE2.

CALCULATING CAPITAL ALLOWANCES
Sole traders and partnerships

For an unincorporated business capital allowances were given as a deduction for the tax year under the old system. They were not given as a direct deduction from profits in calculating the amount assessable in each tax year. This rule is varied for unincorporated businesses set up from 6 April 1994 and for existing businesses from 1997/98 onwards. Capital allowances for these businesses are allowed as a deduction in computing profits for income tax. The result is that if capital allowances are given for an accounting period of more than or less than twelve months, they must be expanded or reduced proportionately to arrive at the correct relief. The examples at the end of this chapter show how this works in practice and how the change is made from the old system to the new system.

Companies

For limited companies and other corporations, capital allowances are given by direct deduction from the profits of the accounting period.

Assets which qualify for capital allowances

Capital allowances are due on capital expenditure on industrial buildings, machinery or plant including motor cars, fixtures and fittings, mineral extraction, research and development expenditure on scientific research, the cost of patent rights and know-how, agricultural buildings and dredging. Each of the types of asset have their own particular capital allowances rules and the main types are described below.

Timing of expenditure

The time when expenditure is incurred is important in ascertaining when a capital allowance is due. Usually that time is obvious and capital expenditure is taken to be incurred on the date on which the obligation to pay the amount becomes unconditional whether or not there is a later date on which it is actually paid or required to be paid. Where the requirement for payment falls on a date which is more than four months after which the date on which the obligation to pay the amount becomes unconditional, the expenditure is treated as incurred on the date on which it is actually required to be paid. Accordingly, if you enter into a contract to buy an asset but do not pay for more than four months, you will not be entitled to capital allowances until payment is made.

Industrial buildings allowance

Industrial building

If you use a building for making goods for resale, for processing any materials or if you store goods or materials that are used for manufacturing or processing it will qualify as an industrial building. But any building which is used as a dwelling house, retail shop, show room, or office will not qualify for allowances.

Certain hotels also qualify for allowances. To qualify, a hotel must be open for at least four months in the season and must have at least ten letting bedrooms and provide services, including the provision of breakfast and dinner. It must also provide services for making beds and cleaning rooms. The four months during which it is open must fall within the months of April to October.

Writing down allowances

The rate of allowance available on expenditure incurred in constructing or acquiring an interest in an industrial building is a writing down allowance of 4% per annum. The building must be an industrial building at the end of the 'chargeable period'. The 'chargeable period' is the period used to find the taxable profits, eg, the business's accounting period.

Balancing allowances

When the industrial building is sold, a balancing allowance or balancing charge is made by reference to the difference between the proceeds received and its written down value. No balancing allowance or balancing charge is made on a sale after 25 years.

Enterprise zones

If the industrial building is located in an enterprise zone an initial allowance of 100% of the expenditure on the building cost (ie, excluding land element) can be claimed instead. If the full 100% allowance is claimed, no further writing down allowance is obtained.

Plant and machinery

Plant and machinery is broadly interpreted as covering most apparatus used in your business, including cars and other vehicles, computers and computer software.

Writing down allowances

Expenditure on machinery or plant qualifies for a writing down allowance of 25% per annum of the 'pooled' cost of the machinery (see 'Pooling' overleaf). Expenditure on the plant or machinery must have been incurred wholly and exclusively for the purposes of the trade and the plant or machinery must belong to the business. You can opt to reduce the 25% allowance to a lower percentage if you so wish.

Pooling

In calculating capital allowances all expenditure on plant and machinery is pooled except motor cars, short life assets (see below) and assets used partly for non-business purposes which are pooled separately. When an asset is sold the proceeds are deducted from the pool and the writing down allowance calculated on the reduced balance. A balancing allowance or balancing charge only arises when the pool is exhausted. The examples at the end of this chapter illustrate how pooling operates.

Motor cars

This pooling rule is restricted where capital expenditure is incurred on motor cars costing up to £12,000. In these cases a separate pool exists for each class of assets, eg, all 'inexpensive' cars have their aggregate costs pooled.

Expensive motor cars

In the case of a motor car costing more than £12,000, the maximum writing-down allowance in each year is restricted to £3,000. When a car costing more than £12,000 is sold, a separate balance allowance or balancing charge will arise based on the comparison of the proceeds with the written-down value. This is done by treating each car as a separate pool.

Short-life assets

Assets which have a very short life can also be excluded from the normal pool of machinery and plant if an election is made for them to be treated as short-life assets. An election must be made within two years of the end of the period in which the capital expenditure is incurred and the election is irrevocable. The short-life asset is treated as falling into a separate pool which means that when it is scrapped or sold a balancing allowance will fall due earlier than would otherwise have been the case. At the end of four years any expenditure on a short life asset which has not by then been fully written off for capital allowance purposes is transferred to the normal pool. It is, therefore, only worth making an election for assets which you anticipate have a life of less than four years.

Tax Alert

Think carefully before you make an election for short-life assets. You will need to keep a separate record of each short-life asset and account for each one separately, which can be a very burdensome requirement. Some assets, including motor cars, do not qualify for treatment as short-life assets.

Long-life assets

A special Long Life Assets regime has been introduced in this year's Finance Act. Capital allowances on expenditure incurred on or after 26 November 1996 on certain assets with a working life of 25 years or more will be reduced from 25% on a reducing balance basis to 6% p.a. There is a 'de minimis' limit of £100,000.

Tax Saver

For all new businesses it is worth noting that qualifying capital expenditure in the first period of accounts can effectively be relieved more than once.

Other qualifying assets

Allowances on other types of capital expenditure are available at the following rates:

Agricultural buildings	4%
Mineral extraction	25% or 10%
Scientific research	100%
Patent rights	25%
Know-how	25%
Dredging	4%

Tax Alert

The intangible costs of drilling oil production wells will no longer qualify for a 100% tax deduction from 26 November 1996 but will qualify for deduction at mineral extraction rates.

TABLE 1

Calculating capital allowances on capital investments by an unincorporated business

Example:
Capital Allowances – Pooling and changing to the new tax system.
Business commenced before 6 April 1994.
Accounts prepared to 30 April

			Capital allowance expenditure £	Profit £
Pool value at 5/4/94			20,000	
Year ended/Period ended:				
30/4/94	Additions		6,000	50,000
30/4/95	Disposal proceeds		(5,000)	60,000
30/4/96	Additions		10,000	40,000
30/4/97	Additions		8,000	80,000

Capital Allowances Pool	£	Year of Assessment	Basis period	
Pool b/f	20,000			
		1995/96	1/5/93 – 30/4/94	50,000
Additions	6,000			
	26,000			
WDA 25%	6,500			
c/f	19,500		CAs	6,500
		1996/97	1/5/95 – 30/4/96	
			Profit (transitional rules)	50,000
			Capital allowances	
Additions	10,000		1/5/94 – 30/4/96	
Disposals	(5,000)			
	24,500			
WDA 25%	6,125		CAs	6,125
	18,375			
		1997/98	1/5/96 – 30/4/97	80,000
Additions	8,000			
	26,375			
WDA 25%	6,594			6,594
c/f	19,781		Profit	£73,406

(CAs = Capital Allowances)   (WDA = Writing down allowance)

TABLE 2

Example:

Business commencing after 6 April 1994		£
Business commences	1/1/95	
Profits to	30/6/95	43,000
Qualifying capital expenditure		24,000
Year to 30/6/96 – Profits		100,000
– Qualifying expenditure		59,000
Year to 30/6/97 – Profits		120,000
– Qualifying expenditure		20,000

Pool	£			£
Period of account 30/6/95				
Additions	24,000		Profit	43,000
WDA				
25% x 6/12	3,000		Capital allowances	3,000
	21,000		Taxable profit	£40,000
YE 30/6/96				
Additions	59,000		Profit	100,000
	80,000			
WDA 25%	20,000		Capital allowances	20,000
	60,000		Taxable profit	£80,000
YE 30/6/97				
Additions	20,000		Profit	120,000
	80,000			
WDA 25%	20,000		Capital allowances	20,000
	£60,000		Taxable profit	£100,000

Net profits taxed

1994/95	1/1/95 – 5/4/95		
	1/2 x £40,000		£20,000
1995/96	1/1/95 – 31/12/95		
	(1/2 x £80,000)	+ £40,000	£80,000
1996/97	1/7/95 – 30/6/96		£80,000
1997/98	1/7/96 – 30/6/97		£100,000
Overlap profits	1/1/95 – 5/4/95		£20,000
	1/7/95 – 31/12/95		£40,000

Tax filing tip

Enter these details on Self Employment: Page SE3.

9 Special considerations for partnerships and sole traders: when your earnings are taxed

The UK tax system for personal taxpayers has undergone a massive upheaval to accommodate the introduction of self assessment. Part of this change relates to the allocation of profits to tax years (the move to current-year basis) and the making of interim tax payments. This chapter describes how this change affects both existing and new businesses.

While sole traders and partnerships must work out the amount of the profit which will be taxed in each year, companies don't have this problem as they are taxed on profits of accounting periods and this chapter relates to the special considerations for sole traders and partnerships only.

BUSINESSES WHICH WERE SET UP BEFORE 6 APRIL 1994

If you have been in business for several years, you will know that you were once taxed on what is known as the 'preceding-year' basis. For instance to work out the amount of profits liable to tax in 1995/96 you had to refer to the tax-adjusted profits of the accounts for the year that ended in the tax year 1994/95. For example, accounts for the year ended 31 December 1994: profits taxed in 1995/96. The 'preceding year' basis has however been eliminated under self assessment.

From 1997/98 all sole traders and partnerships will be taxed on a 'current year' basis. This means that the profit taxed will be that for the accounting period ending within the tax year. Businesses commencing after 6 April 1994 will have already started on this basis (see the section at the end of this chapter dealing with their position).

Example: Accounting period ended 30 April 1997 ends in 1997/98 tax year: profits taxed in 1997/98.

Accounting period ended 31 December 1997 ends in 1997/98 tax year: profits taxed in 1997/98.

1995/96 was the last year that businesses were assessed on the profits of the accounting period ending in the preceding year of assessment.

Example: Accounting period ended 30 April 1994: profits taxed in 1995/96.

Accounting period ended 31 December 1994: profits taxed in 1995/96.

Transitional year – 1996/97

1996/97 is the tax year in which the switch from the 'preceding year' to the 'current year' basis took place.

If the Inland Revenue were to make the switch from preceding-year basis to current-year basis without any special rules the profits of one period of account would not be assessed to tax at all. To combat this there was a special transitional year rule for 1996/97 under which the profits of the transitional period were averaged and that average profit for a twelve-month period was assessed in 1996/97. Broadly speaking, for ongoing businesses which had not newly commenced or ceased, this meant that the profits assessable in 1996/97 were one-half of the profits for the accounting periods ending in the tax years 1995/96 and 1996/97.

Example: A business made up accounts to 30 April 1994, 30 April 1995 and 30 April 1996. 1996/97 will be assessed on one-half of the profits of the two-year period 1 May 1994 to 30 April 1996.

In the case of a partnership in which there was a change of partner but no continuation election made (see *'Joining or leaving a partnership'* on page 149) it is possible that the profits of an ongoing business were not being assessed on a preceding-year basis prior to the transition, but on the actual amount of profits for the tax year. In that case, 1996/97 was also based on the actual profits of the tax year for 1996/97, arrived at by apportionment of the accounting periods if necessary.

Overlap profits

Overlap profit relief is a feature of the new self assessment regime. The concept of the current year basis of assessment which will apply to all businesses from 1997/98 is that profits will be assessed to tax once, and once only. In fact there will be occasions when profits are taxed more than once (this is explained in more detail on page 145 – see the section *'Businesses which were set up after 5 April 1994'*). Relief is then given to 'balance the books' by deducting the doubly-taxed profits from the assessable profit when a business permanently ceases. A proportion can also be deducted if there is an earlier change of accounting date.

If you started in business before 6 April 1994 and continue into the 'current year' basis regime after 5 April 1997, you will not get the benefit of any drop-out of profits, even though when you began some of your profits will have been taxed more than once. Such profits would drop out because, as explained above, the concept of self assessment is to tax profits once only and give relief for any that are double taxed in the early years of a business. To make up for this you are being given an arbitrary form of relief for overlap profits. This 'transitional relief' for overlap profits applies to the amount of any profits or gains of the basis year for 1997/98 which arise prior to 6 April 1997.

Example: Accounts are drawn up for the year ended 30 April 1997 and these will be assessed in 1997/98. The overlap profits will be the profits for the period 1 May 1996 to 5 April 1997 under the transitional rules.

The way in which relief is given is described in more detail in the section *'Change of accounting date'* on page 144. But you will not receive the relief until either your business ceases or you have a change of accounting date. As the figure of overlap relief is not index linked, its value will erode.

Transitional period – planning

A second matter to consider is whether or not there is any planning opportunity available to you in the transitional period.

It is clear that if you have a high income in the basis period under the transitional relief rules for 1996/97, then only one-half of it will be taxed whereas any deductions that you make from your profit will only be effectively relieved to the extent of one-half. There are, therefore, some obvious tax savings to be made by maximising your income and minimising your deductions in the accounting periods which form the transitional period.

Anti-avoidance provisions

To prevent widescale tax avoidance, legislation was enacted in the 1995 Finance Act which aims to prevent abuse of this situation. The legislation will come into effect if you have undertaken one of four different types of transaction. These are known as 'triggers' and are:

- a change of one accounting policy for another or a modification within one policy. For this purpose changing the date to which your accounts are made up is regarded as a change of accounting policy unless the change is to move the accounting date in 1996/97 closer to 5 April 1997. The reason for this exclusion is to encourage you to change to a fiscal year basis of accounting, although there are timing disadvantages for you if you do this

- transactions with persons with whom the taxpayer has some family or proprietorial link (typically connected persons) including partnerships

- arrangements with unconnected persons which are wholly or partly reciprocal or self-cancelling – for example, the sale of stock immediately before the end of the transitional basis period and repurchase immediately afterwards, and

- changes in business practice.

As can be seen, these triggers are very widely defined. Changes in business practice are of particular concern to most businessmen. This includes any change in the timing of invoicing customers, supplying goods or services, or collecting debts. It also includes any change in the timing of buying goods or services, incurring business expenses and paying outstanding debts.

If an event has taken place in your business that falls within one of the triggers, the Inland Revenue will challenge the extra profit result unless one of the following applies:

- the main benefit that can reasonably be expected from the trigger is not the obtaining of a tax advantage arising from an increase of the profits of the transitional basis period or, as the case may be, the transitional overlap relief period, or

- the triggering transaction was undertaken solely for bona fide commercial reasons – obtaining a tax advantage will not be such a reason

■ the absolute and relative amounts of profits shifted into particular periods fall below a prescribed limit or the turnover of the business is less than a prescribed amount.

To make matters worse, the Inland Revenue have decided not to announce what the de minimis limits under the exclusion described will be until nearer 5 April 1997. The purpose of not disclosing this is to discourage businesses from entering into the transactions regardless of size.

Tax Alert

Breach of these rules can have disastrous effects on the business's income tax liability. Not only will the counter measures cancel out the benefit of the 50% relief on any increased profit, but in addition there is an automatic penalty of 12½% of the increased profit to the amount assessable in 1996/97. The effect is that you will pay more tax than if you had not attempted to increase your profits in the first place.

If you also time extra profits so that they fall into the period which qualifies as overlap profits in the transition a similar counter-measure will be applied and there are also special rules to prevent partnerships refinancing themselves so as to obtain additional relief.

These proposals are very wide ranging. Sadly, as with most anti-avoidance rules, they are expected to be somewhat arbitrary in their effect so that they will not only apply to those deliberately trying to influence their tax liability. Even if you are simply trying to run your business more efficiently, eg, by invoicing customers faster, you may still be caught.

Change of accounting date

If you change your accounting date, the change will be disregarded for tax purposes unless you comply with certain conditions. The conditions and the way in which your profit will be divided into the appropriate tax year is the same as for businesses which start after 5 April 1994 and you should refer to the section below which explains this.

Losses

If, after adjusting accounting profits for tax purposes, you show a loss, it may be possible to set off the loss against other taxable income and possibly gains also. Capital allowances can be used to increase the amount of loss.

From 1996/97 the loss that can be deducted from your total income will be calculated in exactly the same way as it is for a business commencing after 5 April 1994 (see below).

If you have just started in business, you can claim a special relief in respect of any loss which you sustain in the tax year in which you first carry on your business or in the next three years. This loss can be set against any of the income you received in the three years before the one in which the loss arose. You must deduct the loss from your income in the earliest of those three years first.

Example: You commenced in business on 6 April 1994 and draw up your second set of accounts to 5 April 1996. If you make a loss you can carry it back and deduct it from your total income in 1992/93 then 1993/94 and finally 1994/95. You must claim the deduction by 5 April 1998.

If your business ceases and you make a loss over the last 12 months of trading (known as a 'terminal loss'), whether or not you made a loss in your last accounting period (which may be different) or indeed the last tax year itself, you can deduct it from the trading profits for the final year and the previous three years.

Example: Your business ceased on 30 September 1996 and you incurred a loss. The loss must first be apportioned to each tax year. The loss for 1996/97 can be set against profits of the business in 1995/96 then 1994/95 then 1993/94.

If you incorporate your business from a sole trader (one which you run yourself) or partnership into a limited company in exchange for shares in the limited company and you receive income from the company either by way of salary or dividend on the shares, then you can deduct from that income any loss carried forward from the years before you formed the company.

Tax Alert

Note very carefully the time limits for claiming loss relief. If you do not claim relief by the two-year deadline the Inland Revenue will not give you the deduction. Table 1 at the end of Chapter 6 provides a list of time limits.

BUSINESSES WHICH WERE SET UP AFTER 5 APRIL 1994
The general rule for businesses set up after 6 April 1994 and indeed for all businesses from 1997/98 is that they will be charged to tax on profits of the twelve-months accounting period ending in the tax year.

Example: Accounts for year ended 30 September 1998 – taxed in 1998/99.

Most businesses will have to apply the new commencement rules. The commencement rules for a new business beginning from 6 April 1994 will result in an amount of profit of the opening period being assessed to tax twice. As with the previous system the opening year is assessed on the actual profits arising in the tax year. You must apportion your accounts as appropriate to arrive at this figure if you do not prepare accounts to 5 April. The following chart illustrates assessment for the second year.

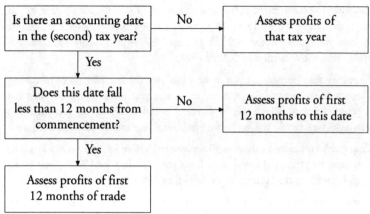

Note: This chart ignores a change of accounting date in the opening period

Example: You start in business on 1 September 1995 drawing up accounts to 31 December 1996. In 1995/96 you are assessed on your profits from 1 September 1995 to 5 April 1996, ie, $^6/_{15}$ of the first accounting period.

In the second year of assessment, 1996/97, you must look to see if you have the end of an accounting period falling in that year which falls at least 12 months after you began trading. If there is, you are assessed to tax on the period of 12 months ending with that accounting date.

Example: You began trading on 1 September 1995 and drew up your first accounts to 31 December 1996. The assessment for 1996/97 is based on the profits from 1 January 1996 to 31 December 1996, ie, $^{12}/_{15}$ of the accounting period.

If you have an accounting date ending in the year but it is not at least 12 months after your commencement date, you are charged to tax on the profits of the 12 months beginning with the commencement date.

Example: You commenced in business on 1 February 1996 and drew up your first accounts to 31 December 1996 and annually thereafter. In 1996/97 you are assessed on the profits from 1 February 1996 to 31 January 1997. You will need to wait until your second set of accounts are available to arrive at this figure.

If there is no accounting period ending in the second year of assessment, you are taxed on the profits of the tax year.

Example: You commence in business on 1 March 1996 and draw up your first accounts to 30 June 1997. In 1996/97 you are assessed on the profits for 6 April 1996 to 5 April 1997.

In your third year of assessment you will usually be charged to tax on the profits of the accounting year ending in that year.

Example: You commence business on 1 September 1994, drew up your first accounts to 31 December 1995 and annually thereafter. You will be assessed to tax in 1996/97 on your accounts for the year ended 31 December 1996.

This rule changes slightly if you did not have an accounting period ending in your second year of assessment.

Example: You commence business on 1 March 1995 and drew up your first accounts to 30 June 1996. In the third year of assessment, 1996/97, you are assessed to tax on the profits of the 12 months ending on 30 June 1996, ie, from 1 July 1995 to 30 June 1996, $^{12}/_{16}$ of your accounts profit.

Tax Saver

Although the period on which profits are assessed twice is significantly shorter than under the old rules, it still pays to reduce your profits of the opening period as much as possible. See Chapter 8 under 'Choosing an accounting date' for a discussion on how you should choose your accounting date.

Change of accounting date

If you are a new business commencing after 5 April 1994 and you change your accounting date, the Table below will help you work out how to tax your profits.

Tax year in which accounts are made up to new date		No accounting date in tax year
Accounting period reflecting change less than 12 months	Accounting period reflecting change more than 12 months	
Tax profits of 12 months ending on new accounting date	Tax profits from end of last accounting period to end of new	Tax profits of 12 months from end of last accounting period

Example: Accounts are drawn up to 31 December 1997 and the accounting date is then changed to 31 March 1999.

Profits for 1997/98 are based on the year ended 31 December 1997. Profits for 1998/99 are based on the accounting period 1 January 1998 to 31 March 1999.

Example: Accounts are drawn up annually to 31 March 1998 and the accounting year is then changed to 30 June 1999.

1997/98 is assessed on the year ended 31 March 1998.

1998/99 is assessed on the period 1 April 1998 to 31 March 1999. 1999/2000 is assessed on the profits from 1 July 1998 to 30 June 1999.

In the unusual situation of changing your accounting date in the same tax year that you begin a business you should take professional advice on how the commencement rules and change of accounting date rules are combined.

For the new accounting period to be adopted for tax purposes, three out of four conditions must be met:

1 the new accounting period must be a period of less than 18 months; and
2 notice of the changed accounting period must be given to the Inland Revenue on or before 31 January next following the year of assessment; and either
3 there must not have been a previous change of accounting date in any of the five years immediately preceding the year of assessment; or
4 alternatively, in giving notice to the Inland Revenue of the change you should satisfy them that the change is made for bona fide commercial reasons.

Obtaining a tax advantage is not regarded as a bona fide commercial reason for this purpose but if the Inland Revenue reject the notice within 60 days of receiving it you can appeal against their decision within 30 days of the Revenue telling you of the rejection.

If the conditions are not met then the Inland Revenue will continue to assess profits based on your old accounting date but of course you can try again to make the change in the next tax year if you can then meet the conditions.

Overlap profits

Note that in the last example the profit from 1 July 1998 to 31 March 1999 is taxed twice. If you look back at the examples of a business commencing, you will see the same thing. For example, if you commenced business on 1 September 1995 and drew up your first accounts to 31 December 1996, the profits of the period from 1 January 1996 to 5 April 1996 will be assessed twice. A profit taxed twice like this is known as an overlap profit. Keep a careful note of this figure. You will be allowed to claim a deduction for these profits when your business comes to an end, even if this is many years in the future (see Chapter 12). You may also be able to claim a partial deduction if you change your accounting date.

To determine the amount of overlap profits that may be deducted on a change of accounting date you apply the following formula to the accounting periods in question:

$$A \times \frac{B - C}{D}$$

In this formula A is the aggregate of all overlap profits net of any previously relieved, B is the number of days in the basis period and C is the number of days in the year of assessment. D is the aggregate length of the overlap periods giving rise to the overlap profits.

Example: Accounts are made up annually to 31 December 1997 and the accounting period is then changed to 31 March 1999. The basis period for 1998/99 is 1 January 1998 to 31 March 1999 which is 455 days. There are 365 days in the year of assessment. Previously overlap profits have arisen for a period equal to 95 days (1 January to 5 April).

The amount of these profits which can be relieved by deduction in 1998/99 is the overlap profits multiplied by

$$\frac{455 - 365}{95} \quad = \quad \frac{90}{95}$$

Losses

In the case of businesses which started after 5 April 1994 you may deduct the loss for the period of account ending in the tax year against taxable income of that year or the previous tax year. This rule for new businesses also applies to all existing businesses from 1996/97. If you adjust the accounting result to fit the tax year (eg, because your business has just started) you adjust the loss accordingly. You cannot get relief for a loss more than once.

Example: You start trading on 1 May 1995 and draw up accounts to 30 April 1996. You incur a loss of £12,000.

In 1995/96, or 1994/95 if you prefer, you can claim a deduction from total income of

$^{11}/_{12}$ of £12,000 = £11,000.

In 1996/97, or 1995/96 if you prefer, you can claim a deduction for £1,000.

For losses incurred in 1994/95 or 1995/96 you must claim the loss as a deduction within two years as for pre-6 April 1994 businesses. From 1996/97 under the self assessment regime, the time limit is reduced to 22 months from the end of the tax year.

Example: Loss incurred year ended 30 June 1998.

Claim loss for 1998/99 or 1997/98 by 31 January 2001.

The other general provisions relating to losses are as for businesses existing before 6 April 1994.

SPECIAL TYPES OF BUSINESS

Special tax rules apply to some occupations, for example farming or underwriting, and you may need professional help to take advantage of these rules.

PARTNERSHIPS

Partnerships are broadly taxed in the same way as sole traders. But there are some special rules to take account of the different nature of a partnership. Additionally with the move to self assessment in 1996/97, partnerships are affected by different rules in some respects.

Joining or leaving a partnership

When you join or leave a partnership, legally one partnership comes to an end and a new partnership begins. As a result, without special rules the tax calculations for partnership would have to take account of frequent commencements and cessations, even though the partnership business itself carried on uninterrupted. To avoid this there is provision in the tax system for all the partners both before and after a partnership change to elect for the business to be treated as though it continued uninterrupted so long as the partnership trade itself has not come to an end. The time limit for making a continuation election, which is strictly enforced, is two years from the date of the change.

Partnerships which commenced before 6 April 1994

Where no continuation election as described above is made, the normal rules for attributing profits to a tax year are amended for partnerships when there is a change in the partners. For the first four years in which the 'new' partnership trades, tax is charged on the actual profits arising in the tax year, allocating the accounts profit where necessary. The partnership has the option to change the profit charged in the next two years to the actual profit of the tax year if it so wishes.

Tax Alert

If, as a result of this rule, a partnership was charged to tax on the actual profits of the tax year in 1995/96, it will not get the benefit of the transitional rule on the switch to the current year basis of assessment. Instead, tax for 1996/97 will be charged on the actual profits arising in 1996/97 and the current-year basis will apply from 1997/98 in the normal way.

Where a continuation election is made a new partner will find that he is taxed on a share of partnership profits for the first tax year in which he is a partner. Normally this will be based on the preceding year, but of course the new partner will not have shared in this profit which arose before he became a partner. Correspondingly a partner leaving a partnership will not be taxed on the last year's profits which are credited to his capital account in the partnership accounts.

Pre-6 April 1994 partnerships are taxed as a separate legal entity and an assessment to tax is issued in the partnership's own name. To work out the tax due a share of taxable profit for each accounting period is allocated to each partner. This is not necessarily the amount of profit he actually receives in the accounts but is the profit allocated to the tax year shared in the proportion in which the partner actually shares profits in the tax year.

Example: For the accounts year ended 5 April 1994 a partner receives $\frac{1}{12}$ of the profits of £100,000.

For the accounts year ended 5 April 1995 he receives $\frac{1}{10}$ of the profits.

His share of the 1994/95 tax assessment is $\frac{1}{10}$ of £100,000, ie £10,000.

A share of partnership profit may include a fixed 'salary', and interest on capital as well as a proportion of profit. These are not deductions from taxable profit but merely an allocation of the profit. In the next chapter we explain how a partnership then pays the tax due.

Post 5 April 1994 partnerships

New partnerships or partnerships who do not elect for continuation on a partnership change after 5 April 1994 also have to divide out a share of profits to each partner.

10 Paying tax on business income

SOLE TRADERS

Businesses which were set up before 6 April 1994

The entry on the tax return for the year ended 5 April 1997 (the transitional year) is taken from the accounts forming the basis of assessment for that year (see Chapter 9).

Tax Filing Tip

Enter these details on Self Employment: Pages SE2 & 3.

Businesses which were set up after 5 April 1994

The entry on the tax return for the year ended 5 April 1997 is the profit for the accounting period which ends in that tax year, unless the new commencement rules apply (see Chapter 9).

Example: Accounts for the year ended 30 April 1996.

Tax Filing Tip

Enter these details on Self Employment: Pages SE2 & 3.

Tax Alert

Care should be taken in putting the information from the accounts onto the tax return, so that the figures on the form properly reflect the figures in the accounts. In addition, where estimates are used in calculating private use elements of expenses (for example, private use of telephone) these should be properly disclosed (on the Additional Information section).

Calculating the tax payments – 1996/97

If your only source of income derives from an unincorporated business, working out the transitional payments in 1996/97 is easy.

Example: You received a 1995/96 tax assessment on trading profits showing tax payable of £10,000. In 1996/97 you will make a payment on account on 31 January 1997 of one-half of your 1995/96 tax liability, ie, £5,000. You will make a second payment on account on 31 July 1997 also of one-half of your 1995/96 liability, ie, £5,000. You will pay the balance of your tax liability for 1996/97 on 31 January 1998 in accordance with your completed tax return.

If you have income from more than one source, the calculation of your tax payments due in 1996/97 is more complex. Broadly speaking you will pay an amount equivalent to one-half of the tax on your 1995/96 trading profits plus an amount of tax equal to the tax paid in 1995/96 (other than that suffered under a tax withholding scheme) on all your other sources of income on 31 January 1997. You will pay a second payment on account on 31 July 1997 equal to one-half of your tax bill on trading profits as charged in 1995/96 and you will pay the balance of your tax due for 1996/97 based on the figures on your tax return on 31 January 1998, after taking account of these payments on account (see Chapter 4).

Tax Alert

The Inland Revenue computer system produced incorrect statements of account for a large number of taxpayers in the autumn of 1996 leading to a good deal of confusion. The details given above are a summary of the correct rules.

Tax Saver

The amount of tax you will pay under the transitional rules in 1996/97 is linked to your actual tax liability in 1995/96. It will, therefore, still pay to minimise your tax liability in 1995/96 as you will get a timing benefit derived from this in paying your tax in 1996/97. In particular, contributions to a retirement annuity or personal pension scheme may still be made prior to 5 April 1997 and carried back to reduce liabilities for the 1995/96 tax year where there are unused reliefs.

Calculating tax payments – 1997/98 onwards

From 1997/98 tax is paid in three instalments for a tax year, being an interim payment on account on 31 January in the year, a further interim payment on account on 31 July following the end of the tax year and the balance instalment on the following 31 January at the same time as the deadline for filing your tax return. Unlike the 'transitional year' 1996/97, however, each interim payment will now be calculated as a straightforward 50% of the 1996/97 income tax liability (see Chapter 4).

Tax Alert

For unincorporated businesses, one consequence of these new rules is that you may have to pay higher amounts of tax earlier than you would have under the old rules. To avoid any adverse effect on your cash flow, you should now estimate what your liabilities will be for 1997/98 based on your business plan and budgets for the coming year and adjust your cash flow accordingly. Remember that you make interim payments of tax for 1996/97 on 31 January 1997 and 31 July 1997 with the balance due on 31 January 1998 with your completed return. The first interim payment for 1997/98 based on the final liability for 1996/97 will also be due on that date.

PARTNERSHIPS

Under the old rules a partnership could complete and file a partnership return (Form 1) each year but in practice the Inland Revenue accepted the lodging of the partnership's income tax computation and accounts, together with an allocation of profits based on the profit-sharing arrangements in the tax year itself. The completion of the partnership return for 1996/97 will however be compulsory and will be on the same basis as for that of a sole trader (see above).

Tax Filing Tip

Enter these details on the Partnership tax return.

However, the Inland Revenue will continue to look at each individual partner's tax return and work out the deductions and tax rates applicable to each partner's share of profit. The figures are all added together and one tax bill is sent to the partnership for payment. Tax is paid in two instalments on 1 January in the tax year and on the following 1 July.

The last tax which the partnership will pay will be for 1996/97. That is also the first year in which you start to assess your own tax liability as an individual. From 1997/98 each partner will be charged to tax in his own right and there will no longer be an assessment on the partnership.

In 1996/97 each partner's share of tax charged by the 1996/97 partnership assessment will be treated as tax deducted at source, so that in computing his own self assessment for 1996/97, he will not need to worry about paying the partnership tax himself.

This applies to the final balancing payment for 1996/97 payable on 31 January 1998 but remember at the same time each partner will also have to make his first instalment payment for 1997/98. At this stage each partner takes over responsibility for paying his own share of tax on partnership income and he will need to know the quantum of his share of the 1996/97 assessment in order to arrive at the interim payment on account for 1997/98 due on 31 January 1998. Where estimates are used these should be properly disclosed on the Additional Information section of the tax return.

Under the new rules even though a partnership will not be a tax-paying entity, it will be required to compute its income and file a partnership return by 31 January following the end of the tax year. The first such partnership return will be required in respect of 1996/97 partnership income and gains. The partnership return will include a statement of each partner's share of income and deductions. Failure to file or the incorrect completion of a partnership return will give rise to significant penalties. The penalty for failing to make a return is £100 plus a possible further £60 for each day the failure continues. For a partnership this applies to each partner and not just the partnership as a whole.

Tax Alert

For a 60-partner partnership failure to render the partnership return on time would therefore mean a minimum penalty of £6,000. If each individual partner's return was also delayed, awaiting the necessary information from the partnership return, the effective penalty would double to £12,000.

If a return is not filed within six months of the normal filing date, the penalty will be increased by a further £100 per partner. If the failure to file continues for 12 months from the filing date, there is a further penalty based on the tax liability shown on the return.

These penalties are subject to the partnership having a reasonable excuse for not delivering the return. Partnerships should be taking steps now, however, to organise themselves so that they can comply with the completion of the partnership tax return by the filing deadline.

If you are a partner you will have to enter your share of profits as shown on the partnership return in your tax return for 1996/97.

Tax Filing Tip

Enter these details on Partnership (Full): Pages P1-4.

Tax provisions

Many partnerships will need to consider their organisation in the light of these new rules carefully. For years up to and including 1996/97 the partnership liability is a joint and several liability of the partnership. Many large partnerships made provisions for tax in their accounts which they debited to each partner's current account. Depending on the basis on which they provided tax, they may have reserved a proportion of their profit for each accounting period and, due to the time lag before tax is payable on profits, this tax provision often provided part of the working capital of the partnership. From 1997/98 partners are responsible for paying their own share of tax and the need for partnerships to reserve an income tax provision ceases.

Large partnerships will need to consider very carefully the timing of the release of tax provisions to partners. Partners will have to be in possession of the funds required to meet their tax liability by the due dates.

As the partnership will no longer be aware of its partners' individual circumstances, it will not be possible to quantify the partnership tax liability of each partner as is done at present. On the other hand, if large partnerships allow partners to draw the whole of their share of profits in each year without restriction, this may adversely affect their working capital requirements and increase their need for overdraft or other facilities.

Partners need to agree how they are going to tackle these issues, building any cash flow impact into their partnership business plan.

Borrowings

Partnerships borrow to finance their capital requirements in one of two ways. Where the borrowing is done through the partnership accounts the deduction for overdraft or loan interest is made on the face of the taxable trading profits computation. In this situation under the transitional rules for 1996/97 only one-half of the interest paid will be relieved. Alternatively, partners borrow individually by way of a loan to contribute capital to the partnership. In this situation each individual partner is given a deduction from his total income for the interest paid in the tax year. Such deductions will not be affected by the transitional relief and individual partners will get the full amount of loan interest which they actually pay in the two years concerned. Partnerships which finance their capital requirements off balance sheet by way of loans from individual partners should be careful not to disturb this arrangement during the transitional period.

Partnerships which currently finance their borrowing requirements through the partnership directly should be careful if they wish to restructure this arrangement as the anti-avoidance measures relating to the transitional period (see Chapter 9) may impact. Unless any new loans are taken out wholly or mainly for bona fide commercial reasons (which does not include obtaining a tax advantage), if a partnership restructures its finance so that partners borrow on an individual basis where previously borrowings were through the partnership, any interest relief will be reduced. The interest affected will be that paid in the period between the end of the 1995/96 basis period under the old rules and 6 April 1997 and the amount paid will be reduced by a fraction. The numerator of the fraction will be twelve and the denominator will be the total number of months in the period. Effectively this averages the interest paid over the entire period so that the partner gets a deduction for the interest applicable to a twelve-month period but spread over a number of tax years.

COMPANIES
Corporation tax
Tax rates
From 1 April 1997 a corporate body with profits of up to £300,000 is liable to corporation tax at a rate of 23% (24% up to 31 March 1997). If profits are above £1.5m the corporation tax rate is 33% of the full amount. If the company has profits between £300,000 and £1.5m, the difference is taxed at an effective marginal rate of 35.5% (35.25% prior to 1 April 1997). The same rates of corporation tax also apply to any capital gains realised by the company.

Pay and File
A limited company files a corporation tax return and pays its tax without assessment under a system known as Pay and File. Under Pay and File a company must pay its corporation tax liability by the due and payable date of nine months and one day after the end of the accounting period. The company must file the completed corporation tax return, together with accounts and computations, by the filing deadline of twelve months after the end of the period of account. At present, when the company's corporation tax liability is finally agreed, the Inland Revenue issue an assessment on the final liability. This will change when companies move to a full self assessment system. The date has not yet been fixed, but will not be before 1 January 1999.

Dividends

A company can choose to retain its profits or distribute them to shareholders by way of dividend. When a company pays a dividend it has to pay advance corporation tax (ACT). For payments of dividends in the tax year 1996/97 the rate of ACT applied to a payment is one-quarter.

Example: A company pays a dividend of £20,000. It must pay ACT of £5,000.

ACT can be offset against a company's mainstream corporation tax liability. The maximum set-off is the amount of ACT that would have been payable in respect of a franked payment, ie, a dividend plus tax credit equal to the profits and made at the end of the accounting period. A franked payment is equal to the dividend paid plus ACT.

Example: Financial year ending 31 March 1997	£
Profits	2,000,000
Corporation tax 33%	660,000
Maximum ACT set-off	400,000
Maximum dividend	1,600,000
ACT thereon	400,000

If the ACT on dividends exceeds the maximum current period set-off then it may be carried back six years or carried forward.

If a company receives dividends these, when added to the tax credit attaching, are known as franked investment income. Dividends received are not liable to corporation tax but can be matched against dividends paid with ACT being calculated only on the excess dividends paid.

Example:	£
Dividend income received	100,000
Tax credit	25,000
Franked investment income	125,000
Dividend paid	£160,000
ACT	40,000
Franked payments	£200,000
Excess franked payments	£75,000
ACT payable – one-fifth	£15,000

Returns of and payments of ACT are made quarterly on Form CT61.

Where franked investment income exceeds franked payments of an accounting period, the excess is treated as surplus franked investment income and is carried forward into the next accounting period.

Example:

Dividend received	£100,000
Franked investment income	£125,000
Dividend paid net	£ 40,000
Franked payment	£ 50,000
Surplus franked investment income	£ 75,000

If a company has incurred a trading loss it can elect to have the loss set off against surplus franked investment income and have the tax credit repaid.

VALUE ADDED TAX

All businesses, whether unincorporated or incorporated, need to consider the impact of VAT on their business and whether or not they require to register for VAT. A business is required to register for VAT if its taxable turnover exceeds £48,000 (prior to 28 November 1996 the limit was £47,000) for any twelve-month period or if there are reasonable grounds for believing that its turnover in the current year will exceed this figure within the next thirty days. However, no registration is required if you can satisfy Customs and Excise that in the year ahead your taxable supplies will not exceed £46,000.

If the business's turnover is less than requires registration, you can still register voluntarily if this would be advantageous. Where a business is registered for VAT it generally has to complete a VAT return each quarter although there are monthly options. The return must show its taxable supplies and its output VAT, ie, the VAT it charges on supplies to customers and its taxable purchases and input VAT, ie, the VAT charged on purchases. If output VAT exceeds input VAT, the difference is paid to Customs and Excise. If input VAT exceeds output VAT, a repayment is due.

In making the decision whether or not to register voluntarily for VAT, you need to consider the impact on your sales and the impact on your costs. If your customers are all registered businesses or are mainly registered businesses, it is advantageous to register for VAT because your customers will incur no additional cost when you charge them VAT as they will be able to recover this in turn against their own taxable supplies. On the other hand, you will be able to recover VAT incurred on your taxable expenditure. If you do not register for VAT, any VAT incurred on business expenditure will not be recoverable, increasing your costs and overheads and possibly requiring you to charge an increased price for the goods you sell, although you will not be required to add VAT to these goods. A further factor to consider is the detailed record keeping and accounting for VAT which is quite an onerous burden, particularly on smaller businesses.

Special VAT problems arise if your business makes exempt supplies, for example by renting land, and you should consult your local VAT office for advice or take professional advice. The amount of input VAT you can recover may be restricted.

If you incur VAT on business expenses and do not recover it because you are not registered for VAT or because the VAT is irrecoverable (for example where you make some exempt supplies), it can be deducted from your taxable profits.

11 Business tax planning strategies

The key to successful tax planning for businesses is accurate forecasting of your current results and future profits. Most businesses will have drawn up a business plan which will include how it intends to develop sales of its goods or services, what capital expenditure will be required to support this and how the business will change in the future. Ideally it will include income and expenditure forecasts. This may be a formal document or an informal outline. Most well-run businesses also budget their profits for one year ahead and monitor actual performance against budget as the year progresses. The better the information in your business plan and budget, the better placed you will be to implement tax planning strategies effectively.

YEAR-END REVIEW

Every business whether unincorporated or not should review its likely profit level near the end of its trading year. A number of opportunities exist to take action to influence the level of profits and ensure their enjoyment. The following paragraphs provide some hints on the specific points to consider:

- timing of income, deductions and payments
- capital expenditure
- extracting cash from companies
- paying costs tax-effectively
- smoothing profits.

Timing of income, deductions and payments

Typically you will wish to time income to periods when tax rates are lower and deductions to periods when they are higher. You can do this by deferring or accelerating sales or purchases. Remember that the earnings basis of accounting requires you to accrue expenditure incurred even if you have not actually paid for it, so you must actually delay incurring expenditure to defer it.

The following suggestions may accomplish this:

- increase or decrease directors' remuneration
- pay extra pension contributions for directors
- accelerate or defer capital expenditure qualifying for capital allowances
- buy rather than lease assets, or vice versa
- employ your spouse in the company.

Tax Alert

Unincorporated businesses will find it more difficult to alter timing of profits as the anti-avoidance rules aimed at the transitional year 1996/97 on the switch to current year basis may penalise them heavily on any profit manipulation. They should examine each transaction carefully to check it doesn't activate one of the anti-avoidance triggers described in Chapter 9.

Timing bonuses

Bonuses and other remuneration are taxable on an employee on the receipts basis as they are paid. However, an employee may be deemed to have received emoluments at a date earlier than when they are actually paid, eg, if they are credited to a director's current account in the company.

An employer cannot claim a deduction for emoluments which are not paid, even if they have been accrued in the accounts, if they remain unpaid more than nine months after the end of the period of account. If actual payment is delayed beyond this date the deduction from trading profits is given in the period in which the emoluments are paid rather than the period in which they have been accrued.

Tax Saver

If you are paying bonuses to employees you should be particularly careful to time the payment both to a tax year which is advantageous to the employee and to a point in time where it is advantageous to obtain the tax deduction for the business paying the figure.

Capital expenditure

Timing

Your business plan will reveal the projected capital expenditure your business needs to incur. Consider carefully when you should spend the money. If the expenditure is of a type which will generate capital allowances, consider whether you can acquire the asset prior to the end of your accounting period but be careful that you pay for the asset in good time so that you do not lose the capital allowances. If your projections show that you will suffer a higher rate of corporation tax in the next year, it might be better to defer capital expenditure until after the end of your accounting period.

Buy or lease

For both incorporated and unincorporated businesses, buying assets outright is not the only option available. You may be able to acquire assets under a hire purchase contract or, alternatively, you may be able to lease them.

Leases which are not hire purchase contracts come in two types.

Operating lease

An operating lease is one where the lessor takes on any risks and rewards. The lessee is charged rentals which are designed to give a profit reward to the lessor in his profit and loss account. The leasing charges are deductible in full for tax purposes in the lessee's tax computation. There is one exception to this – which applies to expensive cars where there is a similar restriction to that which applies to Capital Allowances – see *Calculating capital allowances: expensive motor cars* in Chapter 8. Where an asset is acquired under an operating lease, it is the lessor who is entitled to capital allowances.

Finance lease

The alternative type of lease is known as a finance lease under which most of the risks and rewards of ownership transfer to the lessee. Usually these operate so that initially there is a primary lease period during which the rental paid enables the lessor to recover the cost of the asset plus his associated costs. At the end of the primary lease period the lessee may be able to continue leasing the asset for a much reduced rental. A lessee will usually show an asset acquired under a finance lease on his balance sheet, depreciating it over its useful life and showing a creditor for the sums owed under the finance lease.

In the case of a finance lease, although the lessee shows the asset in his balance sheet, he is still not entitled to capital allowances which fall due to the lessor. The lessee remains able to deduct rentals payable in his tax computation. The rentals paid may differ from the sum charged in his profit and loss account each year in respect of finance charges under the finance lease.

Hire purchase

If an asset is acquired under a hire purchase or lease purchase contract it is the purchaser who is entitled to any available capital allowances. This applies even though he is not entitled to ownership of the asset until the end of the hire purchase period. The purchaser will also be able to deduct interest paid under the hire purchase arrangement.

Tax Saver

In evaluating whether it should lease or buy, a business should take into account the time value of money. Purchasing an asset outright may, for example, increase its overdraft and hence in comparing alternatives, the cost of overdraft interest net of tax should be compared with the cost of leasing rentals or hire purchase charges. The alternative costs and benefits in the form of tax deductions and capital allowances should be compared on a time basis over the expected life of the asset and account taken of any residual value in the asset at the end of that period. By comparing the cash flows prepared in this way it will be obvious which is the better option for your business.

Extracting cash from companies

Family companies

When looking at tax planning for limited companies you must have a very clear idea what your objectives are. For many owner-managed businesses the objective will be not only to minimise the corporation tax payable by the company but also to extract an adequate amount of funds for the owner manager to live on in a tax-efficient way while also providing for his future. There will be a balance to be struck between what should be extracted from the company and what should be left in it to meet the business requirements. It may therefore not be possible to plan for the tax liability of the company in isolation – the personal affairs of its shareholders/directors may also be important.

If your directors are also shareholders, consideration needs to be given as to how much remuneration should be extracted by way of salary and how much by way of dividend.

Salary v dividend

It will usually be more expensive for a company to pay a salary than a dividend. This is because the employer has to meet a National Insurance contribution which is currently 10.2% (reduced to 10% from 6 April 1997). The employee will also suffer National Insurance but his liability is limited by the upper earnings limit.

A further alternative would be for the employee to take benefits in kind out of the company, as many benefits in kind are not liable to Class I National Insurance.

Despite the Class I National Insurance saving of paying a dividend in lieu of a salary, contrary issues must be considered:

- If the employee receives no salary he may lose out on State pension at retirement age.
- If too much is paid by way of dividend rather than salary, the employee's pension entitlement from an occupational pension scheme may be adversely affected or his ability to pay personal pension contributions may be reduced.
- The payment of dividends is a major factor in valuing shareholdings of under 25%. The more the dividends generally the higher the effect on price.
- Companies can pay dividends only if they have distributable profits.

Timing of dividends

Timing payments of dividends to shareholders offers a useful opportunity for planning by companies. Frequently a company's accounting period will not coincide with the end of the tax year. By paying a dividend within the accounting period the company will get relief for the ACT against its corporation tax liability which will be due nine months after the end of the accounting period but the shareholder may not have to pay higher rate tax on any dividend paid in 1996/97 until 31 January 1998.

Tax Saver

Companies should aim to pay dividends as late in their accounting period as possible to minimise the time cost of the early payment of ACT under the quarterly accounting system. If, however, a company expects that income tax rates are likely to increase, it should pay dividends prior to 5 April rather than after that date. If the converse is expected, or rates are expected not to change, dividends should be delayed until just after 5 April so that the shareholders obtain the maximum deferral before they are due to pay any higher rate tax on them.

Retained profits

If funds are accumulated in a limited company they may eventually suffer a double tax charge when the company is sold or wound up.

Example:

Profits earned or gains realised	£100,000
Corporation tax	25,000
Value of company	75,000
Company wound up – proceeds	75,000
Capital gains tax, say	30,000
Net benefit to owner	£45,000

Of course, because a company has an infinite life of its own you do not need to wind it up. It could, for example, be retained and funds accumulated within it and invested. However, whenever the owner tries to extract funds from the company either by way of dividend or salary, a liability to income tax will arise. The best way of dealing with this double tax trap is to take out funds, excess to the business needs, in regular tax-efficient tranches on an annual basis.

Paying costs tax-effectively

Profit-related pay

All employers should give careful consideration to the introduction of a profit-related pay scheme. These schemes allow employees to get part of their pay tax-free and motivate employees by linking part of their pay to the profits of the business. Where a profit-related pay scheme is in operation, the profit-related pay (PRP) element can be paid to the employee completely free of income tax up to a maximum of £4,000 or 20% of salary, whichever is less. For the employees, a basic rate taxpayer can save up to £1,000 per annum whereas a higher rate taxpayer can save £1,600 per annum. These advantages mean that employers can provide substantial increases to the take-home pay of their employees without increasing overall salary costs. Employees can benefit from an increase in take-home pay equivalent to a gross pay rise in excess of 7.5%. PRP schemes can be structured to achieve one or more objectives:

- Giving a cost-free pay rise.
- Providing additional tax-free income related to the performance of the business.
- Providing cost-free bonus payments.

One of the most popular uses of PRP schemes is the so-called salary conversion arrangement whereby employees are offered the opportunity to participate in the scheme by converting part of their existing pay to tax-free PRP.

Tax Alert

If you are an employee of a company, you cannot participate in a scheme if you own 25% or more of the company shares; nor can spouses of such shareholders who are employees.

Income tax relief for PRP will be phased out, over a three to four-year period, as a result of the 1996 Budget.

Smoothing profits

Using service companies

Sometimes the use of a service company can be helpful both in arranging accurate timing of income and deductions and in providing a vehicle which will accumulate funds. A service company can be used for both an incorporated or unincorporated business or partnership. The service company will provide some service to the main business. For example, it may own the building from which the business operates and it may charge rental. It may also own equipment or hire out employees to the main business. The main business will pay a charge for such a service and the Inland Revenue usually permit a small mark-up on cost to be taken, thus enabling profits to be shifted from one entity to another.

Creating a group

For a limited company the introduction of a service company may create a group of companies. A general discussion on the tax planning opportunities for groups of companies is outside the scope of this book but special tax provisions apply to transactions among groups of companies, including the ability to pay dividends from one to the other without ACT, the use of one company's loss against another company's profits and special arrangements for the charging of VAT on management charges, etc.

The limits at which corporation tax is charged at the small companies rate are lowered for each company in a group by dividing the limit by the total number of companies. It is therefore important to ensure that profits are spread around the group to maximise use of the limits in full. Bringing a service company into use for both unincorporated and incorporated businesses involves a certain amount of expense as well as providing certain timing benefits and the costs against the benefits need to be evaluated very carefully.

Avoiding the marginal corporation tax rate trap

Limited companies with small amounts of profits may find that they are in a tax trap if their profits fall between £300,000 and £1.5m. This is because profits above that level attract corporation tax at 33%, while profits below the £300,000 level will, from 1 April 1997, attract corporation tax at 23%. The marginal rate on profits between these two levels is 35.5% and hence it is not cost effective to have profits which fall between these limits. In order to avoid this trap, consider whether deductions can be made. For example, it may be a more cost-effective time to pay an additional bonus to directors or to make additional contributions to pension schemes. Each £100 paid will only cost the company £65.5 as against £77 if it is subject to the small company's rate or £67 if it is a large company.

Tax Saver

If you have a group of companies each additional company lowers the threshold at which the marginal tax rate applies. Consider if it is necessary to have so many companies in the group or whether you could more effectively organise your business on a divisional basis in one company.

12 Disposing of your business

You may wish to dispose of a business for a number of reasons:

- to realise the value of the business (on retirement, sale or wind-up)
- to pass on wealth to the next generation (estate planning)
- to move from sole trader/partnership status into a company (incorporation).

Estate planning, including the transfer of wealth you have built up in your business for the next generation, is covered in Chapter 15. This chapter deals firstly with disposing of a business you carry on as a sole trade. It describes how final taxable profits will be computed and the treatment of gains realised from sale of the business assets. Various capital gains tax reliefs are explained. We then consider some adaptation of these rules for partnerships. Next, the chapter considers disposing of a company by selling shares to a third party, winding it up or by a company purchase of its own shares. Finally it describes the tax issues to be considered on the incorporation of a self-employed business.

SOLE TRADER

When a sole trader ceases to carry on business there is an adjustment to the way profits are allocated to tax years for the purposes of computing liabilities.

When your business ceases

Pre-6 April 1994 businesses

If your business was set up prior to 6 April 1994 and ceases before 6 April 1998, then in the tax year when your business ends you are taxed on the profits from 6 April in that year to the date the business ceased.

Example: Your business ends on 31 December 1996. In 1996/97 you are taxed on profits from 6 April 1996 to 31 December 1996.

Tax Alert

The Inland Revenue can choose to revise the basis of assessment for the two years preceding the tax year when your business ends. Instead of taxing the profits of the preceding year, they will adjust your profits to the actual profits of the tax years in question (arrived at by apportioning the figures in the accounts) if that would create a higher tax bill.

Example: A businessman has the following profits until his business ceases on 31 December 1996:

		Normally taxed in
Year ended 31 December 1993	£10,000	1994/95
Year ended 31 December 1994	£12,000	1995/96
Year ended 31 December 1995	£18,000	
Year ended 31 December 1996	£20,000	

The Inland Revenue will change the taxable profits to:

'Pre-penultimate year' 1994/95	£13,500	($3/4$ x £12,000 x $1/4$ x £18,000)
'Penultimate year' 1995/96	£18,500	($3/4$ x £18,000 x $1/4$ x £20,000)
Final year 1996/97	£15,000	($3/4$ x £20,000)

Notice that the profits for the year ended 31 December 1993 and $1/4$ of the profits for the year ended 31 December 1994 are not charged to tax. However, as tax on the later years' profits is taxed earlier, from the cashflow viewpoint the increased assessments mean you pay more.

Tax Saver

If you have an option when your business ceases, it pays to work out what your closing assessments will be. By deferring the closing of your business from one tax year to another you may restrict the Inland Revenue's right to increase your tax assessments for the penultimate and pre-penultimate years of assessment.

If your business ends between 6 April 1997 and 5 April 1998 the Inland Revenue retain the right to adjust the 1995/96 and 1996/97 tax years to the actual profits based on time apportionment, but you do not get the benefit of the special transitional rules for 1996/97 described in Chapter 9. The tax treatment of the cessation of your business will be exactly as described above. If your business ceases between 6 April 1998 and 5 April 1999 the Inland Revenue retain the right to revise your tax for 1996/97 only, to the amount of the actual profits arising in that year.

If your business ends after 6 April 1999 you cannot effect tax planning through the 'closing year' rules described above as they cease to have effect. Instead your business is taxed in the same way as post 5 April 1994 businesses.

Post 5 April 1994 businesses

Where a business which was set up after 5 April 1994 ends there is no revision of the profits taxed in any tax year prior to the one in which the business ceases.

Assuming the business does not come to an end in the year of start-up or the following tax year, then profits for the final year will be those from the end of the last accounting period already taxed, to the date when the business ended.

Example: A business commenced on 1 October 1994 and makes up accounts to 30 June each year. The business ceases on 1 June 1999. Profits will be attributed as follows:

Accounts period	Profits taxed in each tax year	
1 October 1994 to	1 October – 5 April 1995	1994/95
30 June 1995	1 October 1994 – 30 June 1995	1995/96
1 July 1995 to	1 July 1995 – 30 September 1995	1995/96
30 June 1996	1 July 1995 – 30 June 1996	1996/97
1 July 1996 to	1 July 1996 – 30 June 1997	1997/98
30 June 1997		
1 July 1997 to	1 July 1997 – 30 June 1998	1998/99
30 June 1998		
1 July 1998 to	1 July 1998 – 1 June 1999	1999/2000
1 June 1999		

Note that for 1999/2000 taxable profits are based on an eleven-month period even though the business was carried on for only two months in that tax year.

Overlap profits As explained in Chapter 9 the profits for one or more periods can be used to find the taxable profit for more than one tax year. In the above example the profits for the period 1 October 1994 to 5 April 1995 and 1 July 1995 to 30 September 1995 are each included twice:

1 October 1994 – 5 April 1995 is used in 1994/95 and 1995/96 tax years.

1 July 1995 – 30 September 1995 is used in 1995/96 and 1996/97.

The profits for these two periods are called overlap profits as they are included in two successive tax years. These overlap profits will be treated as a trading expense in the computation of trading profits for 1999/2000, ie, deductible against profits for the period 1 July 1998 to 1 June 1999.

Selling business assets

If you sell your business when you stop trading as a going concern, one consideration is how you should allocate the proceeds you receive to the various assets which you have.

Maximising after-tax proceeds

In a straightforward situation it will usually be apparent to which assets any proceeds relate. However, on a disposal of the business for a single sum, there is the question of allocation of proceeds to various assets. The greater the amount allocated to stock and assets on which capital allowances are claimed then the greater the possibility of income tax due to increased profits or recapture of allowances. If the business was previously run at a loss it may be possible to use up losses by having greater stock, etc, values.

Alternatively, if you are selling the business, you may be eligible for special capital gains tax reliefs, eg, retirement relief or reinvestment relief, in which case it would be preferable for buildings and goodwill to attract more of the sale proceeds.

It is not uncommon for the seller and buyer to have conflicting aims in allocating the sale proceeds. The buyer may wish a higher allocation to plant and machinery in order to benefit from greater capital allowances. The seller may seek a lower value for plant and machinery in order to avoid an increased recapture of capital allowances. So you should negotiate carefully in this area when both buying and selling your business.

Do not forget that the Inland Revenue are able to question the allocation of sale proceeds to various assets of the business, if they consider the allocation to be unreasonable.

Tax Saver

When selling your business consider the allocation of the proceeds over all the assets of the business and the income tax/capital gains tax effects. It may be necessary to seek the services of a valuer to justify allocations should the Inland Revenue query the sale agreement allocation.

Capital gains tax reliefs
As noted in Chapter 7, the disposal of business assets by a sole trader is a personal disposal for capital gains tax. However, there are a number of reliefs that may be available where the business is a trade for income tax purposes. These reliefs can be used to maximise the after-tax proceeds of sale. The main reliefs are:

- rollover relief
- retirement relief
- reinvestment relief.

All these reliefs are given before any personal capital gains tax losses and before the annual capital gains tax exemption. The last two of these reliefs are described in Chapter 2 and you should also refer to Chapter 14 which deals with retirement.

Business asset rollover relief
Where a business disposes of assets used in a trade, any gain arising on the disposal may be deferred if the proceeds of sale are reinvested in new assets which are also used for the purpose of a new trade.

To qualify for rollover relief, both the old assets and the new assets must be within certain categories. Those mainly relevant are listed below:

- land and buildings occupied and used for the purposes of the trade
- fixed plant or machinery which does not form part of a building
- goodwill
- milk quotas and potato quotas
- ewe and suckler cow premium quotas.

You must buy the new assets within one year before, or three years after, the sale of the old assets unless the Inland Revenue allow you further time. They may do so if you can show you had a firm intention to acquire new assets within the time limit but you were prevented from doing so by circumstances beyond your control.

Capital gains arising on old assets not rolled over for capital gains tax purposes until the new asset has been acquired, should be included in the self assessment tax return and the liability paid on 31 January following the tax year end. However, providing you can show your intention to acquire a qualifying asset within the time limit, you can make a provisional relief claim on the tax return.

Tax Filing Tip

Enter these details on Help Sheet IR290 Page 5.

Tax Alert

Care must be taken when applying for provisional rollover relief, as if the claim fails, the deferred tax would be payable from the normal due date, with interest.

Rollover relief works by reducing the cost of the new asset by the amount of the gain on the old asset. Any gain is therefore deferred until the new asset is, in its turn, sold at some future date. In order to obtain full rollover relief the whole proceeds of the old asset must be reinvested and not just an amount equivalent to the gain. If a lesser amount is reinvested in the new asset, the amount of the gain rolled over is reduced by the shortfall in the proceeds reinvested.

Tax Saver

If you are terminating one business and setting up a new business, the ability to roll over your gain may be a decisive factor in the way in which you decide to structure your new business. For example, it may be better to sell the old assets of an unincorporated business and roll over the gain into the new assets of another unincorporated business and then incorporate at a later date. You are not able to roll over gains on an unincorporated business's assets against the cost of subscribing for shares in a company. However, you may instead be able to claim reinvestment relief. See Chapter 2 for details of how reinvestment relief works.

PARTNERSHIPS

If you are a partner in a partnership you may cease to carry on business in one of three circumstances:

- the partnership may cease to carry on business and wind up its affairs
- you may retire or resign from the partnership, although your partners carry on in business
- the partnership may be taken over or may change into another entity.

In each of these circumstances you need to consider:

- the way in which the taxable profits are allocated to tax years
- whether any capital gains accrue to you.

Partnership ceases to trade

If a partnership ceases to carry on business, the rules described earlier in this chapter for sole traders apply in deciding how to allocate its profit to tax years.

Partner leaves

If you retire from a partnership the first matter that you and your partners must decide is whether an election to treat the partnership as continuing should be made. This is described in Chapter 9.

Partnership changes into another entity

Generally this occurs when it incorporates, in which case it is treated as though the partnership ceased to trade.

The summary chart below shows the possible treatments that may apply when you cease to be a partner of a partnership that began either before or after 6 April 1994.

Ending a partnership

Income tax summary

Partnership started	Partner leaves	Partnership ceases
Pre 6 April 1994	**Up to 1996/97** Deemed ending of the partnership business. Ability to elect to be treated as if it had not ended.	**Up to 1996/97** Normal existing cessation rules apply and the Revenue have the right to adjust second and third last years of trading profits.
	From 1997/98 Same treatment as post 5 April 1994 partnership.	**1997/98** New rules or old rules apply at the Revenue option.
		1998/99 Profits computed under new post 5 April 1994 basis except 1996/97 can be changed to the old basis if Revenue elect.
Post 5 April 1994	The partner leaving is treated in the same manner as a sole trader in respect of their share of partnership profits.	All partners are treated as sole traders, therefore treatment is the same as if each partner had left.

Chargeable assets

For capital gains tax purposes each partner is treated as having a fractional share in each partnership asset, normally based on the partner's entitlement to any proceeds. Clearly if the partnership sells an asset for capital gains tax purposes, eg, a building, then the gain or loss will be allocated to each partner based on their share.

Where a partner leaves a partnership there will be a disposal of a share in each chargeable asset retained by the partnership. The disposal proceeds will be equal to the value of the asset reflected in the partner's capital account withdrawn plus any extra payments he receives.

Ongoing partners will find that the capital gains tax cost of their share of the assets will increase by a share of the amount paid to the outgoing partner.

DISPOSING OF COMPANIES

If you own shares in a company, when you cease to carry on business you will wish to realise the value of your shares in one of these ways:

- selling shares to a third party
- winding up the company
- company purchase of own shares.

Selling your shares to a third party

Capital gains tax reliefs

A sale generates a capital gain in the usual way but you may be entitled to retirement relief or to claim reinvestment relief (see Chapter 2) to reduce this.

Generally for capital gains tax purposes where shares in a company are sold in return for shares or securities issued by the purchaser, then any capital gain is deferred until the new shares or securities are sold. It is possible to seek Inland Revenue clearance for this deferral treatment. While it may be advantageous to defer capital gains tax there are a number of disadvantages also:

- the value of the new shares/securities received will be tied into the fortunes of the new owner of the business. If for any reason the new owner has problems the value of the shares may fall
- the shares being sold may have qualified for various capital gains tax reliefs (eg, holdover relief, see Chapter 2) and inheritance tax reliefs (eg, business property relief, see Chapter 15). The new shares may not qualify for such reliefs
- tax rates may be higher in the future than they are now.

If you gift shares to a member of your family, the market value of the shares is used to calculate any gains.

Tax Saver

Gifts of shares in family trading companies may qualify for holdover relief for capital gains tax purposes. This relief is described in Chapter 2 but in essence it means that on gifting no gain arises and the recipient takes over the shares broadly at their market value reduced by the measure of the gain which would otherwise have arisen. Gifts could be made to members of the family or even into family trusts in order to spread wealth to use up annual capital gains tax exemptions and lower/basic rates of tax.

Pre-sale dividend

It may be possible to receive a dividend before any sale of the company in order that the shares have a reduced value. A dividend may be more favourably taxed than the equivalent amount of share proceeds.

Example: A shareholding has a minimal cost of acquisition and is currently worth £200,000. If sold, capital gains tax of about £80,000 (40% tax rate) would be due. Instead the shareholder receives a £100,000 dividend and sells the shares for £100,000. The after-tax proceeds can be compared:

	Straight sale	*Sale and dividend*
	£	£
Proceeds	200,000	200,000
Less tax	(80,000)	(65,000)
	£120,000	£135,000

Sale and dividend tax computed as:

	£
■ capital gains tax £100,000 x 40% on share sale =	40,000
■ income tax on dividend =	25,000
	65,000
Gross dividend (£100,000 + 20% tax credit)	125,000
40% income tax on dividend	50,000
20% tax credit on dividend	25,000
Net tax due	£25,000

However, a pre-sale dividend may not be advantageous if the company has no corporation tax liability against which to offset the advance corporation tax it has to pay to the Inland Revenue on paying a dividend. That advance corporation tax represents the 20% tax credit noted in the above example enjoyed by the shareholder.

Winding up the company

When a company is liquidated it disposes of its assets. That can crystallise a tax charge within the company itself which is liable to corporation tax. The liquidator will then distribute the cash realised for the assets to the shareholders. This distribution is a capital receipt in the hands of the shareholders in exchange for their shares and may also crystallise a capital gains tax charge in the usual way on a 'sale' of shares. As a result the proceeds received from disposing of a business run via a company can suffer a double tax charge on a winding up. This is an important consideration in choosing your business structure at the outset.

Your company buying your shares

Company law

Under UK company law a company cannot own its own shares, but it can purchase its own shares which must then be immediately cancelled. Any purchase must be for cash.

Tax position

For UK tax purposes a company purchase of own shares is generally treated in the same manner as a dividend. The amount paid on the purchase, less the original subscription price paid to the company, is treated as a distribution and advance corporation tax needs to be paid to the Inland Revenue by the company. The shareholder is taxed on the amount received in the same way as if it were an ordinary dividend.

Tax Saver

As you will have disposed of your shares to the company you must work out whether or not there is any capital gain. But in doing so you can reduce the amount received for your shares by the amount that is subject to income tax as a dividend. As a result you will often find that you are entitled to claim a capital loss.

If you have owned the shares for five years or more, it is possible for a company purchase of own shares to be subject to capital gains tax only and not treated as a form of dividend. For only capital gains tax treatment to apply a number of conditions require to be satisfied, and the company will advise you if the purchase qualifies. If in doubt, seek professional advice.

Tax Saver

If you have a choice between 'dividend' treatment or 'capital' treatment consider carefully which results in the lower tax liability taking into account all your reliefs and exemptions. It may be easy to structure the purchase in the manner most favourable to you.

INCORPORATION

At some point in the life of an unincorporated business, the time may come to consider whether it should continue in that form or whether further expansion and growth will be helped by converting it into a limited company for the reasons set out in Chapter 7. The differences between a limited company and an unincorporated business have also been explained in Chapter 7.

Income tax

If you think that incorporation is appropriate, you should consider the timing of the change very carefully. Remember that when your unincorporated business ends you have to apply the 'cessation' rules in force at that time. These attribute the accounting profits to tax years in the last years of the business. Given the changing tax rules described above it may be better to defer incorporation to a time when the Inland Revenue cannot revise your final three years' tax assessments and when you will have obtained the benefit of the 50% transitional relief for 1996/97 (see Chapter 9).

Remember, you will also be able to deduct any overlap relief (described above) when the unincorporated business comes to an end and the new business begins.

Business assets
Think carefully what assets you wish to transfer to the limited company. Because of the potential for double taxation on a limited company, it may not be appropriate to transfer all your assets and you may, for example, wish to retain in your own possession property which is then rented to the limited company.

Tax Alert

Don't forget that any rental income you receive personally will not be earned income and you will not be able to deduct pension contributions from it.

Capital gains tax
A special capital gains tax relief is available when an unincorporated business is transferred to a company as a going concern. This relief is available only if the whole assets of the business, other than cash, are transferred in exchange for shares in the new company. In this case, the company acquires the unincorporated business's assets at their market value.

The shares received are acquired at the value of the assets transferred to the company, but any gain on the disposal of assets is deducted from the cost of the shares.

Example: A sole trader incorporates his business by transferring business assets worth £1m to a company in return for shares. The transfer gives rise to a gain, for capital gains tax purposes, of £400,000. Under the relief the company acquires the assets at £1m and the shares are acquired for £600,000, for capital gains tax purposes. The sole trader's gain is cancelled.

If you do not transfer all the assets used by the business you will sacrifice this relief so you need to consider carefully what chargeable gains arise. All is not lost if the relief is not available as there are two main alternatives. Instead of transferring the assets in exchange for shares, you can gift the assets to the limited company. The gift of assets will be treated as if the assets had in fact been sold at their market value. Gains will need to be computed accordingly. You may then be able to claim holdover relief on any gain. This relief operates by allowing the company in effect to take over any gain, which is then deferred until the company sells the assets gifted. The deferral operates by treating the company as having acquired the assets gifted at their market value less the gain held over.

Another option is to claim reinvestment relief. Provided you can show that you have invested all the gain arising on assets transferred to the company in subscribing for new shares that qualify under the reinvestment relief scheme (see Chapter 2) the gain will be held over and the cost of your new shares will be reduced by the amount of the gain.

In the case of holdover relief on a gift of business assets to a company, it is the asset value to the company that will be reduced so that if the company ultimately disposes of the asset, it will have a higher liability to tax on any capital gain. In the case of reinvestment relief or the relief on transfer of a business to a limited company the company owns the asset at its market value at date of acquisition, but the tax cost of your shares in the company is reduced. It is the shareholder who has the greater exposure to capital gains tax if the shares are disposed of.

Tax Saver

In choosing which of these reliefs to opt for, consider whether it is more likely that the company will dispose of chargeable assets or you will dispose of shares in the company first.

How to improve your financial future

PART

III

Everyone hopes that one day they will be rich enough to do all the things that currently they are unable to afford. In the past in the United Kingdom we have relied heavily on financial safety nets such as our social security system to cushion us if that bright financial future fails to materialise. We have relied on the State pension providing for us in our old age and the National Health Service looking after us when we are ill.

Sadly our safety net is no longer as strong as it once was since many social security benefits have been cut or removed. The State pension has never provided more than a basic income, but had the advantage that it was increased in line with rising prices. State retirement age is already announced to increase from 60 to 65 for women reaching retirement age early in the next century. The cost of the National Health Service is also giving cause for concern and while there are no plans to end free medical care, more of us may feel obliged to take greater responsibility for our own health care in the future, topping up the service provided by the State and also providing our own social care as we grow old and become less able to look after ourselves. The method of provision of long-term care for a growing ageing population is occupying the minds of politicians and the private sector alike. These trends make it desirable that we save at least some of our income to provide a cushion for the future.

Taxes are not the only consideration in planning your financial future, but they are an important one. The best investment plans involve deferring taxes so that more of your money builds a nest egg for the future. At some point, depending on your age and need for income, you may want to consider investments which are tax-free. You need to plan now – not later – how you are going to afford to retire at a time of your choice. And, as unwelcome a task as it may be, you need to consider planning your estate and how you want to provide for your family. In fact, you can enhance the quality of your life by giving serious consideration to what you want to happen to your assets after your death and with the knowledge that your family is secure.

13 Investment planning and your taxes

Before you make investment decisions it is important to be clear about why you want to invest and what you want to achieve in the future. You also need to take into account your attitude to risk. Some people are relaxed about investing in shares, but others feel happier putting their money into lower-risk investments like British Government stocks, bank deposit accounts and building society savings accounts. Generally, the more risk you are willing to take, the higher the potential returns – but the greater the possibility that you will lose some or even all of your original investment.

Tax considerations also play an important part in your investment decisions, because different investments are taxed in different ways. Some investments pay an income which may be taxable or may be tax-free. With other investments you hope that the value of the capital will increase, in which case the gain you make may be liable to capital gains tax – or may be exempt from this tax. Some investments offer both income and potential capital gains. With careful planning it is possible to reduce the total tax you pay on your investments considerably, and thus increase the return you receive.

If you already have investments, it is important to review them from time to time – at least every few years. There are several reasons for this. First, your personal circumstances may have changed. You may have married or divorced, had a child, moved to a larger home or inherited some capital. Second, some investments have a fixed term – five years, say – and when this comes to an end you will need to decide what to do next. Third, changes in the economic and tax situation may mean that the reasons you had for your investment decision a few years ago may no longer hold true. A change of Government with a different emphasis on methods of taxation should mean a review of your investments.

WHERE TO START
The latter part of this chapter explains the main types of investment. Which would be the best for you depends on your personal and financial circumstances now and on your plans and aspirations in the future. An independent financial adviser should take all of these into account when discussing your investment planning with you. Therefore the best place to start is to draw up lists of your current assets and liabilities, income and expenditure, so that he can understand your situation and give you appropriate advice.

Your assets

First, sum up your situation as it is today. Make a list of your own and your partner's assets and write down their approximate current value. You can use Table 1 in Chapter 15 to do this.

Add to these any assets which may materialise in the future. These will include money you expect to inherit, lump sums and income you will receive from pension schemes when you retire, the projected value of endowment policies when they mature, and the amount that life insurance policies will pay out if you die.

Also make a list of what you currently owe – your mortgage, bank loans, credit card debts and any other loans.

Your income

On a separate sheet, list your various sources of income. Write down the gross amount of income you get from each source over the year and add them up. Then subtract the total tax from your gross income to get your net income. You may find it helpful to use Table 1 at the end of this chapter. Include your partner's income if you want to plan your investments jointly.

Your expenditure

You can also use Table 1 to list your expenditure. Work out approximately how much you spend over the year. You will probably think it prudent to add on a safety net for unplanned and unexpected expenditure.

Add up your expenditure and subtract the total from your net income. The result should give an indication of how much of your income you have available for saving over the year.

HAVE YOU ARRANGED YOUR BORROWINGS EFFECTIVELY?

Before putting money into investments, it is worth considering whether you should use it instead to reduce any loans you have and on which you are paying interest. A good rule of thumb is: if the interest rate you are paying on a loan is more than the return you can get by investing the money, then pay off the loan (or reduce it if you can't afford to pay it off). This means, for example, that it is normally worth paying off credit card debts with high interest rates and bank overdrafts which bear both interest and bank charges. But there are two things you need to take into account before you make a decision:

■ Allow for any tax relief you get on the interest you pay on the loan, and any tax you would have to pay on the return from the investment. If the loan you are considering is a mortgage on your only or main home, remember that tax relief is limited to 15% of the interest you pay on the first £30,000 of borrowing.

■ You also need to think about liquidity – ie, how much cash you need to be able to get your hands on quickly. If you pay off a loan, you reduce your liquidity and it may be difficult to raise another loan if you need money in a hurry. If, instead, you put the money on deposit, you could withdraw it at very short notice.

What type of mortgage?

If you are taking out a mortgage, there are a number of points to bear in mind when choosing between a capital repayment mortgage and an interest only mortgage (such as an endowment mortgage):

■ Repayments on an endowment mortgage comprise interest plus the endowment premium. Those on a repayment mortgage consist of a mixture of interest plus repayment of capital and maybe an insurance premium for a mortgage protection policy. In the early years of a repayment mortgage you pay more interest than capital until the capital outstanding starts to reduce by a significant amount.

■ The cost of an endowment mortgage is more susceptible to interest rate changes. When rates rise, the increase in the monthly cost will be steeper than with a repayment mortgage, and when rates fall the reduction will be greater. If stability is important to you, the monthly cost of a repayment mortgage will be more even over the long term.

■ Don't be swayed towards an endowment mortgage just because it has built-in life insurance. You can arrange term insurance (see below) which will pay off a repayment mortgage if you die and is much cheaper than an endowment policy.

■ Because most of the money you pay into an endowment policy is invested, there may be a tax-free cash surplus at the end of the mortgage term after the mortgage has been paid off. There is no guarantee of this, and there have been cases where the proceeds from the endowment policy have not been sufficient to pay off the mortgage and the homeowner has had to pay the difference.

Pension mortgage

If you are not a member of an employer's pension scheme you can opt for a pension mortgage, whereby the home loan is intended to be repaid in full from the anticipated tax-free lump sum you get when you take the benefits from the pension plan. These schemes are very tax-efficient because you currently get full tax relief on your payments to the pension plan (including the cost of any life cover arranged under the plan) as well as partial tax relief on the mortgage interest. However, remember that repaying the mortgage will significantly reduce the amount of the lump sum you get on retirement.

Although pension mortgages are particularly effective for those who pay higher-rate tax, they are not worthwhile if you are likely to become eligible to join an employer's pension scheme in the near future. This is because pension planning considerations may mean you should join the employer's scheme – and this would mean having to re-arrange your mortgage.

PEP mortgage

PEP mortgages (where the capital is repaid from PEP funds) also seek to exploit tax-free growth for the invested funds, pending repayment. However, the return cannot be guaranteed given the exposure of the investments to stock market fluctuations. Therefore, it also makes sense to effect some term insurance to repay the loan in the event of premature death and perhaps consider early repayment of part or all of the mortgage if the returns from the PEP have exceeded expectations.

HAVE YOU COVERED THE RISKS YOU FACE?

No one thinks that they are going to be the victim of a road accident, heart attack, long-term illness or criminal injury, yet every year thousands of people die or endure long-term suffering from such unexpected events. The personal consequences of death, disablement or long-term illness are tragic enough without having dire financial consequences as well. Even if you have no dependants, you could become dependent on others if you were unable to fend for yourself. In planning for a secure financial future, the most important first step is to ensure that you and your dependants are covered against the financial risks which arise from such an event. The main things to consider are as follows.

Death of a breadwinner

You will need to consider what would happen if you (or your partner) were to die. First, check what money your dependants would receive:

- from your employers' pension schemes
- from personal pensions
- from any life insurance cover you may have taken out to pay off your mortgage or other loans
- from other life insurance policies you have arranged
- from the State.

It may well be that you already have sufficient life insurance – particularly if you belong to a good pension scheme (but remember to consider what happens to that cover if you leave the employment). If not, the cheapest way of providing for your dependants on your death is through *term insurance*. This will pay out either a regular income or a single lump sum (which your dependants can invest and draw on) if you die before the policy ends. If you outlive the policy it pays nothing (which is why this type of insurance is cheap). You choose the term of the policy at the outset; many parents cover themselves for the period until their youngest child will cease to be dependent on them. You may have a right to extend the term of the policy. The cost of term insurance depends on your age and occupation, your health, the amount of cover and the term of the policy. The younger you are when you take out the policy, the better your state of health and the shorter the term, the lower the premiums will be.

The two other main types of life insurance are:

- *Whole of life insurance,* which pays out on your death, whenever it occurs. This costs more than term insurance as the insurance company is bound to pay out one day, but there are circumstances in which whole of life policies are useful (eg, for your family to pay inheritance tax on your estate).
- *Endowment policies,* which are primarily investment schemes over a fixed period between ten and 25 years (although the term can be longer). Policies which

have only a small life insurance component are not a good choice if your main need is life insurance.

It is normally advisable to write life insurance policies in trust for your dependants. This means that on your death the money will be paid straight to your dependants rather than becoming part of your estate. This has two advantages:

■ your dependants should receive the money in a few weeks without any delay that may occur in obtaining a grant of Probate (or in Scotland, Confirmation to the estate)

■ the policy proceeds will be free of inheritance tax.

There is more detailed information about this in Chapter 15.

Long-term illness of a breadwinner

If you are in a job and you become too ill to work, your employer will pay you Statutory Sick Pay (which is taxable) for 28 weeks, or you may be able to claim Incapacity Benefit. Your employer may top these up, so that you receive a substantial proportion of your normal salary for the first six months or a year – and possibly up to retirement age. If your employer doesn't have a top-up scheme, or if it runs out after a period, you should consider taking out *permanent health insurance*. This will pay you a tax-free income from the outset for as long as you are too ill to work, right up until retirement age. These policies don't pay anything for an initial period which can be anything from four weeks to one year – the longer this 'deferral period' the lower the premiums.

The main objective of the State's Incapacity Benefit is to significantly reduce the cost to the State of providing sickness benefits and to increase the provision made by employers and individuals.

If you are self-employed, you won't get Statutory Sick Pay, but you may be eligible to claim Incapacity Benefit straightaway.

Because permanent health insurance policies stop paying out at retirement age, it is important that your pension arrangements will still provide you with an adequate income even if you are unable to continue paying premiums. Many personal pension arrangements offer 'waiver of premium' benefit and if this is available you should consider taking it up.

Incapacity Benefit is not taxable in weeks 1–28 inclusive but is taxable from week 29 onwards.

There is no tax relief on the premiums you pay for permanent health insurance. Income paid out to you is tax-free from when it is first paid. However, if the insurance is provided by your employer, any income paid to you is taxable as if it were earnings, and is liable to National Insurance. Unless the policy is taken out in your name the fact that your employer meets the cost of the insurance does not give rise to a taxable benefit (see Chapter 1).

Critical illness

Nowadays there is also a greater chance of suffering a critical illness, such as cancer, a stroke or a heart attack. Often these conditions will still mean that the individual survives after a period of recuperation. However, taking out critical illness cover which pays out a lump sum cash benefit can help you retain financial independence and give the breathing space required before returning to better health. Critical illness policies can be taken out for a specified term or on a whole life basis. Often the lump sum benefits paid by the insurance company are free of income tax.

Disablement or incapacitation

If you or one of your family were to become disabled or need long-term care, the additional costs of care could be enormous. Trying to obtain compensation for accidents through the courts can take years, so it is fortunate that insurance which will pay out a substantial lump sum can be obtained very cheaply. These policies pay out different amounts for loss of eyesight, hearing, limbs, and so on, and a small amount on death. There is no tax relief on the premiums, but the benefits are tax-free.

Redundancy

It is possible to obtain insurance which will make your repayments on your mortgage or other loans for a while if you are made redundant. This may seem worthwhile in the light of the Government's withdrawal of Income Support for mortgage interest in the first nine months of the claim for anyone who took out a mortgage after 1 October 1995.

However, before taking out such a policy, find out what your employer normally pays to staff made redundant and carefully check all the conditions of the policy. These can be very strict, the period for which income is paid can be quite short, and the policies can be expensive. So consider instead saving an amount equal to the premiums in a separate account which you can draw on if you lose your job – or use for a different purpose if you don't.

Medical care

While the National Health Service provides much medical treatment free of charge, if you were able to be treated as a private patient you would in many cases get treatment sooner and be able to select a time and location convenient to you. This could be particularly valuable if your illness affected your ability to work. These advantages may make it worth taking out medical insurance which will pay the costs of private treatment and accommodation in hospital.

You cannot get tax relief on premiums you pay for private medical insurance unless you are over age 60. If premiums are paid by your employer, you have to pay tax on the amount he pays (unless you earn less than £8,500 a year, or the insurance is to cover you while working abroad). The benefits are normally paid direct to the hospital or consultant.

HAVE YOU PROVIDED FOR YOUR FUTURE?

When you consider that if you live into your 80s your retirement is likely to be half as long as your working life it is clear that you need to be setting aside money to live on when you no longer have earnings. Investments are important, but pension schemes are probably the best way of providing a fundamentally secure income, not least because they are a very tax-effective investment. Chapter 14 deals in detail with planning for retirement.

The main disadvantage of most pension schemes is that you cannot get your hands on the money until you reach retirement age. But if you want to have more flexibility, you can arrange some of your retirement saving through other types of investment.

A second possible disadvantage with pensions is that if you die soon after starting to draw your pension, little benefit will be received from it (unless the scheme pays a pension to your surviving spouse or dependants). Some pensions have a guaranteed minimum pay-out, but only in exchange for getting a lower amount of pension. However, remember that the purpose of a pension scheme is to provide you with a secure income in retirement, however long you live; you can provide an inheritance for your heirs in other ways.

YOUR INVESTMENT STRATEGY

Level of risk

Risk is a very subjective issue. Generally, putting your money in a bank or building society is thought of as low-risk because the institutions are regarded as safe and you can be sure of getting your money back in full. At the other end of the scale, commodities and futures are regarded as high-risk investments because there is a very real chance that you will lose some or all of your money.

Categorising investments with regard to risk is not an exact science. People's perception of risk between different investments will vary according to their financial circumstances, level of wealth and good or indifferent experiences they may have had – whether selected by themselves or recommended by an investment manager or stockbroker. Such experiences may influence them when deciding where to invest any future surplus capital or savings out of income.

Notwithstanding the above, against each type of investment shown later in this chapter is a 'categorisation of risk' code denoting:

LR = Low-risk

MR = Medium-risk

HR = High-risk

Some investments may have more than one code reflecting the fact that they may fall into more than one category.

However, there are other considerations to take into account. A major one is inflation. If you had kept a lump sum in a building society earning interest for the last 25 years, your money (including the interest) would be worth far less now than when you had invested it. As future inflation is unknown, to stick doggedly to such a 'safe' investment for a long period of time is unlikely to be a sensible strategy. In the past, the stock market has consistently outperformed interest-paying investments over the longer term.

In this chapter, when we talk about low-risk, medium or high-risk investments, we use the terms conventionally – as in the first paragraph above. Table 2 at the end of this chapter shows a conventional division of investments into the three risk categories.

Tax considerations

As far as tax is concerned, most investments fall into five main groups:

1 those which are tax-free – there is no tax to pay on any of the income you get or capital gains you make

2 those where income is paid with no tax deducted, but taxpayers will have to pay tax on what they get

3 those where income is normally paid with 20% tax deducted, but non-taxpayers can have their income paid gross

4 those where income is paid after 20% tax is deducted or with tax credits, but you can re-claim tax if the amount deducted or the tax credits come to more than you are liable for

5 those where the main return is likely to be capital gain. This may be exempt from capital gains tax: if not, there will still be no tax to pay if you are within your annual allowances for capital gains.

If you pay higher-rate tax, you will have to pay the extra tax on the income you get from investments in groups 3 and 4 separately.

Table 3 at the end of this chapter shows which investments each type of taxpayer will find the most tax-effective.

Tax Saver

If you are a taxpayer, and especially if you pay tax at the higher rate of 40%, investments which are tax-free are particularly valuable to you. Investments which produce a capital gain rather than income can also be tax-free if the gains you make each year come within your annual capital gains tax exemptions.

Tax Saver

If you are over age 65 and entitled to age allowance consider whether tax-free investments will boost your spendable income without jeopardising your entitlement to increased allowances.

Tax Saver

If you are married, investments can be held by whichever spouse would have less tax to pay. So if one of you pays tax at a higher rate than the other or the other pays no tax:

■ *put taxable investments in the name of the one who pays tax at the lowest rate*

■ *put tax-free investments in the name of the one who pays tax at the highest rate.*

The same principle applies to investments liable to capital growth: allocate them so that you each use up your capital gains tax allowances. You should note that this means a gift between you so that assets belong to the other.

Planning to hold assets producing taxable income in the name of the spouse paying the least tax is particularly important since tax on income from savings is limited to 20% for all basic rate taxpayers.

Special targets

Often individuals will decide to start saving for a specific purpose such as:

i) making provision for school fees/further education for their children over a number of years

ii) accumulating a fund to pay for the deposit on a new home which they propose to acquire within the foreseeable future

iii) building up a lump sum to pay for the cost of an anticipated wedding

iv) retiring early

v) becoming independently wealthy.

A number of factors will normally determine the suitability of the investment – attitude to investment risk; tax position; whether the savings are to be made by lump sums or regular contributions or a mix; the time span involved; the 'target fund' required. Features of the investments such as their flexibility and lack of early withdrawal penalties will also be relevant to their suitability for the particular savings objective.

CHOOSING YOUR INVESTMENTS

In addition to the tax considerations above, the following provides some useful pointers when selecting investments:

■ Don't tie all your money up in complicated investment schemes. Make sure you have enough which you can get at immediately if you need to for unexpected emergencies.

■ If you are investing to give yourself an income, you don't have to invest in an income-producing investment. Nor should you just look at the income paid out – it is the total after-tax return that is important. This is because you can often get an income by cashing in capital growth; as long as it is within your annual capital gains tax exemption it will be tax-free.

■ Remember that some investments can fall in value as well as rise. However, these investments can do better than 'safer' investments over the longer term. But it's not sensible to put money which you may need quickly into such investments – in case the value is low at the time you need it.

■ Similarly, if you invest in a scheme which has a fixed term (such as an insurance-linked investment) and you then wish to withdraw in the early years, you may get a very low return and may even get back less than you invested.

- You can reduce your risk substantially by spreading your money between a number of different investments. Buying shares in six companies is much safer than putting all your money into one, but investing in a unit trust or investment trust (which invests in a lot of different companies) reduces your risk much further. Investing in a number of different unit or investment trusts reduces it even further, especially if they invest in different markets. Of course, you still have to pick the right one but having a good independent financial adviser or stockbroker can help. And you spread your risk even more if you invest in a combination of shares, unit and investment trusts, fixed-interest stocks, National Savings investments, interest-bearing accounts, and so on.

- If inflation is projected to rise it could make sense to switch money from interest-bearing accounts to the index-linked investments offered by National Savings and index-linked British Government stock.

YOUR INVESTMENT OPTIONS

Bank and building society investments – LR

From a security point of view, these are regarded as low-risk investments as long as you keep within the limits covered by the various compensation schemes. For a Sterling bank account, if the bank were to fail you would get compensation of 75% of the first £20,000 you had invested. For a building society account you would get 90% of the first £20,000. If you plan to invest more than £20,000, consider spreading it between more than one bank or building society to reduce your risk.

When deciding where to invest, you will need to consider:

- the reputation of the institution
- the interest rate payable for the amount you want to invest
- how much notice you have to give to withdraw money, and whether there is any limit on the number of withdrawals you can make without losing interest.

Current interest rates are published in the financial press and on Teletext. When comparing interest rates, use the gross compound annual rate ('gross CAR'). This tells you the overall return on your money, taking into account the fact that if interest is credited more frequently than once a year you get interest on interest, unless the interest is paid out to you, of course.

Beware of accounts being discontinued, as you may find the interest rate on it is substantially reduced, and the bank or building society may not write to tell you this. So review your accounts regularly and if this happens switch to a new account offering better terms.

Tax Saver

If you believe that someone in your family will not be liable to income tax in the tax year, ask for a form to get their interest paid gross (ie, with no tax deducted). If they haven't done this, make sure they reclaim any tax which has been deducted but for which they are not liable.

If you have a Save As You Earn account, interest on it is tax-free. New Save As You Earn accounts cannot now be opened unless they are linked to an approved savings-related share option scheme.

Tax-Exempt Special Savings Account (TESSA) – LR

This is a valuable five-year investment for people over 18 who pay tax. TESSAs are available from banks and building societies. Refer to Chapter 1 for further details of these accounts.

Building Society Permanent Interest-Bearing Share (PIBS) – MR

This is essentially a loan to a building society on which interest is payable twice a year at a fixed rate. The interest rate is generally relatively high because of the greater risk involved:

- As a PIBS has no redemption date, its value is determined by the market and will reflect current interest yields, so there is no guarantee of how much money you will get back.

- If the building society were to miss an interest payment, it would be under no obligation to compensate investors.

- If the society were to collapse, PIBS holders would rank behind other depositors and creditors, so could get little or nothing back.

PIBS can be bought through stockbrokers. As they are a form of 'qualifying corporate bond', any capital gain you make when you redeem the bond is exempt from capital gains tax. Interest is paid with 20% tax deducted.

National Savings investments – LR

All National Savings investments are regarded as low-risk because they are underwritten by the UK Government. Details of the current schemes and interest rates are obtainable from Post Offices. All National Savings investments are free of capital gains tax, and National Savings Certificates, Index-Linked Savings Certificates, Children's Bonus Bonds and Premium Bonds are also free of income tax. Yearly Plans are no longer available.

Chapter 1 describes the various investments available and their tax consequences.

British Government stock ('gilts') – LR

Gilts can be used as either a low-risk or a medium-risk investment. Most gilts have a redemption date on which the UK Government guarantees to repay the stock at its face value, so you will know the precise income and capital return if held until maturity. However, from the time you buy stock until its redemption date, its price can (and almost certainly will) rise and fall, depending on the prevailing trend of interest rates. So it is possible to make short-term gains if you are fortunate enough to buy stock before a price increase and sell it at a peak. On the other hand, you will make a loss if you need to get your money back at a time when the price is lower than you initially paid.

The Government pays interest on the stock twice a year. Each stock has an interest rate which may be as low as 1% or 2% ('low coupon'), or as high as 12% or more ('high coupon'). If the coupon is lower than current interest rates, you can expect to buy the stock at less than its face value, so that what you miss in interest is made up in capital gain. As gains you make are exempt from capital gains tax, low coupon stocks are the best choice for higher-rate taxpayers (and also for people over 65 who want to avoid their age allowances being reduced). Non-taxpayers, on the other hand, can often get a good income from high-coupon stocks, although bear in mind that if you pay more than the face value for stock you are effectively cashing in some of your capital.

Over the longer term you should remember that inflation will eat away at the capital value of your stocks. A way of preventing this is to choose index-linked gilts, where both the redemption value and the interest payments are increased in line with the Retail Price Index. This is not a free benefit, however, as the perceived present value of these increases are, of course, built into the price. And note that there is an eight-month time lag between the index and the increases, so the increases will never match inflation exactly.

Some gilts are on the National Savings Stock Register and you can buy and sell them through a Post Office subject to a maximum nominal value of £25,000 of any one stock on any one day. Interest is paid on these stocks with no tax deducted. This is not only good for non-taxpayers, it also provides a cash flow advantage for taxpayers. Tax will be due unless your income (including the interest) is less than your available allowances, so that you do not pay tax.

All other gilts are bought and sold through stockbrokers and other share dealing services. These gilts have 20% tax already deducted from the interest payments. If the tax deducted is more than you are liable for, you can reclaim the difference. If you are liable to higher-rate tax, you will have to pay extra, but if you are a basic rate taxpayer no additional tax is due.

There is a charge for buying or selling gilts. Generally it will cost less to trade smaller amounts of stock through the National Savings Stock Register and larger amounts through a stockbroker. However, the National Savings system works only by post so there is always a few days delay between ordering your purchase or sale and the actual transaction – so there is a risk that the price could move against you in that time. You can instruct your stockbroker, on the other hand, to trade in any amount whenever you want to.

Insurance company investments – LR/MR

Guaranteed income bonds

A guaranteed income bond is an investment which pays interest at a fixed rate for a fixed period. They tend to be offered by smaller life insurance companies. Interest rates depend on the amount you invest and the length of time you invest for, usually from one to five years. From a security viewpoint, provided the life company is a member of the PIA (the Personal Investment Authority) or is directly regulated by SIB (the Securities and Investment Board) 90% of your investment is covered under the Policyholders Protection Act 1975.

These bonds are usually unsuitable for non-taxpayers or lower-rate taxpayers as basic-rate tax is deemed to be deducted at source from the income but this tax cannot be recovered. Higher-rate taxpayers pay an additional 17% (from 6 April 1997) tax on the income they get and on the profit when the bond reaches the end of its term. However, allowing the interest to accumulate by purchasing a guaranteed growth bond (instead of a guaranteed income bond) rather than having it paid out defers the tax to the maturity date, and this can be advantageous if you are likely to have a lower tax rate at that time.

Most guaranteed income bonds are very illiquid and in an emergency not all companies will return the full amount of capital until the bond matures. Those that do often impose steep penalties. The bonds are therefore inflexible if you need emergency funds at short notice. Also check the level of charges levied on such bonds – these can be high.

Investment bonds – MR/HR

These are single premium life assurance policies which provide a return which is dependent on the performance of the insurance fund to which the policy is linked. They are similar to unit trusts in that the insurance company will select and manage the underlying investments. The main feature of these bonds is their tax treatment which can be a useful planning tool for higher-rate taxpayers. Each year (for up to 20 years) you can withdraw an amount equal to up to 5% of the premiums you have paid so far without incurring a tax charge. This is an ideal way to defer or time income so that it falls into years in which your tax rate is low.

The withdrawal is treated as already taxed at 23% (from 6 April 1997), so if you are liable to tax at the basic rate only, you can withdraw more than 5% each year without incurring a tax charge as long as the excess, when added to your other income, remains within the basic-rate band. But be warned: if the underlying investment performance of the bond fails to keep pace with the withdrawals you make, you will effectively be living on your capital.

There is no general tax relief if you suffer a loss on the bond (ie, if your withdrawals eventually prove to exceed the appreciation) although you can use a deficiency in the final year in which the bond matures to reduce your income for the purposes of computing higher-rate tax only, to the extent that you have paid higher rate tax on previous chargeable withdrawals (exceeding 5% of premiums).

Some investment bonds offer returns linked to a percentage of any growth in the Financial Times Stock Exchange 100 index typically over a period of five to six years with a guaranteed rate of return (often less than would have been obtained from a building society account) if the value of the index is less at maturity compared with that at the outset. You should check carefully what the guarantee covers. If it only covers capital growth, remember that you will be missing out on any dividends you would receive if you were to invest directly in stocks and shares.

Look carefully at the level of charges and consider what return you would get if you had to surrender your investment early. Often early surrender values are very low. Investments of this type which offer a high annual income may do so at the price of giving you a low capital return in the future if the underlying fund cannot produce an income of the level required. In effect, your income will be derived from your own capital – you are turning non-taxable capital into taxable income. These comments do not mean that these products don't serve a useful purpose – but in evaluating them you should consider the risks as well as the benefits.

The Inland Revenue issued a consultative document on 27 November 1996 with regard to the reform of policyholder taxation for various types of life insurance policy. The proposals, upon which comments have been invited by 30 April 1997, are wide ranging and represent a major review of the way life assurance policies are taxed during their currency, on partial withdrawal, final surrender or on prior death.

Annuities – LR

An annuity is a contract under which you pay a lump sum to an insurance company and they pay you a regular income either for a fixed number of years (a temporary annuity) or for life (a life annuity). Many pensions are in fact life annuities. A couple can take out a joint-life annuity which will pay an income for as long as either is alive.

The main advantage of a life annuity is that the insurance company takes the risk that you might live to a ripe old age and it will have to keep on paying out – unlike other investments, the money can never run out. On the other hand, if you die soon after buying the annuity, the money you have paid over won't go to your heirs unless there is a guaranteed minimum pay-out.

The older you are when you take out an annuity, the higher the income you are likely to receive for each £1 you hand over. If you are much under age 70 you may find that the income will not be enough to compensate for the main disadvantage of a life annuity – that you can never change your mind and get your money back.

The amount of income you get also depends on the current level of annuity rates (mainly determined by yields on Government stock when the annuity is purchased) and your age (and that of your spouse in the case of a joint life annuity) at the time you buy the annuity, and this reflects the return the insurance company expects to get by investing your money. Each company sets its own rates so it is worth shopping around to find the most favourable.

You can opt to have either a level annuity which pays the same income throughout, or an increasing annuity, where the income starts at a lower amount but increases by a fixed amount (eg, 5%) each year to help cope with inflation. This is a difficult choice. If inflation is high, the purchasing power of a level annuity will quickly be eroded. But because an increasing annuity starts lower, it can be ten or fifteen years before you have received as much as from a level annuity. An alternative is to go for a level annuity but save and invest part of the income paid out in the early years for use later on (or to go to your heirs if you die).

For tax purposes, part of the income you get from an annuity is regarded as repayment of part of the capital you invested and so it is tax-free. This means that it cannot reduce the age allowances given to people over age 65. The older you are when you take out the annuity, the higher the capital element is likely to be. The rest of the income is treated as interest and normally has 20% tax deducted. Higher-rate taxpayers will have extra tax to pay on the interest element.

When you die, the money you paid for your annuity does not count as part of your estate (unless part of it is repaid under a guarantee), so annuities can be a useful way of reducing inheritance tax.

Equity investment – MR/HR

The values of stocks and shares quoted on the stockmarket can – and do – rise and fall over time. For example, many shares fell in value during 1994 but have since recovered. Shares are therefore regarded as a high-risk investment. The overall return in capital and income depends not only on which shares you choose to buy, but also on the time when you decide to buy and to sell. As a short-term investment shares are very high risk – you may be lucky and make a large profit or may be the victim of a crash.

Over the longer term, however, statistics show that an investment in shares can produce a significant appreciation of capital and a rising level of income from dividends. It can thus provide a long-term hedge against inflation and falling interest rates which fixed-interest investment cannot match. If this is what you are seeking, you can reduce the risk by having a spread of different shares and a good way of achieving this is to invest either in unit trusts or investment trusts which are themselves holders of an underlying portfolio of stocks and shares.

Unit trusts – LR/MR/HR

A unit trust is an investment fund which is open-ended, expanding or contracting in size depending on the level of demand from potential investors. As more investors wish to invest, more units are issued to accommodate them and the fund size will increase. If more unit holders are selling their units, the fund is reduced to produce cash to buy back the units.

Collective investment schemes, such as unit trusts, offer a good way to invest small sums of money since the investor's cash can be 'pooled' into a much larger fund.

The fund managers make the underlying investment decisions.

An investor can achieve a balanced portfolio because the fund managers will invest in a range of investments. Lump sum and/or regular savings schemes can be effected.

Investment trusts – MR/HR

These are not trusts at all but are quoted companies which must conform to regulations laid down by the Companies Acts, the Stock Exchange and the Inland Revenue. Their business is to invest in the shares of other companies. They are limited liability companies whose size is determined by the initial share capital when they are floated on the stock market. Once investors have subscribed for shares, the shares are then bought or sold on the stock market and hence the price of investment trust shares is influenced not only by changes in the value of the company's own investment portfolio, but also by the supply of and demand for the shares in the company itself. Because an investment trust can borrow (unlike a unit trust), it can gear up to increase its investments. This can make it a more volatile investment than a unit trust.

Investment trusts can issue various types of shares and loan stock, which separate the ownership of income and capital. These are commonly referred to as split capital investment trusts which have a limited life span of up to ten years. After this they are wound up and the different classes are repaid in priority, assuming sufficient assets are available. Shareholders are not locked into the trust for this period; they can buy and sell shares of split capital trusts at any time, just like a conventional investment trust. In an investment trust therefore you can buy ordinary shares, income shares, capital shares, preference shares and zero-coupon preference shares. A tax-effective arrangement is to put together a package of split capital investment trust investments to meet your specific requirements. For example, by selecting a portfolio of zero-coupon preference shares which mature in successive years, you can obtain a return which may be tax-exempt if your annual capital gains tax exemption is available to offset the profit on disposal. By allocating your investment appropriately, the final redemption from your portfolio may be designed to give you your original capital back. This type of arrangement is complex and you would be well advised to take a stockbroker's advice on which investment trusts to buy and the appropriate structure. Nonetheless, for more sophisticated investors this can be a very tax-efficient way of using investment trusts.

Split capital investment trusts can also be used to reduce the tax paid by a husband and wife without giving away capital. In this case, income shares which give no capital return should be in the name of the spouse with lower income, while the spouse with higher income should retain shares which pay no income but will mature with a return of capital. As an outright gift of income-bearing shares can be made, these are not caught by the income tax anti-avoidance rules which affect gifts between husband and wife (see Chapter 6 'Married couples transferring income') and therefore the income can be passed tax-effectively to your spouse. Split capital investment trusts can also be used as a part of a school fees funding exercise.

Personal Equity Plans (PEPs) – MR

If you are investing in equities, look carefully at using a Personal Equity Plan (PEP) to hold your investments. This enables you to realise any profits tax-free. Choose the type of PEP that is appropriate to your circumstances. You can pick from a discretionary PEP where the fund manager chooses the stocks and shares, an investment trust PEP where the investment is made in shares in the investment trust, unit trust PEPs which operate in the same way as unit trusts, or self-select

PEPs where you choose which stocks and shares are purchased and sold. In deciding between these, look at the investment spread and the investment performance of the underlying fund. Consider both the income return, the potential for capital growth and the statistics showing the capital growth the fund has achieved in the past.

Also find out about the charges. These can take a variety of forms – there may be an initial charge as well as an annual charge. Some PEP managers are now moving away from an initial charge to exit charges which reduce the longer you hold the PEP investment. Compare the fees that the fund managers charge on buying and selling shares, and for unit trusts look at the bid/offer spread, ie, the difference between the cost of units and their sale price. Compare these charges with the tax savings you will make by reason of the tax-free income return. Sometimes the charges can outweigh the income tax benefit, but remember that capital growth is also free of tax in a PEP.

When you make regular savings into a scheme such as a PEP which invests in shares, you benefit from 'pound cost averaging'. As you invest the same amount each month, your savings will buy fewer shares when prices are higher and more when prices are lower. Therefore the average price you pay for the shares will be lower than if you had bought them all at a time when the market was high.

If you already use your annual capital gains tax allowance, a PEP offers an additional tax shelter which should be fully exploited. If you don't use the allowance you don't require the capital shelter of a PEP since you can realise profits of up to £6,300 for 1996/97 and £6,500 for 1997/98 without incurring capital gains tax.

Corporate Bond PEPs – MR

A PEP fund can be held in preference shares, convertible shares and corporate bonds. This type of asset often provides a higher fixed income than ordinary equity shares, so a fund which concentrates on this type of holding can maximise the income tax advantage of a PEP. You should bear this in mind when choosing the appropriate PEP investment to suit your circumstances.

Corporate bonds are issued by companies or corporations and are fixed interest securities, which pay a fixed amount of income half-yearly and usually have a final repayment date.

The most secure type is a debenture, which gets first call on a range of assets or specific assets should the company go into receivership. Unsecured loan stock is not so highly placed but ranks above all types of share capital and therefore merits a higher yield than for debenture holders.

The yields from corporate bonds (and preference shares and convertibles which can also be purchased in a corporate bond PEP) tend to be higher than building society gross interest rates. However, the money effectively lent to each company in purchasing corporate bonds, is more at risk for example if the company fails to honour the eventual repayment of the capital borrowed.

Nevertheless Corporate Bond PEPs are intended to appeal to individuals who are more risk averse. With such PEPs it is also important to consider whether the fund charges are taken out of income or capital.

Approved employee share schemes – HR

Your employer may have a scheme which gives employees the opportunity to invest in the company on what would normally be advantageous terms. There are tax benefits of doing so if the scheme complies with certain Inland Revenue rules and has had its approval. The types of scheme commonly used and their tax effects are described in Chapter 1.

If you stay with the same company for many years you may build up a very significant entitlement under options you are given, and if the share price has been rising steadily these options may have a high value. However, as investing in the shares of a single company is inherently risky, you should consider spreading your risk by making other investments too.

Your entitlement under a share option scheme will generally lapse after ten years, so it is important to keep the options granted to you under review to make sure you don't lose a valuable asset simply through the passage of time. You should draw up a strategy for exercising your options, within the time frame allowed by the scheme rules, with a view to disposing of the shares and reinvesting elsewhere. Unless you intend to dispose of the shares immediately, it is normally preferable to retain the option rather than the shares. You will then have less exposure to stock market fluctuations and in the event of a serious decline in the share price you can simply choose not to exercise the option. Conventional wisdom is therefore to exercise your option only when you intend to dispose of the shares.

Tax Saver

Try to time the exercise of share options so that if you sell some or all of the shares acquired you pay the minimum capital gains tax on your profits. Remember that you (and your spouse) can each make gains of up to £6,300 for 1996/97 and £6,500 for 1997/98 without incurring any tax. You can transfer shares to your spouse and time disposals in different tax years to achieve this. As the example below shows, a married couple can make gains of £25,600 without a tax charge by using the 1996/97 and 1997/98 exemptions.

Even if you will be liable to some tax, if you are married you may be able to reduce it by transferring some shares to your spouse if his or her tax rate is lower than yours.

For example:

	1996/97 tax year £	1997/98 tax year £	Total £
Share disposal, 1 April 1997			
Husband makes profit	6,300		
Wife makes profit	6,300		
	12,600		12,600
Share disposal, 10 April 1997			
Husband makes profit		6,500	
Wife makes profit		6,500	
		13,000	13,000
Total profit, all within CGT allowances:			25,600

The Enterprise Investment Scheme (EIS) – HR

This scheme offers income tax relief at 20% on investments of up to £100,000 in each tax year in shares in unquoted trading companies which were issued after 1 January 1994. The tax relief means that a sum equal to 20% of your investment is deducted from your income tax bill. As long as the investment continues to qualify there is no capital gains tax on the disposal of the shares, and any losses are deductible for either capital gains tax or income tax purposes. However, it is a high-risk investment and also a longer-term one as you will lose your tax relief unless you keep the shares for five years.

This investment offers additional tax benefits if you have made capital gains on other assets disposed of since 29 November 1994. The tax payable on the gain can be deferred by rolling it over into the cost of shares subscribed for under the EIS. This means that the initial tax relief on an EIS investment can be as high as 60% ie, 20% income tax relief and 40% capital gains tax postponement.

The sponsors of the scheme will tell you if a company qualifies under the EIS. The rules applicable to 'qualifying companies' are described in Chapter 3.

If any of the conditions relating to the company cease to be satisfied within three years of the issue of the shares (or of the commencement of trading, if later) the relief is withdrawn.

When evaluating these investments you should consider:

- the tax reliefs obtained and hence the reduced cost in real terms
- the nature of any asset backing and hence the relative security
- the period for which you are locked in (five years)
- your eventual potential exit routes.

Venture Capital Trusts – HR

These new forms of investment, similar to investment trusts, should also be considered by investors over age 18. They are required to invest at least 70% of their assets in unlisted trading companies. The time limit for doing so is within three years of each new share issue raising funds. Not more than 15% of its assets may be invested in any one company. Dividends are received free of income tax and VCT investment disposals are capital gains tax free for investors over 18. See Chapter 3 for further details of tax reliefs.

Venture Capital Trusts can make total annual investments of up to £1m into each company within the trust, provided the gross assets of the particular company do not exceed £10m immediately before the investment.

Enterprise zone investment – HR

This is a high-risk investment into commercial property situated in designated enterprise zones. The attraction is that the full unlimited investment should qualify for income tax relief, but it will only do so if the investment property is let out and qualifies for industrial buildings allowances. The return on the investment will depend on the rent obtained, and if no tenants can be found who carry on a trade, you may find yourself locked into the property long-term with no tax relief. You should therefore only invest if you can do without the funds in the event of being unable to get your money back.

Tax Saver

If you have to dispose of your investment in an enterprise zone at a time when your original tax relief is clawed back, consider transferring the investment to your spouse before disposal if he or she pays tax at a lower rate than you. A transfer between husband and wife does not give rise to the clawback and enables the spouse with the lower tax rate to dispose of the property.

TABLE 1
Income and expenditure schedule 1997/98

	Self	Partner

Income you expect over the year

Earnings (employment/self-employment)

Fringe benefits/overtime/commission/bonuses/tips/PRP

Pensions

State benefits

Rents

Investment income

Other income or receipts

Gross income (add up figures above)

Less tax*   (   )   (   )

Non-taxable income

Total income

Expenditure over the year (joint)

Mortgage/rent

Building and contents insurance

Life assurance

Pension contributions

Gas, electricity and water

Telephone

Car tax, insurance, servicing

Petrol

Loan repayments

Council Tax

Maintenance payments

School fees

Regular savings and investments

TV licence

Subscriptions

Food and drink

Magazines/newspapers

Spending money

Clothes

Holidays

Presents

Other

Add a safety net for unplanned expenditure

Total expenditure

Subtract total expenditure from your total income to leave:

Amount available for investment:

*Use Table 2 in Chapter 6 to find this figure.

TABLE 2

Risk factor of various investments

Low risk		Medium risk		High risk	
	Bank deposits	+	Unit trusts	+	Unit trusts
	Building society deposits	+	Investment trusts	+	Investment trusts
#	TESSAs		Corporate bonds	+	Equities
	National Savings accounts		Local Authority	*	Unquoted shares
	National Savings Bonds		bonds	*	Currency
#	National Savings	+#	Endowment policies	*	Traded options
	Certificates	+	Growth bonds	*#	Venture Capital
#	Save As You Earn schemes	+	Maximum		Trusts
#$	British Government		investment plans	*#	Enterprise
	stock (Gilts)	+	Guaranteed income		Investment
+$	Index-linked gilts		bonds		Scheme
#	Premium Bonds	+	Single premium	*	Futures
#+	Pension provision		bonds	*	Lloyd's
#+	Unit trusts	+#	Personal Equity	+	Offshore funds
			Plans (PEPs)	+	Industrial
		+	Offshore investment		buildings
			funds	+	Warrants
		+	Employee share	+	Overseas
			schemes		property
			Capital conversion		
			plans		
			Convertible stock		
		+#	Permanent Interest		
			Bearing Shares (PIBS)		
		+#	Pension provision		

*   particularly high risk

+   can respond to inflation

normally tax-free or benefits from special tax concessions

$ low-risk if held to maturity; medium-risk in the shorter term.

Some collective investments appear in more than one category since their risk exposure will depend on the nature of the underlying investments.

TABLE 3

How investments are taxed, and who they are tax-effective for

Group	Investments	Effective for
1 *Tax-free*	National Savings Certificates, Children's Bonus Bonds and Premium Bonds Save-As-You-Earn schemes (being phased out) TESSAs PEPs	LRT, BRT, HRT Over 65s

2
Interest paid with
no tax deducted
	National Savings
	   Ordinary Account,
	   Investment Account,
	   Capital Bonds,
	   Income Bonds
	British Government Stock
	   bought through National
	   Savings Stock Register
	Deposits with overseas banks
		NTP,
		LRT,
		BRT,
		HRT,

3 *Interest paid with* *tax deducted* *(except for* *non-taxpayers)*	Bank accounts Building society accounts British Government stock bought through a stockbroker	NTP, BRT, HRT,
4 *Interest paid with* *tax deducted* *or with* *tax credits*	National Savings First Option Bonds Dividends on shares Distributions from unit trusts Gains on non-qualifying life insurance policies [1]	BRT, HRT,

5
Investments for
capital gains
	Gains liable to capital gains
	   tax (unless within annual
	   exemptions):
	Shares
	Unit trusts/Investment trusts
	Gains exempt from
	   capital gains tax:
	National Savings Bonds
	British Government stock
	Proceeds from qualifying
	   life insurance policies
	Enterprise Investment Scheme
	   shares and most Business
	   Expansion Scheme shares
	All those in Group 1
		BRT,
		HRT,
		
		Over 65s

Key: NTP: *Non-taxpayer*   BRT: *Basic-rate taxpayer*
        LRT: *Lower-rate taxpayer*   HRT: *Higher-rate taxpayer*

[1]   Non-taxpayers and low-rate taxpayers cannot reclaim any tax on the proceeds from these policies

14 Retirement planning

As more and more people are living longer and an increasing number are retiring early, many of us can look forward to 20 or even considerably more years of retirement. But the income we live on in these years needs to be provided for during our working lives. Making the arrangements for this is one of the most important aspects of personal financial planning, and this chapter offers you ideas to help you develop your retirement strategies. It is divided into four main sections:

- Long-term retirement planning
- Preparing for retirement
- When you retire
- After retirement.

LONG-TERM RETIREMENT PLANNING

It is never too early to think about planning for your retirement. When you are young and single and just starting in work, saving for your retirement may be furthest from your mind. But savings that you make early in life are likely to produce the biggest benefit when you eventually retire because they have the longest time to grow in value. So the general rule is the earlier, the better. If you leave it to the last minute, you will make it much more difficult to accumulate the necessary funds.

As with all financial planning, you should reassess the provisions you have made for retirement when your circumstances change. For example, if you marry it is important to ensure that you and your spouse will both have adequate provision in later years.

The cash flow analysis process we describe below should help you establish your objectives and then achieve them effectively.

How much will you need in retirement?

As with all personal financial planning, the starting point is to identify your needs and objectives so you need to know how much income you will require after retirement. One way to do this is to run through the exercise described at the beginning of Chapter 13 to quantify your outgoings, but this time consider what expenditure will be appropriate in retirement. For example, you may have paid off your mortgage and so have no more repayments to make. Your car expenses may fall if you have less commuting to do or stop running two cars. On the other hand, some expenditure may rise – you may wish to take holidays more often and your fuel bills may be higher if you are at home for more of the day.

Retirement may bring other changes which may affect the amount of income you require. For example, you may no longer have to support children or other relatives who are currently dependent on you, and this can in turn reduce your life insurance needs. You may decide that your home is bigger than you need and move to a smaller one, releasing some additional capital for investment (though retirement flats and houses are sometimes more expensive because they are in high demand). You may also decide to move to a different part of the country, in which case you should allow for any differences in the cost of living in that area.

How much will you have in retirement?

The above considerations will help you establish – in present day values – how much income you will need in retirement. You then need to establish how much income you will have (again, in present day values) from the arrangements you have already made and what extra steps you need to take. There are two main things to consider – pensions and investments.

Pensions

You will probably be entitled to pensions from the State, from your current and previous jobs and from personal pension plans to which you have contributed. If you don't have recent statements showing the pensions you can expect from each source you can ask the pension providers for figures (for State pensions, you can obtain details from the Contribution Agency by completing form BR19). This will result in a pension forecast being sent to you or it can be sent to your financial adviser upon your authority. The figures you are given will normally show the amount of pension (in today's money) that you would get if you were to carry on contributing to the scheme until your retirement age and, in the case of many employers' pension schemes, if you were to retire on your current salary. Having this information will make sure you don't over-estimate the amount of pension you will receive.

Investments

It can be more difficult to estimate the income you will receive from investments. If you have investments with a fixed maturity date (such as an endowment policy or British Government stock) you will need to make assumptions about what you do with the proceeds (and with an endowment policy you will need an estimate of how much you get from the policy). If you have investments which produce an income (such as a second home you let out, shares you hold, or savings accounts which pay out interest) you will need to estimate how much income you can expect them to produce.

As you have estimated your expenditure and income from pensions in today's monetary equivalent, you should do the same for income from investments, so ignore the fact that rents or share values may be higher in the future than they are now. It is sensible also to make conservative assumptions about future interest rates and dividend levels.

You may want to assume that you will turn some of your capital into income by periodically selling assets or cashing in investments in stages. But be aware that reducing your capital is a risky strategy, because if you live to a ripe old age you will be reducing your future income. A safer course depending on your personal circumstances may be to use some of your capital to buy a life annuity from an insurance company, as this guarantees you an income for life (see Chapter 13).

Making further provision for retirement

Comparing the income you will need in retirement with the income with which you have already provided yourself will give you an indication of whether you need to provide for additional income – and, if so, how much.

The two main ways of increasing your retirement income are through pensions and through making investments. In the next few pages we look at the main considerations affecting each.

Pension schemes

The main advantages of pensions over other investments are their security and their tax-efficiency. Generous tax concessions are given for pension arrangements which are approved by the Inland Revenue and which comply with strict rules about how they are set up and run.

There are two main types – pension schemes run by companies for their own employees, and personal pension plans. With certain exceptions, you cannot contribute to both a company scheme and a personal plan at the same time (but you can belong to different schemes and plans over your working life). There is more information about each type of scheme below.

Tax Saver

Pensions – both employers' schemes and personal pension plans – are not only a wise investment, they are also a very tax-effective one, because:

- *you normally get full tax relief on the contributions you make*
- *the pension fund grows in value free of tax*
- *when you retire, the pension you are paid is taxed like earnings but you can give up part of your pension in exchange for a tax-free lump sum.*

Employers' pension schemes

If you are a member of a company pension scheme, your employer will pay money into the scheme's fund. Unless the scheme is 'non-contributory' you will also have to contribute a few per cent of your pay. When you retire, a pension will be paid to you until you die and you will have the option of receiving a lower pension and a tax-free lump sum. The scheme may also provide other benefits such as life insurance and a pension for your spouse or other dependants on your death during your employment or during retirement. There should be a booklet explaining the main features of the scheme and the benefits to which you are entitled.

The fund of money is invested mainly in shares, Government stocks, property and other assets. It is completely separate from the company's assets. Its money and investments are held in a trust administered by trustees who have a legal obligation to act within the rules set out in its Trust Deed and only in the interests of the scheme members.

Benefits from employers' pension schemes are normally payable from age 60 although they can be taken from age 50 upon 'early retirement' with the employer's consent. Exceptions exist for those in special occupations (who would normally retire earlier) and where a member is seriously ill.

There are two main types of scheme – 'final pay' schemes and 'money purchase' schemes. The difference is important.

'Final pay' schemes The amount of pension you get is based on the number of years of 'pensionable service' and on the amount you are earning just before you retire. For example, a generous scheme might pay you a pension of $^1/_{60}$ of your 'final pay' for each year you are a member. So if you are a member for 40 years, you would get a pension of $^{40}/_{60}$ ($^2/_3$) of your 'final pay'.

At retirement 'final pay' will be defined by the scheme rules – it may mean your salary in your last year of work but may have a more complicated definition – the average of the best three years out of the last ten years you work.

A final pay scheme is likely to provide you with a good pension if you work for the same employer for many years – especially if your final salary in that job is close to the salary on which you retire. If you move jobs you can either have a transfer payment made into a new employer's scheme or an insurance company plan, or you can have your pension 'preserved' within your former employer's scheme. In the latter case, the pension you get when you retire will be based on the number of years you were in the scheme and on the amount you were earning at the time you left. This 'preserved pension' broadly has to be increased each year by the rate of inflation (or 5% a year if less) to work out how much pension is payable when you come to draw it. This means that after you leave the job your pension gets some protection from inflation, but if your future earnings increase faster than inflation (as may be likely), the pension you get from those years will be lower than if you had stayed in the job.

But don't let this deter you from joining an employer's final pay pension scheme. The contributions you pay are eligible for full tax relief and are topped up by your employer, so they should provide a good return on your money.

Money purchase schemes A money purchase scheme works much like a personal pension, but is run by your employer. In effect, each member has a separate 'account'. The contributions that you and your employer pay into your account are invested and when you retire the money that has accumulated is used to buy an annuity which pays your pension (though you can give up part of your pension and instead take a tax-free lump sum). Thus how much pension you get depends on the performance of the investments in the fund and on the level of annuity rates at the time the pension is bought.

The main disadvantage of a money purchase scheme is that it is you who take the investment risk. With a money purchase scheme the employer's contribution is usually fixed as a percentage of your salary, and there is no certainty in the amount of pension you will get.

The only potential advantage of money purchase schemes over 'final pay' schemes is that you don't lose out by changing jobs frequently, because the amount of money in your 'account' can in most circumstances be transferred to the next scheme. However, the effect of any penalties on transfer or early surrender must be taken into account in judging whether such action should be taken.

Hybrid schemes A few employers' pension schemes give you the best of both worlds. They have a formula for working out what your pension would be both on a 'final pay' basis and on a money purchase basis, and you get whichever is higher.

Topping up your pension You are allowed to pay up to 15% of your remuneration (subject to the 'earnings cap' if appropriate as described on page 209) each year into your employer's pension scheme, but most schemes ask you to contribute much less than this. If you want to top up your pension, you can do so – and save tax.

Tax Saver

A good way to boost your pension, especially if you haven't belonged to schemes for all your working life, is to pay extra in Additional Voluntary Contributions (AVCs), either to the scheme itself or to an insurance company on a 'Free-Standing' basis. You get full tax relief on what you pay in. AVCs paid for the first time after 7 April 1987 only provide additional pension and not extra tax-free cash.

'Final pay' schemes usually impose an 'actuarial discount' to the benefit built up where the member decides to draw his/her pension early. Payment of AVCs or Free-Standing AVCs can help to mitigate such a penalty. Furthermore, because the majority of such schemes base benefits on basic salary, other pensionable elements of remuneration such as bonuses or taxable benefits such as a company car can be taken into account in providing the maximum pension. AVCs and Free-Standing AVCs can hence be used to take advantage of this, although free-standing AVCs are not available to company directors who own at least 20% of the ordinary share capital of their company.

Employer's pension or personal pension?

If you have the choice between joining your employer's scheme and taking out a personal pension, which should you do? In most cases it would be better to join your employer's pension scheme, because the company normally pays most (sometimes all) of the cost, whereas most employers won't contribute to personal pensions. In an increasing number of situations employers now operate 'Group' Personal Pension Plans.

Personal pension plans

A personal pension plan is ideal if you are self-employed or work for a company which doesn't have a pension scheme. The plans are operated by insurance companies and other financial institutions. The money you pay in is invested by the insurance company until you decide you want to start drawing the benefits from the plan, which you must do between the ages of 50 and 75 (it doesn't have to be when you retire). Part of the money which has accumulated can then be given to you as a tax-free lump sum but at some time before you reach age 75 the rest has to be used to buy an annuity which will pay you a pension for life (though part can be used to provide a pension for your surviving spouse and certain other benefits). The Finance Act 1995 introduced flexibility in the timing of the purchase of the annuity to give individuals the ability to defer purchasing at times of poor annuity rates and the option to wait for rates to improve.

You can also use a personal pension plan to 'contract out' of the State Earnings Related Pension Scheme (SERPS), where your employer's occupational scheme is not already 'contracted out'. SERPS is the second tier of State Benefit over the basic State pension. Benefits from such a personal pension arrangement can only be used to purchase pension (not cash) between the ages of 60 and 75. In respect of the 'contracted out' period, no SERPS entitlement accrues. With the planned introduction of age-related National Insurance rebates from 6 April 1997, employees who are not members of their company's 'contracted out' occupational scheme should review the position and consider whether they should 'contract out' for the first time with a personal pension plan, remain 'contracted out' with a personal pension plan or decide to 'contract back in' to SERPS.

Contributions to personal pension plans are allowable deductions against your income for tax relief at your highest rate of tax. Even if an employed person is not liable to tax, basic rate tax relief will still have been given at source on each contribution. However, no clawback of such relief will be made by the Revenue. The self-employed pay contributions gross without the immediate cash flow advantage of automatic basic rate tax relief. Careful timing of payments can improve the position.

Personal pension plans (and retirement annuity contracts) offer a 'Waiver of Premium' option on a regular premium policy only. If taken up, the pension provider will credit regular premiums to the policy if the policyholder becomes unable to contribute due to lack of earnings owing to incapacity. This is a valuable option worth considering.

There is a very large number of plans available. Some are single premium, others are regular premium and others are completely flexible (you pay in what you like when you like). With some, the money is invested in a unit-linked fund which works like a unit trust (so the value of the fund can go down as well as up); some are on a with-profits basis where there is a minimum guaranteed pension or accumulated fund which is increased as the insurance company makes profits on the investments; others are different again. You should consult a good independent financial adviser for advice on which plans would be most suitable for you.

There are limits on the amounts you can pay into personal pensions each year, and these are given in Chapter 3. The rules are complicated but your financial adviser should be able to guide you. Part of what you pay can be used to provide life insurance – which means you get tax relief on your life insurance premiums too.

One of the changes to take place under 'self assessment' is the way in which relief is given for personal pension plan (or retirement annuity contract) premiums paid in one tax year but related back to the previous tax year.

Under the new rules, relief will be given not by reducing the assessment for the earlier year but by reducing the tax liability for the year in which the premiums are paid by the amount of tax relief computed by reference to the previous year. One effect of this is that where an individual normally pays and then relates back premiums to the previous tax year there will be a gap year, 1996/97, in which the tax liability will not reflect any relief for those premiums.

This method of giving relief for the relating back of premiums will affect the level of tax payments to be made on account for the following year as, under 'self assessment', such tax payments are based on the tax liability of the previous year (see Chapter 3).

Another change from 1996/97 onwards is that the time limit for relating back premiums has been extended from 5 July after the end of the tax year (in which premiums are paid) to the following 31 January to coincide with the latest date for the filing of Tax Returns.

You can have any number of personal pensions at the same time. If you have a range of policies you can choose to implement a technique called 'staggered vesting'. Instead of buying an annuity when you retire you phase the encashment of your policies so that each year you build up your pension, making up the shortfall of what you would otherwise receive by taking a tax-free lump sum. This gives you more flexibility and could mean a higher retirement income, because the later you start taking the benefits from a plan the higher the pension you should get from it (because your money will have been invested tax-free for longer, and the pension will be paid for fewer years). There is another advantage too. If you were to die before you start taking the benefits from a policy, your heirs would normally get the value of the fund that had built up tax-free. Once you have started taking the benefits they may get nothing at all (unless you have opted for a lower pension in order to provide some return in this eventuality).

There are many variations on the principle. For example it may be more convenient just to buy three annuities at age 60, 65 and 70 rather than each year. An important consideration would be the current level of annuity rates at the relevant times.

Note that, while you will always have more flexibility with a number of policies, there is no guarantee that you will be richer with 'staggered vesting'. Annuity rates and investment returns do not remain constant throughout. In practice, you could lose out if annuity rates fell, or a stockmarket slump reduced the value of the investments in your fund (though you could protect against the latter by having your pension fund linked to cash or fixed-interest funds). Up to 25% of the accumulated fund value can be taken as a tax-free cash lump sum from a personal pension plan (with retirement annuity policies it is often a higher amount).

To save you having a lot of different personal pension plans, many insurance companies offer plans which are set up as a 'cluster' of policies, often 100, so that you can start taking the benefits of any number of policies at any time between age 50 and age 75. You could switch your current plan to one of these, but be aware that the charges for switching may be high.

The Finance Act 1995 introduced the concept of 'pension withdrawal' allowing you to defer most of the annuity purchase (as noted earlier) but in the meantime to take regular withdrawals (within limits) from your personal pension plan. These are liable to income tax. The annuity purchase can be deferred to any age up to 75 whether or not the 'tax free' lump sum is taken. Meanwhile, 'pension withdrawals' are made. The scheme will be reviewed every three years to ensure withdrawals are not depleting the fund too rapidly.

Investing for retirement

Pensions undoubtedly provide a tax-efficient way of building up a retirement income, but there are circumstances in which you may want to save more. For example, you may have contributed to pension schemes for only a part of your working life; you may be paying the maximum allowed in contributions to personal pension plans or Additional Voluntary Contributions to your employer's pension scheme; or you may have no earnings from which to make pension contributions.

Tax Saver

Check whether the ability to contribute could be augmented by entering into a 'salary sacrifice' arrangement with your employer, whereby you reduce your earnings and in turn your employer's pension contribution is increased, although such an arrangement has to be agreed by both employer and employee in advance in order to be effective. This has both income tax and national insurance tax savings, although pension benefits will be based on your reduced earnings after taking account of the 'salary sacrifice'.

If retirement is still a long way off, you will need to consider investments which should give you a good return over the long term. Use the information about different investments in Chapter 13 and consult an independent financial adviser before making decisions. Remember, too, that the main worry about long-term investment is that high inflation could substantially reduce the value of your savings. Investments which produce a fixed return won't help you build a good retirement income if the return doesn't compare well with inflation. So you should consider investing in assets that have historically provided good protection against inflation, such as shares. To spread your risk you should invest in a range of different shares or a number of unit trusts or investment trusts.

Probably the most suitable investment is a Personal Equity Plan (PEP). Indeed, it can be a good alternative to a pension scheme. Although you don't get tax relief on what you pay into a PEP, the money invested grows in value free of tax, just as in a pension scheme. And PEPs have the advantage that there is no tax on any withdrawals and you can encash them when you want.

Tax Saver

If you can, make maximum contributions to both pension schemes and PEPs. If you cannot afford this, choose the investment medium that is most appropriate to your own requirements. If you are not eligible to pay pension contributions (because you have no earnings), saving by way of a PEP can provide similar benefits at retirement age. The value of PEPs can fall as well as rise and should be regarded therefore as a medium to long-term investment.

PREPARING FOR RETIREMENT

Will you get the maximum State pension?

In the approach to retirement, check that you have paid enough National Insurance contributions to entitle you to the maximum State retirement pension. This is particularly important if you have had a break in paying contributions, eg, if you have been working abroad for a while. Women who have taken a career break to have families may also find that their contribution record is inadequate, although Home Responsibilities Protection may cover most if not all of the gap by reducing the number of years' contributions that you need for a full pension. If you do have a shortfall, you may find that making a payment of Class III National Insurance contributions (£6.05 per week as from 6 April 1997) to top up your contribution record will produce an increased State pension well in excess of the cost of the additional contributions.

Reducing investment risk

Having a good spread of investments will be even more important in retirement than before, so you should try to diversify your portfolio as you approach retirement. This will not only reduce the risk of one investment failing, but will also increase your options if you need to get at your money.

In particular, it makes sense to protect the capital values your investments have built up against a sudden fall in share prices, for example. This is particularly important if you intend to use a large amount of your savings to buy an annuity in the near future. The normal way of protecting your capital is to move your money (or change the investment risk in a unit trust or personal pension plan, for example) from a higher-risk fund (such as shares) to lower-risk assets (such as cash investments).

If you own your own business

If you run your own business, the ten years prior to retirement can be very important in maximising your pension entitlement. If you are the owner manager of a limited company and have provided yourself with an 'exempt approved' occupational pension, the Inland Revenue's pension limit is based on a proportion of your 'final pay' (or 'final remuneration'). If, however, you are a 20% shareholder or earn more than £100,000 a year, your 'final remuneration' must be calculated as an average of the best three or more consecutive years remuneration ending not earlier than ten years before leaving 'pensionable service'. You can inflation-link this remuneration if your pension scheme rules allow benefits to be calculated on this basis. However, it will be clear that maximising your remuneration in this period will increase your ability to take the maximum lump sum cash benefit of 1½ times 'final remuneration' or maximum pension of ²/₃ of 'final remuneration', subject to the limits set by the scheme rules. Of course, you cannot have more than can be bought with the value of the pension fund, but if you have maximised your pension fund you want to be sure that all of it can be used to provide you with pension benefits.

'Final remuneration' will be restricted to the 'earnings cap' – £84,000 from 6 April 1997 – for members who joined existing Inland Revenue approved occupational schemes after 31 May 1989 (where such schemes were in force before 14 March 1989), or where members joined any new schemes set up after 13 March 1989.

If you plan to sell your business on retirement, you need to prepare early for the sale. If, for example, there is surplus cash in the business, it may be worth withdrawing this before the sale and the most tax-effective way of doing this may be to pay out dividends or increase pension contributions over a period of two or three years rather than waiting until the last minute.

Generally speaking, when you sell or wind up a limited company, double taxation of the underlying worth of the company is avoided by stripping out dividends wherever possible. Any income not distributed in this way gives rise to a capital gains tax liability, although if you have capital gains tax exemptions or reliefs (such as retirement relief) available, you might wish to do the opposite. Remember that most reliefs for business property only apply where the assets are genuine business assets. Excess cash and investments in a company may jeopardise some or part of the reliefs.

Early retirement
Retiring early will have attractions for many, but it can mean having a somewhat lower income for the rest of your life. Most pension schemes are geared to providing a good pension at normal retirement date – if you retire earlier you may find that your pension cannot be paid early or that the income is substantially lower. If you are asked by your employer to retire early, it is worth asking them in return to pay you an increased amount of pension.

With personal pension plans, the date that you stop work is unimportant. All that matters is the date when your plan says you can start taking the benefits. The Inland Revenue won't allow you to take the benefits of a personal pension plan before you are age 50 unless you are seriously ill. If your pension is provided through retirement annuities, the minimum age is 60 (though you could get round this by converting your policies into personal pension plans).

Certain professionals (eg, sportsmen) customarily retire early. But if you are not in this position and have not had to retire early through ill-health, you need to look at the financial equations carefully before deciding to retire early. Remember that you cannot start drawing State retirement pension until you reach State retirement age. And if you are more active because you are younger, you may find that you incur more expenditure.

Late retirement

With most employers' pension schemes you stop paying contributions when you reach the scheme's normal retirement age, even if you continue working. Personal pension plans let you defer taking the benefits until you are age 75.

If you continue to earn after reaching State pension age, you don't have to pay any more National Insurance contributions, and your earnings don't affect your entitlement to State pension in any way. If you want to, you can defer drawing your State pension for up to five years, in which case the amount you ultimately receive will be higher. However, it pays to work out how many years it will be before you have received the same total amount in pension. It could give you more flexibility to take the pension and invest it rather than defer it.

WHEN YOU RETIRE

Pension schemes

Pension schemes to which you have belonged and personal pension plans you have taken out may offer you a number of options about the type of pension you have and other benefits. You may be offered the choice of a level pension or one which increases annually, normally at a pre-set rate, but starting at a lower amount than a level one. Work out how many years it will be before you have had as much total income from the increasing pension as you would have had from the level one. You could have more flexibility if you opted for a level pension and saved what you didn't need.

There is no particular need to start taking the benefits of all your pension entitlements at the same time. The different schemes and plans to which you have belonged will probably have different rules about when you can do so, and you may decide to leave some of them invested for a few more years. Indeed, you may have deliberately planned a 'staggered vesting' arrangement as described earlier.

As briefly noted above, new personal pension plans available from 2 May 1995, and other such plans taken out beforehand where the rules have been amended subsequently, offer the option to defer taking a specified proportion of your pension until not later than age 75 – a useful option if you expect annuity rates to improve at the time you retire.

Should you take a tax-free lump sum?

Most employers' schemes and personal pensions will offer you the option of giving up part of your pension in exchange for a tax-free lump sum. How should you choose?

The simplest way is to compare the net amount of pension you would give up with the net income you would receive if you used the lump sum to buy a life annuity.

(Remember that part of a purchased life annuity is treated as a repayment of capital and is not subject to tax.) Often you will find it is better to take the lump sum. Remember, if you don't take the lump sum you lose control over it.

Taking a lump sum also gives you more flexibility. If you invest it in some other way than buying an annuity, you can get at the capital if you need to and it will be there for the benefit of your heirs if you die.

Do you need to provide other benefits?

Find out what benefits are provided by the scheme on your death to your spouse or any other dependants. If there are none, you may want to use part of the lump sum to provide some. If a widow/widowers pension is provided it is generally lower than a full pension, so you may need to increase it in order to leave your spouse with sufficient income to live on after your death.

If your pension scheme has provided you with life insurance, you may find that this ends as soon as you retire. You should therefore consider whether you need to replace it.

What to do about your investments

While you are saving for retirement, you should have been building up tax shelter investments such as National Savings, PEPs and TESSAs. This may be the time to use these investments and convert them into tax-free income. You can do this, for example, by cashing in savings certificates each year (see Chapter 6) – though beware of depleting your capital too much.

You don't need to encash the whole of a PEP at one time. You can simply choose to sell so many investments each year as to give you your required income (no tax will be payable on what you get). And, of course, if you have been accumulating income within the PEP you should now choose to withdraw it, whether or not you also need to draw capital.

Reducing investment risk

If you have not already done so, you should reduce the amount of risk in your investments. If a risky investment fails while you are still in work you have more opportunity to replace the funds lost. But if there is a failure once you have retired, your income may be permanently affected.

Liquidity

You don't want to be forced to sell assets at inconvenient times once you are retired. You may also find that your need for liquidity increases. For example, if you can no longer look after yourself and need to move into a retirement home, you may need regular high income or capital to maintain yourself or your spouse and meet the fees. Rather than risk having to cash in investments at a time when they may have accrued high capital gains tax liabilities, you could transfer them to more liquid assets such as cash deposits and gilts, at a time which suits you from a tax point of view.

Disposing of a business

If you own a business, your retirement may be the occasion to dispose of it or to pass it on to the family for future generations to run. From a capital gains tax point of view, remember that retirement relief is only available on the disposal of shares in a family company if you are a full-time working officer or employee of that company at the time of disposal (see Chapter 3). If you defer disposing of your business until after you have retired you may, as a result, sacrifice entitlement to retirement relief. If you prepare for retirement by reducing your working hours, you may still be entitled to retirement relief provided that you spend at least ten hours per week working for the company in a technical or managerial capacity.

The decision to give business assets to the family on retirement is made more difficult as business property relief for inheritance tax purposes is available if you retain the investment (see Chapter 15). If you own a business this can mean that holding it until death would enable you to leave it to your family free of capital gains tax and inheritance tax. Of course, tax savings are not the only consideration and whilst there is no tax incentive to give away business assets, you should bear in mind that the current beneficial tax regime in this connection may change in the future. There could, therefore, be a significant advantage in giving the asset away in your lifetime using hold-over relief for business assets (see Chapter 3) to defer any capital gains tax liability and relying on business property relief to exempt the asset from inheritance tax. However, if you die within seven years of giving the business property to your children and meanwhile they have sold it without using the proceeds to buy new business property, the business property relief in the original gift for inheritance tax purposes will be withdrawn (see Chapter 15).

Continuing to hold shares

Another incentive to retain business assets after retirement is that they may continue to provide you with an income. Although you are no longer drawing salary you may still, for example, be able to take a dividend from shares in a limited company. You may have to consider what other incentives there are for non-shareholding managers working in the business to build it up to the same extent, but there is no reason why you should not employ managers to run the company for you rather than selling it.

Company buying its own shares

If you are not the only shareholder in a company and there is a limited number of people with funds to buy you out, one way of disposing of your shareholding might be for the company to buy back its own shares. If you have owned the shares for five years or more and the purchase can be shown to be for the benefit of the company's trade (a criterion which a retirement situation will usually satisfy) then provided certain other conditions are met the disposal will be treated as giving rise to a capital gain. See Chapter 12 for the tax treatment.

AFTER RETIREMENT

Tax planning for married couples

Routine financial planning requires you to look at your own levels of income and those of your spouse to ensure that you make best use of income tax rates and allowances.

Once you retire, you may need to carry out a more fundamental review. You should try to make sure that neither of you creeps into the higher-rate tax band, and there may be an advantage in restricting one spouse's income to below the threshold at which you cease to qualify for age allowance (see Chapter 3). Generally it will be better if the husband's income is restricted because this may then entitle you not only to an increased personal allowance, but also to an increased married couple's allowance. However, practical limitations, such as a pension being paid to the husband, often prevent this.

From an income tax viewpoint there may be an apparent advantage in having all the investments (including investment of lump sums from pension schemes) in one spouse's name, while the other spouse continues to receive a pension. However, this strategy may be quite wrong from a capital taxation point of view. First, you would only be able to use one annual capital gains tax exemption, whereas if you each had some investments you would each get an exemption. Second, it may restrict the ability of one spouse to make tax-free transfers for inheritance tax purposes. As in all tax planning, you must strike a balance and you should make the choice that most suits your individual circumstances.

Residential homes

If you are admitted to a residential home, part of the cost of your care will be met by the Department of Social Security, whilst the cost of your accommodation will be met by the local authority. You may also be entitled to various social security benefits. The amount which the State will pay will generally be reduced if you have 'capital' exceeding £16,000. Your 'capital' includes all your assets, with a few exceptions. You can ignore personal items such as a car or furniture. You may be able to deduct 10% of the value of an asset if realising it would incur expenses. At present, the value of your home is disregarded if your family is living in it. If you live alone the value of your home will be disregarded for up to six months while you take steps to dispose of it.

You cannot get round these rules by giving things away, as the authorities may still regard them as belonging to you when they are working out your benefits. So if you are planning to make gifts to your family, don't wait until you are no longer able to care for yourself.

Giving away surplus assets

If you have been in the habit of saving or accumulating income, when you finally retire you may feel that you have accumulated more than you require. If you carry out a review of your affairs for inheritance tax purposes as explained in Chapter 15, you may also be concerned about your potential liability to inheritance tax and consider making lifetime gifts of assets to reduce exposure to this tax.

Do, however, look at your capital requirement projections very carefully as you may be retired for a very long time. At some stage your health may fail and you may need to pay for nursing care. Remember that inheritance tax is your heirs' problem, not yours, so don't give away more than you can comfortably afford to without affecting your standard of living.

For these reasons, a sensible strategy can be to keep your investments and only give away assets which don't produce an income. For example, if you have a holiday home which you don't let out to provide an income, giving it to your family makes sense if you no longer plan to use it.

However, capital gains tax is a major barrier to making gifts in retirement. On death, all assets that you hold are deemed to be disposed of and re-acquired at their market value at that time. Any notional gain is not subject to capital gains tax. Thus, at a stroke, all accumulated capital gains on your investments and other assets will be wiped out. If you gift assets during lifetime you may crystallise these gains, offsetting any inheritance tax benefit of making the gift as well as jeopardising your financial security.

Should you give away your home?

Many retired people think about the home in which they live and wonder if they should now give this to their children. Think about this very carefully. If you continue to live in the home it may not have the inheritance tax result you expect. Because you will continue to receive a benefit by living in the home, it will remain part of your estate for inheritance tax purposes.

It is possible to devise a method of giving your home to your family but often this is not income tax-efficient. For example, your family could grant you a lease of the property at full market rent, but your children would pay income tax on the rental due and if you did not pay full market rent you would have a reservation of benefit which would negate any inheritance tax advantage (see Chapter 15 on inheritance tax).

An alternative arrangement would be to gift your family cash for them to buy the home from you. You would have to be particularly careful that the price was set at full market value, and it would be unwise to make the gift of cash conditional upon them using it for this purpose. Indeed, the arrangement would be less likely to be challenged by the Inland Revenue if there were a time lag of several years between making the cash gift and buying the home, and if the amount of cash gifted were not equal to the price paid for the home.

Apart from the inheritance tax issue, you may be exposing your property to capital gains tax. If you occupy it as your own principal private residence any capital gain on sale is exempt. Additionally, there is no capital gains tax on your death when your family would inherit it at its full market value. If, however, you give your home to your children and they sell it without living in it, they will be liable to tax on the appreciation from the date of the gift.

Finally, you should consider the security aspects. If you have given your home away, there is nothing to stop you being evicted from it and there could be increased pressure on you to move into a retirement home. While you may be very friendly with your children now, families can fall out. Worse, if your children were to die, your home could be inherited by their spouses who could then remarry. Your financial security may then fall into the hands of strangers. Ideally, you should seek to retain your home for as long as possible.

15 Estate planning and your taxes

Most people would prefer to leave their assets when they die to their family, heirs and friends rather than a substantial sum being paid to the Government in tax. This chapter discusses inheritance tax, the tax which applies to your estate on death and also to gifts and other transfers made during lifetime. It contains some ideas and techniques used in estate planning that may help you make plans for the future and minimise the amount of tax that will ultimately be paid on your estate.

As with any financial planning, once you have drawn up an estate plan you need to review it regularly – at least every five years. Frequent changes in taxation rules can undermine your planning. In addition, family circumstances change – young children grow up and become independent and your family may expand with the addition of grandchildren. Your health may deteriorate, you may retire and for many other reasons your financial needs during lifetime may change. Reviewing your plan will enable you to take account of these changes and help you assess whether you are still on target to minimise your tax liability.

This chapter is intended as an introduction to estate planning and before looking at the tax issues considers some of the practical issues that you need to consider. You should seek professional advice if your financial or family situation is complicated; if you own shares in unquoted companies or own businesses, farms or other substantial interests in land or if you or your spouse are not domiciled in the UK. Domicile is an important concept in estate tax planning and is explained in Chapter 5.

GETTING STARTED
When you fill in your tax return every year you probably automatically review your income position and give some thought as to how it may be improved. You probably spend a lot less time appraising your inheritance tax position. Yet an annual review of the following questions will help you decide when is the appropriate time to update or review your estate plan more fully:

1 Are you aware of any changes in the tax legislation that might adversely affect your present estate plan? Do you check the financial press?

2 Have you sufficient assets to take care of your debts, funeral expenses and other liabilities on death?

3 Have any of your assets grown in value or has your estate increased in the course of the year, eg, by inheritance or for other reasons?

4 Have there been any changes in your family circumstances – births, adoptions, deaths, marriages, illness, etc, that might call for revisions in your estate plan?

5 Are you in a position to give away some of your assets to your family or charitable institutions?
   - If you have already been making lifetime gifts, should you continue to do so?
   - Which assets are most appropriate for such a gift programme?
6 Have you made a will leaving all your assets to friends and relatives of your choosing? Or are you relying on statutory rules to do this for you, and are you sure that they will?

DO YOU NEED A WILL?

A will is a legal document that regulates your estate after death in three respects:

- It appoints executors whose job is to administer your estate.
- It sets out who you wish to inherit your assets on death.
- It stipulates the terms and conditions on which the assets are to pass to your chosen heirs.

Generally, everyone should have a will, even if their estate is modest. Apart from achieving the objectives above, a will makes it easier and cheaper to wind up someone's estate after they die. Not many people realise that if you do not have a will it is necessary for the Court to appoint administrators to wind up your estate. The administrators are chosen from those who are legally entitled to receive your assets. They may not be the persons most suited to that task or may not be willing to assume those responsibilities. As a result the costs involved in winding up your estate could be greater than they would be if you had a will.

Making a will has another advantage – it can help you to distribute your estate in a tax-efficient manner, thus ensuring that more value passes to your heirs. If you don't have a will, your estate passes under predetermined rules known as intestate succession. The distribution of an estate under intestacy is different depending on whether you are domiciled in England and Wales, or in Scotland when you die. See Chapter 5 for an explanation of 'domicile'.

A summary of the intestacy rules in England and Wales and in Scotland can be found in the tables on pages 218 and 219. If the order of intestate succession described in the tables is not how you wish your assets to be divided, making a will is absolutely essential to override the statutory rules.

Providing for dependants

The intestacy rules provide a mechanism for dividing an estate where the deceased has left no instruction. However, the law also requires that you make adequate provision for those who are financially dependent upon you. Therefore, even a will may not ensure that your assets pass in the way you wish. In England under the Inheritance (Provision for Family Dependants) Act 1975 application can be made to the Court by anyone who was financially dependent on someone who has died for an order which directs that part of the estate should be transferred to them or held for their benefit. The category of claimants under this Act has been extended by the Law Reform (Succession) Act 1995 to include an unmarried cohabitant

ENGLAND AND WALES: YOUR ESTATE ON INTESTACY

	SPOUSE AND CHILDREN [1] SURVIVE YOU	SPOUSE SURVIVES YOU BUT NO CHILDREN OR GRANDCHILDREN	NO SPOUSE SURVIVES YOU
PERSONAL EFFECTS	SPOUSE	SPOUSE	–
LEGACIES	£125,000 TO SPOUSE	£200,000 TO SPOUSE	–
RESIDUE	(2a) 1/2 On trust to provide income to spouse for life then capital to children equally following death of spouse (2b) 1/2 To children in equal shares at 18 years old and on trust until that time (surviving grandchildren take the share of a deceased child)	1/2 To spouse outright 1/2 To parents outright If none: To brothers/sisters outright (or their children) If none: To spouse outright	Whole estate in order of priority to the exclusion of all others: 1 your children or grandchildren 2 your parents 3 brothers and sisters (nephews and nieces, if they have predeceased) 4 half-brothers and half-sisters (their children, if they have predeceased) 5 grandparents 6 uncles and aunts (their children, if they have predeceased) 7 half-brothers and half-sisters of your parents (and their children) 8 the Crown

1. From 1 January 1996, if your spouse survives you but dies within 28 days of your death, the intestacy laws will apply as though your spouse had not survived you. 2. A trust is created and the assets are held for the benefit of the beneficiaries by third parties who are trustees of the fund. In the case of the trust at (2a) the spouse receives only the income and the children eventually receive the capital. In the case of the trust at (2b) statutory provisions require that the funds are held on behalf of the children while they are under the age of majority. They then receive the assets outright.

SCOTLAND: YOUR ESTATE ON INTESTACY

		SPOUSE AND CHILDREN SURVIVE YOU	SPOUSE SURVIVES YOU BUT NO CHILDREN	CHILDREN SURVIVE YOU BUT NO SPOUSE	NEITHER SPOUSE NOR CHILD SURVIVES YOU
1	Matrimonial Home	To spouse up to a value of £110,000. Balance per 5	To spouse up to a value of £110,000. Balance per 5	–	–
2	Contents of Matrimonial home	To spouse up to a value of £20,000. Balance per 4 then 5	To spouse up to a value of £20,000. Balance per 4 then 5	–	–
3	Legacies	£30,000 to spouse	£50,000 to spouse	–	–
4	Balance of estate excluding land/buildings	1/3 to spouse 2/3 to children	1/2 to spouse 1/2 per 5 below	To children	–
5	Balance of estate (land and buildings)	To children	1/2 to surviving parents (All if no brothers/sisters) 1/2 to brothers/sisters (All if no parents) If none: All to spouse	To children	1/2 to surviving parents (All if no brothers/sisters) 1/2 to brothers/sisters (All if no parents) If none all to: 1 aunts and uncles (or children of those who predeceased) 2 grandparents 3 brothers and sisters of grandparents (or their descendants) 4 remoter ancestors 5 the Crown

financially dependent on the deceased. Where such a direction is made, inheritance tax is charged as though the deceased had left his assets as the Court directs.

Scotland

In Scotland the position is entirely different and your spouse and children or grandchildren have automatic rights in your estate without application to the Court, whether you have a will or not. These rights are known as legal rights and cannot be displaced, although your family can disclaim their legal rights in favour of anything you leave to them in a will if they prefer. To do this they would formally advise the executors. They cannot both claim their legal rights and accept a gift under a will.

If you have no children, under Scots law your surviving spouse is entitled to one-half of your moveable estate (ie, all of your assets excluding land and buildings). If you have no spouse, your children are entitled to one-half of your moveable estate. If you have both spouse and children, the spouse and the children (jointly) are each entitled to one-third of the moveable estate. The balance of the estate passes according to the provisions set out in your will.

If you are not happy with your family's entitlement to these legal rights under Scots law, then the only way to defeat their claims is to give away the assets during lifetime and here trusts can be a useful tool (discussed later in this chapter).

Tax Saver

If you are entitled to legal rights in the estate of a Scot and you want to disclaim them, make sure you do so within two years of the death. Inheritance tax will then be levied according to how the estate passes under the will.

Practical considerations

One practical consideration you should address in deciding whether you need a will relates to your children. If you have minor children you may wish to appoint guardians for them in your will. If you don't and they have no surviving parent, it will be up to the Courts and the local authority to decide who will have responsibility for your children in the event of your premature death.

Making a will is not only tax-efficient but as noted above there may be many non-financial reasons why you wish to have a will drawn up. You may have preferred burial arrangements or wish to donate organs to science. In order to ensure that these kinds of issues are addressed you need to include them in your will.

A word of warning. You can prepare your own will or even acquire a prepared form from a stationers as a 'do it yourself' kit. If your affairs are at all complex there are great dangers in preparing your own will and you would be well advised to take your solicitor's advice and to pay for a professional will to be drafted. You should also take care that your will is signed and witnessed in accordance with the law as the formalities which must be followed to create a valid will are stringent.

Marriage and divorce

Getting married automatically revokes an existing will unless it specifically states that it is made in contemplation of your marriage to a particular person. All newly-married couples should therefore make new wills as soon as possible to avoid the intestacy rules applying.

Divorce has a different effect in that the will is not revoked but all references to the spouse are treated as if he or she had died before the will takes effect so that the other gifts made still stand. Unless this is what you want to happen, you should make a new will.

Enduring power of attorney

One final matter that should not be overlooked is that of an enduring power of attorney. A power of attorney is a legal document which authorises someone to act on your behalf and at your direction. Normally this authorisation would cease once the person appointing the attorney became incapable of authorising the actions of the attorney (for example in the case of illness or mental incapacity). An enduring power of attorney is a special power which continues to exist even after the person executing it has become incapacitated. Such a power can be drawn up at the same time as a will to ensure that a spouse or relative has the ability to look after your affairs should a serious illness befall you, or later at the onset of old age. This avoids the otherwise cumbersome legal procedure necessary to deal with your affairs. An enduring power of attorney should in particular be drawn up by all of those who have any history of debilitating illness in their family.

INHERITANCE TAX FUNDAMENTALS

When does inheritance tax arise?

Contrary to what its name implies, inheritance tax does not just apply to assets passed on when you die. It applies to transfers of assets (or more precisely 'transfers of value') which include the transfer of your entire estate when you die and, in addition, to certain transfers or gifts you make during your lifetime.

Inheritance tax applies to property situated anywhere in the world but if you are not domiciled in the UK, property situated outside the UK is not subject to inheritance tax. Such property is known as excluded property. Certain designated British Government Stock (see Chapter 13) owned by non-UK domiciled individuals is also treated as excluded property.

Inheritance tax applies not only to certain gifts of such property made during lifetime but to any other transaction as a result of which the value of your estate immediately after the transaction is less than it would otherwise have been. This would include, for example, failing to exercise a valuable right causing a depreciation in your estate. The amount of the reduction in the value of your estate counts as a 'transfer of value'.

The tax is cumulative so that the value of all gifts made within the previous seven years which do not qualify for exemptions or reliefs, are added together. However, no tax is charged on the first £215,000 of this total (£200,000 for transfers made before 6 April 1997). This is referred to as the 'nil-rate band', and is the level of the band from 6 April 1997. (The band for the period from 6 April 1996 to 5 April 1997 is £200,000 and references to the sum of £215,000 in the remaining part of this chapter should be read as £200,000 as regards any taxable events occurring between those dates.)

The long-term intention of the Conservative Government is to abolish this tax; in comparison, the Labour Party are committed to retaining and extending it.

Although the £215,000 limit is normally linked to the movement in the retail price index and should increase annually, index linking was suspended between 9 March 1992 and April 1995. As a result the value of the nil-rate band has hitherto not kept pace with inflation. This position was significantly redressed in the 1995 Budget when the nil-rate band was increased from £154,000 to £200,000.

What lifetime gifts are taxable?

Gifts you make in your lifetime fall into three broad categories:

1 *Those which are tax-free* These include gifts to your spouse (subject to the caveat mentioned below), to UK charities and to certain public bodies. These gifts are completely ignored for inheritance tax purposes.

2 *Gifts you make to certain types of trust and gifts to companies* These always count as 'chargeable transfers' meaning that inheritance tax will be payable at the time you make them if the total value of such gifts you have made in the past seven years (after deducting any amount covered by exemptions) exceeds £215,000.

3 *Other gifts you make – eg, to your relatives or friends or non-charitable organisations* These will not incur any liability to inheritance tax in your lifetime (but you should watch out for capital gains tax – see Chapter 2). However, when you die, the value of such gifts you have made in the last seven years of your life (after deducting any amounts covered by exemptions) is added to your estate and, if the total comes to more than £215,000, inheritance tax is charged at a rate of 40% on the excess. These gifts are called potentially exempt transfers or PETs for short. Seven years after you have made such a gift it falls out of account if you are still alive and essentially is forgotten for inheritance tax purposes.

Do you need to be concerned about inheritance tax?

Basically, the answer is yes if any of the following applies to you:

- your estate when you die is likely to be worth more than around £215,000 in today's monetary terms

- the total value of gifts you have made to trusts and companies in the last seven years when added to your estate exceeds £215,000, or you are planning to make such gifts which will bring the seven-year total to more than this

- you benefit from certain trusts which give you the right to the income and the total value of the trust assets, when added to your estate, exceeds £215,000 (such trusts are quite commonly found in wills).

Do check the total value of your assets

Do check the total value of your assets – you may be worth more than you think. Many people now own homes which are worth in excess of the £215,000 limit without taking into account other assets. Even if your assets do not exceed £215,000, they may do so at the time of your death.

Note that the proceeds of any insurance policies which will pay out on your death will be included in your estate unless the policies are written in trust for your dependants so that the proceeds are payable to them directly.

If none of the above applies to you, you do not need to be concerned about inheritance tax at present. But if you are near one of the limits, it could be worth making sure that any gifts you make come within the many exemptions (see below) in case an unexpected inheritance or win adds to your estate in the future. The advice and in particular the Tax Savers in the remainder of this chapter are aimed at those who want to reduce their exposure to inheritance tax. However, it is worth remembering that unless you make gifts to trusts or companies, it is not you who will pay this tax, but the donee or your personal representatives after your death, and your only reason for planning is so that your heirs get more. So don't do anything which threatens your own financial security just to reduce the tax paid by others.

Tax on 'chargeable transfers' made in your lifetime

If the total of 'chargeable transfers' (category 2 above) which you have made in the last seven years and which don't qualify for reliefs (see below) exceeds £215,000, inheritance tax is charged on the excess at 20%.

If the person making the gift or transfer also pays the tax, that tax is calculated both on the transfer value and the amount of tax payable as a result. Working out the value on which tax is payable in this situation is known as 'grossing up'. If the recipient of the gift agrees to pay the inheritance tax due on the transfer, there is no need to gross up.

For example: You have already made chargeable lifetime gifts in the last seven years of £215,000 and used all of your annual exemptions. You now want to make a discretionary trust (see later) with £60,000.

	You pay the tax		*Trustees pay the tax*
Trustees receive	60,000	Trustees receive	48,000
Tax on gift (20% x £75,000)	15,000	Tax on gift (20% x £60,000)	12,000
Cost to you	75,000	Cost to you	60,000

Tax Saver

If you are currently considering making gifts in excess of £200,000 to a discretionary trust defer the transfer until after 6 April 1997 when the 'nil rate band' increases. Assuming no other chargeable lifetime gifts have been made, a gift of £215,000 can be made with no lifetime charge to tax post 6 April 1997 but prior to that date would give rise to a tax charge of £3,750 if you pay the tax or £3,000 if the trustees pay the tax.

Tax when you die

When you die, certain assets you leave are tax-free and are disregarded. They include the gifts mentioned in category 1 above and the proceeds of life insurance policies which are written in trust for your dependants. If you die before retirement, lump sums paid directly to your dependants at the discretion of the trustees of a personal pension plan or an employer's pension scheme are also normally tax-free. (You should request that they make such a payment by lodging a letter of wishes with them.)

Tax Saver

If you are entitled to a death in service benefit, make sure that you have sent an expression of your wishes to the pension scheme trustees. You could consider directing that any death in service benefit is paid to your children instead of a surviving spouse so that your surviving spouse's estate is not inflated, giving a higher inheritance tax liability on their subsequent death. Before you do so you should consider carefully whether or not your spouse can afford to be without the death in service benefit. If not, the same beneficial tax treatment can be secured by creating a trust to receive the death in service benefit and making your spouse a beneficiary (see the description of discretionary trusts later in this chapter). If you are unmarried you should certainly direct the trustees to pay the death in service benefit to someone other than your estate to ensure that it is not subject to inheritance tax on your death.

To calculate whether inheritance tax is due, the total value of the rest of your estate is added to the value of the PETs and chargeable transfers you made in the last seven years of your life, plus the proceeds from life insurance policies which were not written in trust and certain trust funds in which you may have an interest. Normally any loans or debts you owed are deducted from this total, as is the cost of your funeral expenses. If the remaining amount is less then £215,000 there is no tax to pay. If it is more than that, tax is charged at 40% on the excess.

If tax is due on part of your estate, PETs and chargeable transfers you made in the last seven years of your life have to be re-assessed on your death. Tax may now be due on them at 40% but none was paid on PETs when they were made and only 20% was paid on chargeable transfers. The extra tax is paid by the person who received the transfer.

Tax Saver

Because your death within seven years of a gift may give rise to an inheritance tax liability for the recipient of the gift, consider seven-year decreasing term assurance to cover the potential liability. This can be very cost-effective.

Tax Saver

If you are the recipient of a significant lifetime gift and the donor does not take out term assurance (see Chapter 13), consider doing this yourself. You will have an insurable interest in his life and the cost should be much less than any tax you may have to pay on death within the seven-year period.

Date for payment of tax

On chargeable transfers, other than on death, made between:

6 April and 30 September   –   payment due on 30 April in next tax year

1 October and 5 April   –   payment due six months after end of month in which the chargeable transfer was made.

On transfers following death, and extra tax becoming payable on chargeable transfers and potentially exempt transfers within seven years of death – payment due on earlier of:

- six months after end of month in which death occurred, and
- delivery of account by personal representatives.

TAX–FREE GIFTS
Lifetime gifts which are tax-free

The types of gifts you can make in lifetime which are exempt from inheritance tax are as follows:

Spouse exemption

Transfers to a spouse, whether during lifetime or on death, are totally exempt without limit. The only exception applies where the spouse receiving the gift is not domiciled in the UK and you are. Exempt transfers to such a spouse are limited to £55,000.

Annual exemption

This is the main exemption in this category. A gift (or gifts) of up to £3,000 made in any tax year ended on 5 April is exempt. If you don't use all the exemption in one tax year you can use the remainder the following year (but not after that). The current year's exemption is always used first.

Example: You make a gift of £5,000 in the year ended 5 April 1997. You have not previously made any lifetime gifts. Your annual exemptions available to set against the gift are £3,000 for 1996/97 plus up to £3,000 brought forward from 1995/96. Therefore the whole gift is exempt.

Small gifts

You can give any number of individuals gifts worth up to £250 per person in each tax year.

Tax Alert

This exemption is designed to cover Christmas and birthday presents and other small gifts that you may make during the year. If total gifts to any one person in any year exceed £250 you have lost this exemption but the whole gift can count towards the £3,000 annual exemption.

Marriage gifts

Each parent of a couple getting married can give them presents totalling £5,000 in value free of inheritance tax. A grandparent can give £2,500 and anyone else £1,000. The couple can give each other gifts worth up to £2,500 before the wedding (but any amount afterwards).

Tax Saver

Since both parents of both bride and groom have this exemption, up to £20,000 may be given tax-free for a single wedding.

Normal expenditure out of income

Transfers of value which fall within this category are also exempt. To determine if payments you make qualify, you must compare your income over several years against the annual outgoings of your usual standard of living to determine if there is an excess. If there is, the excess can be given away. However, such a gift must form part of your normal expenditure and you must therefore establish a habitual pattern of making gifts before the exemption will apply. It is not necessary that they be made to the same people or that they are of similar sums. Establishing a pattern usually involves repeating gifts for a three or four-year period but where the intention to make recurrent gifts is established at the outset, eg, on payment of a life assurance policy premium, the exemption will be available for the first gift even if none follow (for example in consequence of death). This is a valuable exemption for people with a high income but with few capital assets which they feel able to give away during their lives.

Tax Alert

Many people assume this exemption will apply to gifts without carefully checking the position. Normally any question of whether this exemption applies will only arise after your death when the onus of proof will lie with your executors or the recipients of the gifts. They will have to provide the necessary details of your income and expenditure. Make sure you document all the necessary information to prove the exemption applies. Remember too that income means just that – it does not, for example, include the capital element of an annuity even though you may treat that as income in meeting your expenditure.

Waivers
If you are entitled to wages or salary and decide to waive that remuneration, the waiver will not be treated as a transfer of value. Nor will the waiver of any entitlement to a dividend, provided you waive it within the twelve months before your legal entitlement to the dividend arises.

Bad bargains
There is also an exemption from tax for any reduction in the value of your estate which arises in consequence of your making a bad bargain. If you can show that your transaction was not intended to create a gift to any person and either it was made between you and someone with whom you had no relationship or association, or that you did have an association but you had no intention to confer favourable terms on them, then any 'gift element' will not be treated as a taxable transfer of value.

Family maintenance
Payments which you make in maintaining your spouse and children up to the age of 18 or while they are undergoing full-time education or training are ignored, as are any payments you make which provide for them under your pension arrangements and which you can deduct for income tax purposes.

Gifts which are tax-free both in lifetime and on death
The following types of gift are exempt from inheritance tax whether you make them in your lifetime or in your will.

Gifts to a UK registered charity or a housing association
Gifts to a UK registered charity or a housing association are exempt without limit. Take care not to leave assets to a foreign charity which has no registration in the UK as this will seriously reduce the value of the gift you make.

Gifts to political parties
Gifts to political parties are exempt without limit but the political party must be a qualifying one. To qualify, at the last General Election before the gift at least two members of the party must have been elected to the House of Commons, or at least one member must have been elected and not less than 150,000 votes cast for members of the party.

Gifts for national purposes
Gifts for national purposes to certain specified museums or national institutions are exempt. If you own assets which are important works of art or antiques, for example, you may be able to take advantage of this exemption.

Gifts for the public benefit
Gifts for the public benefit are also exempt where the property transferred is land of outstanding scenic, historic or scientific interest, buildings which the Treasury deem should be preserved because of their outstanding historic, architectural or aesthetic interest, any pictures, prints, books, manuscripts, works of art or scientific collections which are of national, scientific, historic or artistic interest and any property given as a source of income for the upkeep of such property.

BUSINESS AND AGRICULTURAL PROPERTY RELIEFS

In addition to the exemptions mentioned above there are two other very important reliefs which apply to special categories of business or agricultural property. These depend not on the identity of the person who receives the gift or the nature of the gift, as the above exemptions do, but on the character of the assets which are the subject of the transfer. The decision trees on pages 229 and 230 illustrate the criteria for and measure of the relief which may be available to you from 6 April 1996 onwards. For the rules in operation before this date see *'The Ernst & Young Tax Saving Strategies Guide 1995'*.

To qualify for business property relief assets must have been owned for a minimum period of two years immediately before the transfer. However, this period is extended if you dispose of one property and replace it with new assets or if you have inherited it from your spouse. Any business which deals in securities, stocks or shares, land or buildings, or making or holding investments, is not eligible for business property relief. If the assets of a business or company include anything which was neither used wholly or mainly for the purposes of the business throughout the whole of the last two years before the transfer, nor was required at the time of the transfer for future use for the purposes of the business, the value of that asset is excluded from relief. The extension of 100% Business Property Relief from 6 April 1996 to all shares in qualifying unquoted companies (irrespective of voting control) has significantly increased the availability of this relief and will for example make investment in the Alternative Investment Market (AIM – which replaces the USM) considerably more attractive for those with an appropriate risk profile.

Agricultural property also qualifies for an important relief known as agricultural property relief. Agricultural property is valued on the basis it can never be used for any purpose other than agriculture. This means that you can ignore the development value of any agricultural land. Again, the decision tree on page 230 illustrates the criteria for and measure of the reliefs. These two generous forms of relief may be subject to scrutiny and restriction under a Labour Government.

HOW TO VALUE YOUR ESTATE

Valuation principles

The value of any transfer for inheritance tax purposes is not the value of property given away but the value of the difference in your estate before the transaction was made and its value afterwards. To arrive at the value of your estate at any time, you must include all the assets you own valued at their market value at that time.

When valuing your assets you must value not only your own assets but also any assets which are treated as 'related property'. Related property means any assets owned by your spouse or which, in the last five years, have been the property of a charity, political body or museum or other institution because you gifted them using one of the exemptions mentioned earlier. You only include the value of your own share of related property in your estate but it may be that consideration of the larger holding for valuation purposes places a premium on the assets valued. The example below explains.

Qualifying business property relief

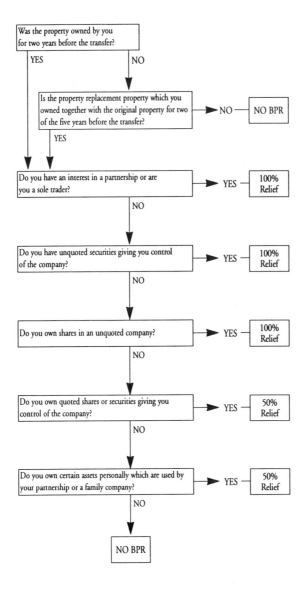

Qualifying agricultural property relief

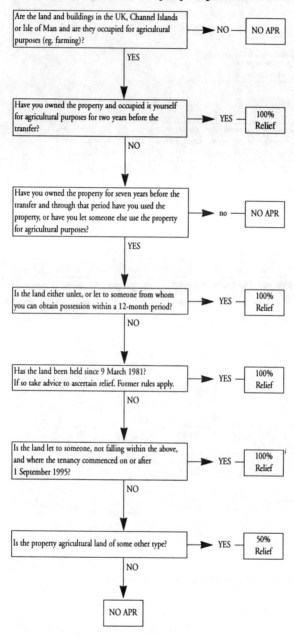

Are the land and buildings in the UK, Channel Islands or Isle of Man and are they occupied for agricultural purposes (eg. farming)? → NO — NO APR

YES

Have you owned the property and occupied it yourself for agricultural purposes for two years before the transfer? → YES — 100% Relief

NO

Have you owned the property for seven years before the transfer and through that period have you used the property, or have you let someone else use the property for agricultural purposes? → no — NO APR

YES

Is the land either unlet, or let to someone from whom you can obtain possession within a 12-month period? → YES — 100% Relief

NO

Has the land been held since 9 March 1981? If so take advice to ascertain relief. Former rules apply. → YES — 100% Relief

NO

Is the land let to someone, not falling within the above, and where the tenancy commenced on or after 1 September 1995? → YES — 100% Relief

NO

Is the property agricultural land of some other type? → YES — 50% Relief

NO

NO APR

Example: You own 25% of an unquoted company. Your wife owns 26%. The value of a 51% interest is worth much more than the value of either 25% or 26% held separately since the aggregate holding gives control of the company and hence carries a premium. The value to be included in your estate is $^{25}/_{51}$ times the value of a 51% holding.

Quoted investments

The open market value of quoted stocks and shares is found using special rules. You must obtain the prices at which the shares were quoted on the stock exchange daily official list. This price will be different from that quoted in national newspapers. The value to be used is either the lower of the two prices shown in the quotations for the day, plus one-quarter of the difference between the two figures (known as the 'quarter up' value), or half-way between the highest and lowest prices at which bargains were recorded in shares on the relevant date. If you are valuing shares on a Saturday or Sunday, you can use prices for the previous Friday or the following Monday, whichever gives the lower result.

Unquoted shares

It is harder to value shares in unquoted companies. You will need professional help in arriving at the valuation. The value that is assessed to inheritance tax in respect of unquoted shares is reduced by business property relief (see earlier in this chapter).

Life policies

Life policies are also valued at their open market value when transferred during your lifetime. This usually equates to their surrender value. That value is subject to a de minimis limit in that the policy is deemed to be worth not less than the total of the premiums paid under the contract. If the policy is unit linked then the value is the value of the units allocated to the policy. These rules do not apply to term assurance which has no value as it only pays a benefit if you die before the expiry of a specified term. Nor do they apply to the proceeds received from a policy on death where it is the actual sum received that matters. This counts as part of your estate unless the benefits are subject to a trust in favour of your dependants.

HOW TO ESTIMATE YOUR TAX LIABILITY

Use Table 1 at the end of this chapter, entering the value that would be used for inheritance tax purposes against the items which form part of your estate. If you are entitled to the income of any trust as of right, this is known as an interest in possession in a trust. To arrive at your total taxable estate, you must add together the value of all assets in such a trust as well as assets which you own outright. The trust will, of course, pay its own share of the total inheritance tax liability calculated on the total value of the trust fund and your own assets.

The value of any taxable gifts which you have made within seven years of death will also form part of your estate. Your death within that period may cause extra tax to be paid. Don't forget to include any PETs made within the last seven years as these will become chargeable on death within the seven-year period. Chargeable transfers must also be included (for example, gifts into discretionary trusts). Gifts made within seven years of death use up the band of £215,000 taxed at the nil-rate in priority to the remainder of the estate. However, don't forget to reduce them by the amount of any annual exemption that would apply for that year if the annual exemption has not been used elsewhere. Any lifetime gifts in excess of the nil-rate band will then attract a tax charge of 40%. If, however, your death occurs more than three years after you have made a gift, the tax payable on that gift is reduced by tapering relief.

No. of years after gift made	Percentage of tax at 40% payable
0 – 3	100%
3 – 4	80%
4 – 5	60%
5 – 6	40%
6 – 7	20%
Over 7	0%

If you have made a taxable lifetime gift such as a transfer to a discretionary trust you may have paid some tax at half the normal rate, ie, 20%. The tax is recalculated on death within the seven-year period and the tax rate is increased to 40%. The increased tax (if any) is payable by the donee. Once you have worked out the extra tax payable on gifts made during your lifetime, you will be able to see how much, if any, of the nil-rate band applies to the estate retained on death. Any excess is taxed at 40% and this represents your potential exposure to inheritance tax.

Table 2 at the end of this chapter will help you work out the potential tax liability on your death.

THE USE OF TRUSTS

We have mentioned trusts throughout this book and they are very useful vehicles in financial and tax planning for many reasons. They do however, more importantly, provide a practical vehicle by which you can ensure your assets are preserved for the future and for the longer term security of your family.

When you form a trust you give the full legal ownership and administration of the property you transfer to independent parties whom you appoint as 'trustees'. They normally hold this property on terms set out in a written trust deed for the benefit of people you specify and who are known as 'beneficiaries'. When you transfer assets into the legal ownership of trustees you immediately end your unrestricted control over those assets (though in some cases you can be a trustee or a beneficiary and retain certain rights in that capacity).

A trust should be created by means of a written trust deed and it is essential that you ask a solicitor to prepare this on your behalf. The terms of the trust specify not only which beneficiaries are entitled to income and which beneficiaries are entitled to capital, but also when and in what circumstances they obtain their entitlement. Trustees are generally not allowed to be paid for their services unless the trust deed states otherwise and are bound by strict legal rules which ensure that they act in the best interests of the beneficiaries and not in their own interests. A trust deed can vary from a simple one-page document to a deed comprising tens of pages depending on the complexity. Although a trust deed can provide more or less what you wish it to, there are legal parameters in which you must operate, particularly as to the potential duration of the trust.

Most solicitors draft modern trust documents which allow a great deal of flexibility in dealing with trust property. This enables account to be taken of changes in legislation or family circumstances which could not be foreseen when the trust was established. The most common forms of trust are :

1 *Interest in possession trusts (or life interest trusts)* Under this type of trust the beneficiary is entitled to the income of the settlement as of right. He may become entitled to the capital on attaining a specified age or if the trustees have a power to make distributions to him, or alternatively the capital may be held for other beneficiaries on the income beneficiary's death. The income beneficiary is sometimes referred to as the life tenant in England or the liferenter in Scotland.

2 *Discretionary trusts* A discretionary trust is any trust where a beneficiary is not entitled to the income as of right. Usually these trusts give wide powers to trustees to distribute income and/or capital in such proportions and at such times as they think fit, subject to any specific directions given in the trust deed.

3 *Accumulation and maintenance trusts* This is the name given to trusts which receive favourable tax treatment. They have virtual exemption from inheritance tax. The trust is something of a hybrid between the above two types of trust. To qualify as an accumulation and maintenance trust the terms of the trust must meet certain conditions:

- It must be established for one or more persons who must be under the age of 25.
- The beneficiaries must be entitled to the capital at age 25 (ie, the trust ends) or to the income of the trust as of right by that age.
- Either the trust must be created for a single generation (all beneficiaries must have the same grandparent) or it must not exist for more than 25 years.

The trust must be discretionary at the outset – ie, no beneficiary can have the right to demand payment of the income at that time. However, during the life of the trust the trustees can pay out income for the maintenance, education, or other benefit of the beneficiaries. To the extent it is not paid for these purposes the income must be accumulated and added to capital.

Within the confines of these conditions there is scope for great flexibility. For example, the trust deed may provide for children to become entitled to income at age 21 and capital at age 25 but the trustees could be given a power to defer payment of the capital if the child had not demonstrated an ability to handle money by the time he or she reached age 25.

Each of these different types of trust is subject to a different inheritance tax regime which is explained in more detail below.

Purpose of using a trust

There may be many reasons why you may wish to use a trust. Commonly they are used to hold assets where the beneficiaries are not considered capable of looking after the assets themselves – for example, in the case of minor or disabled children. They can be used to provide security for a spouse, to circumvent succession rights such as legal rights claims, and to protect against claims in various circumstances. For example, a gift to a child on the occasion of marriage through a trust, rather than outright, may protect division of those assets on divorce. They might also be used to give a second spouse rights in an estate but to preserve the capital for the children of a first marriage. In short there are many practical uses for trusts.

From an estate planning point of view, trusts are often used as a means of making lifetime gifts so that property is gifted at a time when it does not attract an inheritance tax liability and so that any growth in the value of assets arises outside your estate. The use of a trust may be necessary in particular if you are not yet in a position to decide who should get the assets or where you feel that your beneficiaries are not yet sufficiently responsible or mature to receive the assets.

Taxation treatment

Interest in possession trusts

Gifts to an interest in possession trust are treated as PETs. In addition, if a beneficiary who has an interest in possession gives up or makes a gift of his interest, this too may qualify as a PET. If a beneficiary who has an interest in possession dies, the whole value of the trust fund is added to his estate on death and is charged to inheritance tax. Thus the assets of an interest in possession trust are treated as though they were owned by the beneficiaries entitled to the income. There is, however, no ten-year inheritance tax charge on such a trust, as there is with the discretionary trust (see below). If assets are transferred to the trust rather than cash, this may cause a capital gains tax exposure on making the gift since the gift is treated as a taxable disposal of the assets.

Discretionary trusts

Discretionary trusts are much more harshly taxed than accumulation and maintenance trusts. When you create a discretionary trust it does not qualify as a PET. This is one of the few occasions when you may incur a lifetime charge to inheritance tax at the rate of 20% if the value of assets you give over a seven-year period exceeds the post 6 April 1997 £215,000 nil-rate band. In addition, inheritance tax charges arise throughout the life of a discretionary trust. Whenever capital is distributed from a discretionary trust, there is a tax charge. Additionally, tax is charged on the value of the trust assets every ten years whether assets are distributed or not. The calculation of the tax charge on distributions is extremely complex and rises throughout the ten-year period until its maximum at each ten-year anniversary. Under current legislation, however, the ten-year tax charge cannot exceed 6% of the fund value and on distributions from the trust between ten-year anniversaries, it is often significantly less. This maximum 6% tax charge compares favourably with the position of an interest in possession trust. Broadly this charge is intended to raise the same amount of tax as one would expect to raise in one generation if the assets had been owned outright.

A discretionary trust is also useful to enable you to make gifts of assets which contain a measure of appreciation (eg, company shares purchased some years ago). This is because you can elect to 'hold-over' any gains which would otherwise arise when you made the transfer to the trustees (unlike the position in an interest in possession trust). This then defers the tax charge until such time as the trustees sell the assets. See Chapter 2 concerning holdover relief.

Tax Saver

You can set up a discretionary trust which will not attract any inheritance tax charges for at least ten years using your nil-rate band of £215,000 and you can defer any capital gains tax which would arise on the gift. Even if the asset has appreciated significantly since you created the trust, the trust can be broken after nine years without any inheritance tax charge and assets can be passed to the next generation. For example, you own company shares which are likely to appreciate but you believe your son is too young to receive a gift of them so you create a discretionary trust. If you decide that he has matured sufficiently within the next nine years, the trust can be brought to an end without a tax charge. The appreciation bears no inheritance tax when the trust is wound up and the capital gains tax can be held over so that no tax arises until the beneficiary sells the assets.

Accumulation and maintenance trusts
The transfer of funds to an accumulation and maintenance trust qualifies as a PET. No inheritance tax is chargeable during the lifetime of the trust, nor when the trust comes to an end and the beneficiaries become absolutely entitled to the assets or to the income rights described above at the specified age. If a beneficiary of an accumulation and maintenance trust dies before these capital or income rights mature, there is no charge to inheritance tax on the trust assets. Thus on transfers into and out of accumulation and maintenance trusts and throughout the lifetime of the trust (whilst it is still in discretionary form), there is a total exemption from inheritance tax.

Will trusts
While many trusts are created during lifetime, it is equally possible to create a trust in your will. Any of the trusts described so far can be created in your will, but two particular types of trust lend themselves to will planning.

One of the most significant tax-saving provisions of the inheritance tax legislation is the exemption for gifts to a spouse. As described above, in most cases an estate is allowed an unlimited deduction for the value of property transferred to the spouse of the deceased. In effect, the exemption permits a couple to postpone paying any inheritance tax until the surviving spouse dies.

Tax Saver

You can take advantage of the spouse exemption by leaving your property in your will so that your spouse receives the benefit of any income during lifetime but on subsequent death the terms of your will determine who eventually receives the property. You can ensure property stays in your family by this route, where your spouse remarries after your death or where you have married twice and wish your capital to be preserved for the children of your first marriage.

Two-year will trust

Since no one knows exactly when they are going to die or what the financial circumstances of their family will be at that time, it can often be difficult to take advantage of tax exemptions and reliefs in your will in case you deprive a dependant of much needed income or capital simply to save tax. If you have this problem, you could consider setting up a two-year discretionary will trust. Under this arrangement you leave all your assets to the trustees of a discretionary trust where you specify the potential beneficiaries but your trustees decide who gets what and in what proportions. The onus will be on your trustees to evaluate the family's circumstances at the time of your death and to deal fairly with your estate with a view to reducing tax liabilities sensibly. Provided that the trustees make their decision within two years of your death, the redivision of assets is treated as though it had taken place at the time of your death. The inheritance tax consequences are computed on that basis. If you wish to use a will trust in this way you must be careful to make sure that your trustees are aware of your intentions – a letter would normally be deposited with your will to explain to your trustees how you wished them to exercise their powers.

Tax Saver

Using a two-year discretionary will trust can be a good way of reducing tax liabilities. For example, your trustees can take into account gifts made within seven years of death in deciding how much of the nil-rate band is available for legacies to children, while leaving the rest of the estate direct to a surviving spouse, taking advantage of the spouse exemption.

Tax Alert

Assets left to a two-year will trust will bear inheritance tax. However, if the trustees give assets to your spouse within two years of your death, any inheritance tax paid can be reclaimed taking advantage of the spouse exemption. You should not forget, however, that your trustees will have to pay inheritance tax initially, possibly selling assets to do so. In deciding if this course is right for you, you have to balance the cash flow disadvantage of paying the tax initially against the potential tax savings and flexibility a two-year will trust can offer.

Trust interests not liable to inheritance tax

Two types of interest in a trust are outside the scope of inheritance tax. The first relates to settlements which were created by someone who was not domiciled in the UK at the time the settlement was made. See Chapter 5 for tax planning for non-UK domiciled people.

Tax Saver

If you are a non-UK domiciled settlor of a trust and you want to include UK assets in the trust, consider setting up an offshore company to hold the assets. Shares in the offshore company will be situated outside the UK, so creating an excluded property trust. However the underlying assets of the company, such as land or stocks and shares quoted on the London Stock Exchange, can be held by the company without losing the inheritance tax exemption.

The second trust interest outside the scope of inheritance tax is a reversionary interest. Broadly a reversionary interest is a future interest under a settlement, ie, your interest cannot be enjoyed until that of someone else has ended. For example, if your father is entitled to the income of the trust and on his death you become entitled to the capital you have a reversionary interest. Reversionary interests are not liable to inheritance tax.

Tax Saver

If you have a reversionary interest in a trust and will become entitled to the assets on the death of an elderly relative, consider whether you should make a gift of the interest now, directly to your children or into a trust for their benefit. If you do this, the assets will not form part of your estate nor will the gift of the reversionary interest count for inheritance tax even if you die within seven years of transferring it.

WHAT HAPPENS ON DEATH

Deductions from the estate

When you die your executors add together all the assets of your estate. The value of your assets is the value the instant before you die but if that value increases or decreases as a result of your death, the change is treated as if it had occurred immediately before the death. Typically this might apply to the value of an insurance policy which only pays out if you die as a result of an accident. The value of such a policy immediately before your death may be very low but if your executors are entitled to the proceeds, the benefits payable under the policy will be added into your estate because it will have become more valuable as a result of your death.

Your executors can deduct from your estate most bona fide liabilities which exist at the time of your death. Liabilities will include any income tax or any capital gains tax liabilities that are due up to the time of your death and inheritance tax payable on transactions made during your lifetime but not the inheritance tax payable as a result of your death.

Reasonable funeral expenses can be deducted from your estate. Funeral costs include the cost of the funeral itself, the cost of a gravestone and a reasonable amount for mourning for your family. If your estate includes property situated outside the United Kingdom your executors can also deduct expenses for administering or realising the property which are shown to be attributable to the location of the property up to a maximum of 5% of the value of the property.

Payment of tax

Strictly speaking, your executors are liable to pay tax due on your death six months after the end of the month in which you die. In practice, tax often has to be paid earlier. This is because your personal representatives (who administer your estate) must pay the tax at the same time as they lodge with the Probate Registry in England and Wales an inventory of your estate. In Scotland the inventory is lodged with the local Sheriff Court or the Commissary Office in Edinburgh. This must be done in order to obtain formal authority to administer your estate – a grant of representation.

In England and Wales obtaining authority to administer your estate under the provisions of a will is known as a grant of Probate while in Scotland your executors obtain Confirmation to your estate. Your personal representatives have twelve months from the end of the month in which you die to submit to the inheritance tax authorities an account of the assets in your estate. For all practical purposes however it is the case that a grant of representation needs to be obtained much earlier as your assets will be frozen until such time as your personal representatives can prove their proper title to them.

As a result, at a fairly early stage your personal representatives will need to consider how they are going to pay the liability to inheritance tax. Commonly funds are not available from your estate both because your assets are in non-liquid form and because they cannot be sold until after the grant of representation has been obtained. This cannot be done until the tax is paid. To defeat this impasse, it is usual to arrange borrowing facilities with a bank to bridge the period while they obtain title and sell assets in your estate.

Tax Saver

Executors should always borrow to pay inheritance tax by means of a bank loan and not by means of a bank overdraft. Interest on a bank loan for this specific purpose will be deductible from the income of the estate for income tax purposes. While interest on an overdraft will be an expense of administering the estate, no relief will be obtained from tax at the basic and lower rates and only beneficiaries of your estate who are liable to tax at the higher rates will effectively obtain relief from higher rate tax on overdraft interest (by reason of receiving less income).

Paying tax in instalments

Some assets in your estate may not be easily converted into cash. Typically this applies to land and buildings and also to shares in unquoted companies or interests in unincorporated businesses. Recognising this problem, your personal representatives can elect to pay inheritance tax due on such assets by ten equal annual instalments. The instalment option applies to land of any description wherever it is situated. In the case of shares in a company, it applies to shares which gave you control of the company, whether they are quoted or unquoted. In the case of unquoted shares which do not give control, the instalment option is also available provided that not less than 20% of the total inheritance tax bill is attributable to the value of such shares. Bearing in mind that business property relief will often be available to eliminate or substantially reduce any tax liability, the instalment option should significantly reduce any difficulty in paying tax on unquoted shares. If, however, there is still tax payable on unquoted shares and your executors can satisfy the Inland Revenue that the tax attributable to their value cannot be paid in one sum without undue hardship, they will also allow the instalment option to apply.

Interest on tax

Unpaid tax carries interest from six months after the date of your death. Tax which is paid by instalments in relation to an interest in a business or to any shares or securities (save those of an investment holding company), only carries interest from the date on which the instalment is payable. This also applies to tax payable on woodlands but tax payable by instalments on other land or property does bear interest from the normal six-month date when it first becomes due for payment and not just from the date the instalment is due.

Funding the tax liability

For many people, a crucial part of an estate plan is to make sure that the liability on your death can be funded in such a way that assets do not have to be sold in order to meet it. This is particularly true if the assets will continue to be needed by your family, eg, the family home, or there are assets which you do not wish to be sold, for example shares in a family company. If you cannot reduce your liability by gifting assets during lifetime, one option is to think ahead and provide funding for the liability.

Tax Saver

Consider funding any inheritance tax liability payable on death with a whole of life insurance policy. The policy should be written in trust for the persons who will inherit your estate, particularly those who will have to suffer the tax liability. This way the policy proceeds will fall outside your taxable estate and be paid directly to them. Each life insurance premium you pay will be a gift when a policy is written in trust but you will usually be able to cover the payments with one of your exemptions. Exemptions commonly used are the annual exemption or the normal expenditure out of income exemption, provided you have sufficient surplus income. On your death the beneficiaries will receive the policy proceeds which they can lend to your personal representatives in order to obtain their grant of representation. This avoids the cost of bank borrowing and the funds should be available swiftly.

ESTATE PLANNING TECHNIQUES

Inheritance tax lends itself to four main planning strategies which you should try to build into your estate plan:

- reduce your estate by making lifetime gifts if you can
- make full use of exemptions and the nil-rate band
- invest in tax-favoured assets such as those qualifying for 100% business property relief or agricultural relief
- make arrangements to fund the payment of tax outside your taxable estate.

In the following pages we suggest a range of ways in which you may be able to reduce your tax liability.

Reservation of benefit

Because it is so easy to avoid inheritance tax by giving away assets during lifetime, there are rules to ensure that you gift assets fully and don't retain use or enjoyment of the asset, making the gift a sham. The rules provide that where you have reserved a benefit in an asset gifted, the asset is treated as if it remained in your estate at the point of death. A liability to inheritance tax therefore arises on assets given away where a benefit is reserved. A reservation of benefit applies if the recipient of the gift does not immediately possess and fully enjoy the property given to him. A simple example illustrates the point.

Example: If you purport to give a painting to one of your children but it remains hanging on a wall in your house, your child will not have begun to enjoy the property and so there will be a reservation of benefit. The painting will not be regarded as having been given away for the purpose of calculating inheritance tax on your estate.

There is also a reservation of benefit if at any time since you gave the asset away, the property is not enjoyed by the recipient to your entire exclusion or benefit whether by formal contract or any other informal arrangement between you. The Inland Revenue have published some examples of how they will apply these rules.

Example: You give a house to one of your children which becomes their residence. Subsequently, you make visits and stay with your children. The Inland Revenue will regard a reservation of benefit as existing if you stay with your child for more than one month each year or, you stay in the house for more than two weeks each year while they are away.

Example: You give a motor car to a grandchild. If you are given an occasional lift in the car, there will not be a reservation of benefit unless the lifts are more frequent than three times a month.

Example: If you give a holiday home which you and the recipient both use on an occasional basis, this will be regarded as a gift with reservation.

These Inland Revenue examples illustrate how broadly they interpret the gift with reservation rules. The only safe course is to give an asset away completely. If you have made a gift with reservation and subsequently the reservation is released, the rules operate as though you had made your gift at that time. Taken together, these rules can mean that the same gift would be subject to tax more than once and there are provisions which ensure that an asset gifted with a reservation is only subject to one tax charge.

There is normally no reservation of benefit in a gift of cash but if you give cash on condition it is used to purchase an asset which will be available for you to use it is likely that the Inland Revenue will regard this as a gift with reservation. There is no reservation of benefit if you pay a full market rental for your use of property or for the use of an asset which you have given away but this strategy can be expensive in income tax terms. You are making payment out of your taxed income and the donee is paying tax on the sums he receives from you as they are also part of his income. It is important to realise that the full market rental must be charged and paid – even an underpayment of £1 would be sufficient to reserve a benefit in the whole asset.

Equalisation of estates for married couples

In the case of a married couple, it will be impossible to know which spouse will die first. But if your combined estates are large, the total inheritance tax bill will obviously be much lower if you each make use of the lifetime exemptions and the £215,000 nil-rate band on death. Married couples with large estates can reduce the total tax liability by equalising their estates at least to the extent that each has £215,000 of assets to leave to the family on the death of the first to die. They can then leave a total of £430,000 of assets on death without any inheritance tax.

Tax Saver

Remember that leaving assets to a discretionary trust for your family means that you can include your spouse as a beneficiary. The nil-rate band of £215,000 can be used (saving £86,000 in tax) without depriving your spouse of access to the assets but without passing assets into his or her estate for tax purposes.

Although equalising estates sounds an easy technique, there are some points to watch. From an income tax planning point of view remember it may be desirable for the spouse with lower income to hold investments enabling full use of their lower and basic rate income tax bands. If this strategy is more important to you it may start to dictate which assets should be owned by which spouse. Assets can be transferred between spouses without giving rise to a liability to capital gains tax.

Tax Alert

Take care that your strategy doesn't jeopardise other exemptions, for example, retirement relief through holding family company shares in the name of the non-working spouse.

If your combined estates are large, it is probably worth seeing that each spouse's estate is rather more than £215,000, as this will also allow for future increases in the nil-rate band and also allow each spouse to support a regular policy of lifetime giving. If each spouse has assets that can be given away, you can double up the value of exemptions such as the annual exemption. However, if both spouses want to take advantage of the normal expenditure out of income exemption, remember that both must have sufficient income to cover their net expenditure including income tax in order to support a claim that this exemption applies.

The family home

The family home often features in equalisation plans. Deciding how you should own your family home is an important issue since in many cases it will be the most substantial investment you make. There are two ways to hold property. **Joint tenants** own their home on the basis that the survivor will become entitled to the property automatically by law. **Tenants in common** own their home on the basis that each person has the right to leave their share in the property by their will. If you want to consider leaving a share in a property on a will trust for the benefit of your family you must own the property as tenants in common and not as joint tenants.

Tax Saver

If you own your home as joint tenants it is easy for you to convert this to a tenancy in common by a simple notice. Ask your solicitor how to go about this when reviewing your will.

If you own property in Scotland it is common for the title to be held in the joint names of spouses with a 'destination' to the survivor which enables the surviving spouse to have access to the property immediately on the death of the other spouse. In addition there are other legal protections which mean that if you want to leave a half share in the family home to your children on death, Scottish legal advice is essential.

There are many non-financial reasons linked to family security why the home should be in the joint names of husband and wife, and these will usually outweigh the benefit of reducing the tax payable after your death. Ask yourself whether the family home really is a suitable asset to be left to family on the death of the first to die, purely to take advantage of the nil-rate band. As you and your spouse grow older the need for independence and security from owning your own home may be crucial and it is not always a good idea to rely on the goodwill of your family to permit the surviving spouse to reside in the house for the rest of their life. Tax considerations should always be subsidiary to the practical disadvantages of particular courses of action.

If you want to leave an interest in your home to your children by will, rather than to your spouse, check with your lawyer that the way in which the legal title is held will allow you to do this.

Lifetime giving

Giving away assets during your lifetime achieves two ends in reducing your inheritance tax bill – the value of your estate decreases by the amount given away and any growth in value of those assets arises outside your estate.

Tax Saver

Try to give assets with the greatest growth potential as these will reduce your tax liability the most. In addition, even if you die within seven years of making a lifetime gift, only the value at the date of gift will be taxed and not the growth within the seven-year period.

Two factors may discourage you from making lifetime gifts. The first is your personal financial security – once you have given the assets away there is no obligation on anyone to apply them in looking after you if you have given away too much. Think carefully about what will happen if you are unable to care for yourself in the future. Might you need expensive nursing home care? How will your spouse cope after your death? Always err on the side of caution and don't give away too much. The second factor is capital gains tax. Most assets which you give away during your lifetime other than cash will attract capital gains tax and if you are a higher rate taxpayer the rate will be 40%. Contrast this with the inheritance tax rate of 40% payable on death. There is no point in making lifetime gifts of assets which incur a tax liability earlier than would otherwise be the case if you retained the assets until death. On the other hand, remember that it is only the gain that is subject to capital gains tax whereas the value of the whole asset is subject to inheritance tax.

Gains on gifts

If you adopt a policy of giving assets to the value of your annual exemption each year, you may well find that the capital gain is within your annual capital gains tax exemption, although you will have to take account of other capital disposals that you make in the year. It may be a good policy to make lifetime gifts of assets which are exempt from capital gains tax – chattels (tangible assets) worth under £6,000 are one example – but remember you must give them away completely. You cannot retain possession of an asset given away and enjoy its use during your lifetime.

If, despite the considerations above, you decide to give away your home, there is no capital gains tax to pay if it has been your principal private residence. However, the principal private residence exemption only applies to the owner of the home and if your children own a second home, any future growth in value will be subject to capital gains tax. And if you intend to continue living in the house it is likely that the gift will not be valid for inheritance tax since it will be a gift with reservation of benefit. The most suitable assets to choose to give are therefore those which generate no income and which you no longer require. Holiday homes, yachts, antiques, works of art, etc, may all fall in this category.

Tax-favoured assets

Under current rules, business property relief and agricultural property relief mean that you can wholly or partly protect your estate from inheritance tax by investing in appropriate assets. These assets may continue to generate an income during your lifetime, eg, dividends from unquoted family companies – and on death any capital gains tax liability will be removed as your assets are revalued at market value when acquired by your heirs without any capital gains tax being payable. These advantages would seem to dictate that you should retain such assets in your estate as long as possible and invest in more. There are other incentives to invest in sheltered assets – for example, if you incur a large capital gain you may be able to qualify for capital gains tax reinvestment relief by subscribing for shares in an unquoted company. This will also qualify for inheritance tax relief, reducing your total taxable assets and ensuring that an increased amount passes to your family on your death.

Remember, however, that the current tax regime is particularly benign and the availability of 100% relief may disappear in the future under a different government. A contrary school of thought is therefore that advantage should be taken of this regime to make transfers now. The assets can be transferred directly to your family or put into trusts where the inheritance tax relief can continue to shelter them from future liabilities.

Non-tax reasons may also encourage you to gift assets to the family during lifetime. For example, if your children take over the family business from you it will often encourage them to greater efforts if they have a financial stake in the form of shares in the company than if the shareholding remains in your possession.

Gift and loan back arrangements

It would be attractive if you could give away assets and then simply borrow back to meet your spending requirements and various insurance arrangements try to achieve this objective.

The following example illustrates the type of scheme typically marketed by insurance companies.

You start by taking out a single premium life insurance policy, either on your own life or on the joint lives of yourself and your spouse. The policy is then given to your chosen beneficiary, usually using a simple trust. The next step is to make a substantial interest-free loan, repayable on demand to the trustees of the trust. At that stage your estate is not reduced at all because the cash asset which you had previously is replaced by a loan asset. The trustees make a substantial additional payment into the single premium investment bond using the funds they have borrowed. They can then begin repaying the loan to you annually by making 5% withdrawals from the bond over a period of 20 years. You use the funds to live on. Any growth in the value of the bond itself falls outside your estate and the appreciation is instead held for the benefit of the beneficiary.

The taxation of life insurance products is currently subject to review and the facility to make tax-free withdrawals may be short lived. See *'Changes in the Tax Law you should know about when planning in 1997'.*

The use of a life insurance policy has enabled this arrangement to be neatly packaged. However, similar arrangements have been put in place using personal trusts and without the need to invest in an insurance policy.

Deeds of variation

Sometimes, despite the best will in the world, it is not possible to organise your affairs perfectly to take advantage of the tax environment and the family financial circumstances as they exist at the time of your death. In this situation your family may wish to implement a deed of family arrangement or deed of variation over the assets in your estate. Under such an arrangement your will is effectively rewritten to suit the family's circumstances and wishes. Provided this is done within two years of your death by a written agreement and providing a valid tax election is made within six months of the deed of variation, it takes effect as though your will itself had made the revised gifts. There is no additional inheritance tax to pay unless you divert assets from a spouse and, indeed, the deed of variation can be used to reduce a tax liability by taking advantage of the spouse exemption or exemption for gifts to charity. A valid election must be signed by everyone making the variation and, if it results in additional tax being payable, by the personal representatives as well.

Although a useful tool for making sure that your affairs are structured so as best to take advantage of the inheritance tax regime at the time of your death, it is unwise to rely on a deed of variation to implement your estate plan. Your family or friends may be reluctant to disturb your will out of respect for what they see as your last wishes. If you wish the family to implement a deed of family arrangement if that is more tax-efficient after your death, you should make sure that all those involved know your feelings on the matter while you are still alive. There are other reasons why it is unwise to rely on a deed of family arrangement. Firstly the tax legislation may be vulnerable to change and, secondly, the variation requires the co-operation of all potential beneficiaries involved. If anyone did not co-operate it would not be possible to restructure the will and indeed if the interests of minor children were affected by the proposals no variation would be possible since they are unable to give a valid consent. For this reason you should try to ensure that your will is as accurate as possible and only rely on a deed of variation to tidy up any loose ends or take care of any unforeseen or changed circumstances.

Deeds of variation are also equally applicable for beneficiaries of an estate subject to the rules of intestacy where no will has been prepared.

Tax Saver

You should remember a deed of variation if a relative dies and leaves you assets you would wish to pass on to younger generations of your family. This will be an efficient means for you to make a gift without tax implications. You should also note that through a deed of variation you can create a discretionary trust of which you can be a beneficiary, thereby preserving your access to the assets but with no inheritance tax consequence for your estate.

Making gifts to minors

The cheapest form of lifetime gifting is to make an outright gift but this is often not suitable for minor children where you may not want to put them in control of funds at too young an age. In this situation you should consider making gifts for minor children into an accumulation and maintenance settlement discussed earlier in this chapter. The tax advantages of such a trust give complete inheritance tax protection. Where grandparents or someone other than a parent makes the gift, the trustees can spend income for the child's benefit at their discretion and if the child is not subject to income tax, the income tax which is paid at 34% (both for 1996/97 and 1997/98) on the trust income can be recovered for the child. This makes it an excellent vehicle for providing for school fees. If a parent wants to make a gift to a minor child, by making the trust irrevocable, any income arising within the trust will not be added to the parent's income provided it is not spent or distributed until the child is at least 18 years old. Parents should look on accumulation and maintenance settlements as being good savings vehicles for children or as a means for providing university education or passing on family businesses.

Generation skipping

If you are going to make gifts to your family, think carefully who should be the recipient. Often the first candidates will be your children but if they have significant assets in their own right it may be more beneficial to make gifts to grandchildren, thereby skipping a generation. On the death of your children the assets will not suffer an inheritance tax charge which will therefore be deferred for two generations. If you are from a wealthy family it is an ideal plan through the generations if grandparents always provide for grandchildren so that each generation in turn passes its assets down two generations.

ESTATE PLANNING CHECKLIST

This summary will ensure that you have considered the main estate planning measures open to you.

- You and your spouse should review your current financial situation, including your personal financial plan and retirement plan.
- Check you have organised your affairs and documented the location of all your important financial and legal papers.
- Check you have a valid will and that it is up to date.
- Check that your assets are balanced between you and your spouse, having

regard to your income tax plan, capital gains tax plan, and retirement plan, as well as your estate plan.

- Check that any death in service benefits under pension plan arrangements are directed so that they arise outside your estate. Make sure that your spouse is adequately provided for before directing these benefits to children.

- Evaluate the potential inheritance tax liability on the death of you and your spouse. Consider how the liability will be funded and, if necessary, update your life insurance arrangements.

- Make sure that you have adequate financial provision for your surviving spouse and minor children and other dependants and ensure that your arrangements cover the guardianship of minor children.

- Check what scope you have for making lifetime gifts and how best to structure these. If you can, begin a programme of lifetime gifting sooner rather than later.

- Consider making gifts to charity during lifetime or on death to reduce the tax payable on your estate.

- Have you anticipated any significant inheritances by you and your spouse? It may pay to take steps for these to bypass your estate direct to your children.

If you have considered all these points thoroughly then you have done everything you can to put your financial affairs in order.

FINALLY – ARE YOU ORGANISED?

One of the most difficult tasks that a family faces when someone dies is going through their personal affairs and trying to sort out their finances. Grief at someone's death can be made worse by worries and concerns about whether or not you know the full extent of the deceased person's assets and where they are located. It is a good idea to sit down at some stage and draw up a list of all relevant papers and assets and their location. This will make it quick and easy for your family to begin the process of winding up your estate after your death.

If you have a will, make a note of the date of the will, the last time you updated it and where it is. Often it will be held by your solicitor but if you have it in a deed box in a bank or elsewhere, note this down.

Make a note of your funeral wishes – do you wish to be buried or cremated and is there a particular location that you have in mind? Make a note of who your solicitors and accountants are and the address of your tax office and your tax reference number. If you have appointed executors of your will, make a note of who they are and where they can be contacted. The name and address of your insurance broker, banker, doctor and dentist is also useful information.

Now turn to your assets. Make a note of any property you own, if it is mortgaged who the lender is and who holds the title deeds. If you have a portfolio of stocks and shares, keep a list of the companies and the number of shares held. If you hold the share certificates yourself, make a note of the numbers and list them down. If they are held by your stockbroker, solicitor or banker, make a note of this instead.

Don't forget to include non-taxable assets such as National Savings Certificates, premium bonds, etc. Make a note of any bank and building society accounts you have and don't forget to list all your life assurance policies and where they are kept. It helps if you can make a note of how much life cover the policies provide and in the case of endowment policies, what the estimated bonuses or value of the policy is to date. Make a list of your pension policies or, if you are a member of an occupational pension scheme provided by your employer, give details and make a note of who should be contacted in this connection in the event of your death. Don't forget to make a note of your liabilities – if you have borrowed any money write down the amount you have borrowed and the terms of the loan. It also helps to make a list of your credit and store card accounts so that not only can these be settled on your death but so that the cards can be cancelled. You may at the same time wish to list any subscriptions to organisations which should be cancelled on your death, eg, health insurance such as BUPA, motoring organisations and professional associations.

Don't forget to make a note of the whereabouts of title documents to physical assets such as motor cars. If you own a lot of jewellery or there are valuable antiques or works of art amongst your personal possessions, it is helpful to leave a note of the items and their approximate value together with any insurance details.

If you are the beneficiary of a trust, leave a note of the trustees who should be contacted in the event of your death. If you have settled any trusts you should also make a note of these so that the trustees can be notified.

As you pull together this information, you will be able to create a list of your personal assets and a note of their current market value. Jot this down and add it up to get a feel for the size of your estate. The table at the end of this chapter may help you to do this.

TABLE 1

Your estate

Personal Assets – Current Market Value

	Self (£)	Joint (£)	Spouse/Partner (£)	Total
Home (main residence) (after deducting outstanding mortgage)				
Contents/effects/motor vehicles				
Works of art/jewellery				
Second home				
Investment property				
Agricultural property acres				
Woodland/forestry acres				
Stocks & shares				
Personal Equity Plans				
Unit trusts				
Insurance bonds				
Building society deposits				
TESSAs				
Bank accounts				
BES/EIS investments				
Enterprise Zones				
National Savings issues				
Share options				
Funds at Lloyd's				
Life policies payable to your estate				
– mortgage endowment				
– other				
Other assets (specify)				
Total of your personal assets	£	£	£	£

1(a) Deductible liabilities

	Self (£)	Joint (£)	Spouse/ Partner
Mortgages on property (other than your main home)			
Other qualifying loans			
Overdraft/loans(s)			
Other liabilities			
	£	£	£

1(b) Assets not part of your free estate

	Self	Joint	Spouse/ Partner
Pension death in service benefits			
Life policies on your life written in trust			
Interest under trusts			
Anticipated inheritances			
	£	£	£

TABLE 2 Inheritance tax ready reckoner

Estate	Value £	Tax Attributable £	Notes
Total of your personal assets under Table 1			
One half of any jointly owned personal assets			
Total estate	(a) _____	(g) $\dfrac{a \times (f - i)}{a + b}$	
Add			
Assets held in a trust from which you receive income as of right	(b) _____	(h) $\dfrac{h \times (f - i)}{a + b}$	
Assets which you have given away in the last seven years (less annual exemptions)	(c) _____	(i) (c − d) x 40% _____ *	* If (c) does not exceed £215,000, the figure for tax here should be replaced by zero. If the gift was made more than 3 years before the death you will need to reduce the resulting tax by the percentage shown in footnote 2 below.
Gross estate for tax (a + b+ c)			
Less nil-rate band	(d) (£215,000)		
	(e) _____ @ 40% =	(f) _____ Tax	

FOOTNOTES
1. If all assets have been left to your spouse the tax charge is most likely to arise on the second death. You should therefore complete the above by inserting the total values of your joint estates shown in Table 1.
   The tax will arise on the death of whichever of you dies last. By using the technique of the nil-rate band will trust you can reduce this liability by £86,000.
2. Taper relief is applied to the tax liability at the following rates depending on the years between the gift and the death: 3-4 – 80%; 4-5 – 60%; 5-6 – 40%; 6-7 – 20%. Tax reduced to nil after 7 years.
3. The £215,000 'nil-rate band' applies from 6 April 1997.

Index

Note: Definitions of individual terms are to be found in the Glossary on pages xxxvi-xl.

bank investments 28, 186-7
bare trusts 41
beneficial loans 5
benefits in kind 5-6
    self assessment xxii
    tax-free 6-8
blind person's allowance 58
bonds xxix, 27, 48-9
bonuses 159
borrowings see loans
bridging loans 13, 68
building society investments 28, 186-7
business entertainment 14, 131
Business Expansion Scheme 112
business gifts 131
business property relief 228, 229, 244
business travel xxix, 9-10, 130-31
    spouses 12
businesses
    accounting periods 128-9
    capital allowances see capital
        allowances
    choice of structure 121
    disposal
        companies 170-74
        partnerships 124, 168-70
        retirement planning 212
        sole traders 122, 164-8
    incorporation 172-4
    limited companies
        see limited companies
    partnerships see partnerships
    preparing accounts see accounts
    retirement planning 208-9, 212
    sole traders see sole traders
    trading or investing 127-8

C

canteen facilities 6
capital allowances
    calculation 139-40
    companies 135
    industrial buildings allowance 136-7
    motoring expenses 10-11
    partnerships 135
    plant and machinery 136-7
    qualifying assets 135, 138
    sole traders 135

    timing of expenditure 135-6
capital expenditure 159-60
    cars 137
capital gains
    allowing for inflation 44-6
    assets of negligible value 53
    'bed and breakfasting' transactions
        xix, 48, 102, 109
    calculation 42-4
    charitable gifts 74
    declaration 42
    dividends and 36-7
    employer share schemes and trusts 46
    exemptions xxxiii, 47-51
    gifts in retirement 213-14
    holdover relief 51, 170
    incorporation 173-4
    investments for children 40
    lease premiums 24
    lifetime gifts 243-4
    non-UK domiciliaries 103
    non-UK residents 102
    partnerships 169-70
    pre-sale dividends 171
    purchase of own shares 171-2, 212
    Qualifying Corporate Bonds xxix
    reinvestment relief xxviii, 52
    retirement relief 51-2, 212
    rollover relief 53, 167-8
    sale of a business
        partnerships 169-70
        sole traders 167-8
    sale of shares to a third party 170
    tax assessment 85
    time limits for tax elections and
        claims 115
    transfer of assets xix
    trusts 54, 93
    working out tax due 53-4
    year-end planning 108-10
capital losses 46-7
car benefits xxix, 5
    motoring expenses 10-11
    rates xxxi
cars
    capital expenditure 137
    leasing 131
    parking expenses 6

unit trusts 33, 191
unquoted shares xx, 47, 231

V

value added tax 157
Venture Capital Trusts xxviii, 76-7, 196
vocational training 7, 77-8
vouchers
  goods and services 6
  meals 6

W

wages 4-5, 130
waivers 205, 227
war pensions 19-20
wedding presents 226
widow's bereavement allowance 58
widows' pensions 20, 211
will trusts 236-7
wills xx, 217
  deeds of variation 245-6
  do-it-yourself kits 220
  enduring power of attorney 221
  funeral arrangements 220, 247
  guardianship arrangements 220
  intestacy 218-19
  marriage and divorce 221
  providing for dependants 217, 220
  Scotland 219, 220
winding up 171, 209
working abroad 12
        (*see also* domicile; residence)
  double tax relief 78
  foreign earnings deduction 14-16
writing down allowances: industrial
        buildings 136

Y

year-end planning 105
  age-related issues 107-8
  annual allowances 110-11
  capital gains 108-10
  capital expenditure 159-60
  children's allowances and reliefs 107
  claiming reliefs 112, 114-15
  family companies 160-61
  married couples 105-7
  pension contributions 113

personal tax time limits 114-15
profit-related pay 162
remuneration versus dividends xix, 161
retained profits 161-2
reviewing existing investments 112-13
smoothing profits 163
timing of dividends 161
timing of income, deductions and
        payments 158-9
timing personal income 111-12
worksheet to estimate 1996/97
        income tax 116-17